CHANGING FACES

The Consequences of Exposure to Gene and Thyroid Disrupting Toxins

Judy Hoy

Scientist, Biologist, Naturalist, and Wildlife Rehabilitator

Disclaimer

No information contained herein is intended as medical or veterinary advice for humans or animals, nor is it intended to be a training manual for wildlife rehabilitators. The electrolytes, uses of which are mentioned in stories in this book, are not in any way considered drugs and are readily available to anyone. Everyone should be aware that the handling of wild animals can be dangerous to both the handler and the animal without appropriate knowledge and equipment. Also, regulations regarding caring for wildlife may vary greatly in each state in the United States. Every country has their own laws regarding wildlife. In all cases of handling and/or caring for wild or domestic animals, advice from relevant government officials and medical or care providers with appropriate licenses and permits is recommended before any action is taken. The author and publisher are not responsible for any adverse effects or consequences resulting from the use of any ideas or activities included in this *Changing Faces* book.

Printed by CreateSpace, an Amazon.com Company

Dedication

This book is dedicated to my wonderful husband Bob, who provided patient, loving support, encouragement, and vital technical assistance for our long-term wildlife studies and to Bob's brother, Jack, who provided funding for the publishing and promotion of this book. It is also dedicated to Jenny, our Pembroke Welsh Corgi, and all of our other animal friends who died too soon from exposure to environmental toxins, and to all the animals, wild and domestic, especially the young ones who helped me learn how to mitigate specific birth defects.

Because of the animals whose stories are told in this book, many other animals, including humans, have been helped. Also, I would like to thank my very helpful sister Pamela Hallock Muller, my other colleagues, and all others who have each worked diligently in their own way to save the biodiversity of our only planet. You are my inspiration and my heroes.

Changing Faces was written to help young animals like this mule deer fawn to be born normal, grow up, and have young of their own to sustain their species.

CONTENTS

ABOUT THE AUTHOR
By Pamela Hallock Muller

Judy was born on January 3, 1940. The wars in Europe and Asia had brought an end to the Great Depression as metals, explosives, food, and fibers were in demand on the battlefields. She was a scrawny baby, looking something like the wrinkled baby birds she would one day foster. But she was strong and determined to thrive; her parents were proud of their firstborn. She was Daddy's girl, following him around his South Dakota prairie ranch from the time she could walk or cling to a horse's back.

Judy connected with animals from the crib. Buff, the ranch dog's name, was her first word, to the chagrin of her parents. Buff was her best friend until he died. Her younger years were busy ones, exploring the wide-open South Dakota grasslands on her Dad's horse Nifty, another of her best friends. When she was 11 years old, she got her very own horse, Flicka, Nifty's sister, named after the filly in the book *My Friend Flicka*. Mostly Thoroughbred, Flicka loved to run. After Judy broke her to ride they would go for miles over the prairie. Judy also helped with the many outside chores like bringing in the milk cows, milking them by hand, feeding orphaned calves, pigs, baby chicks and other animals, weeding the garden, watching over her two younger brothers, and eventually, two sisters, and of course helping her mother with household chores.

School was interesting and a place to read books, lots of books. But Judy's favorite classrooms were the barnyard filled with animals and birds, and the prairie with all the wondrous wild birds and small mammals, reptiles, and amphibians that lived in the beautiful native grasses and forbs, in themselves fascinating subjects for study. She wanted to know the names of everything. Her favorite wild animals were the ones everyone else hated, the feisty little badgers, the dog-like coyotes, and the beautiful spotted skunks. She always cheered for the coyotes when killer-planes flew low over the open prairie carrying men with guns, blasting away at their vulnerable fleeing victims.

Judy was a perfectionist and liked to draw. She spent hours perfecting her curves and perspectives. She loved to draw horses; they reared and galloped across her pages. But drawing was not just an interest or even passion. It was another teacher through which she learned to observe detail – the kind of detail that escapes most others, even trained scientists.

Her eye for detail contributed to her artistic talents and drawing developed her powers of observation. The wide Dakota prairie provided plenty to observe. She found petrified wood in the pastures, petrified bone and teeth in clay banks, and arrowheads exposed by the wind, lying in the sandy soil between the bunch grasses. She watched the Meadowlarks, Bobolinks, and Lark Buntings taking food to their young, marveled at the graceful Red-tailed Hawks hanging in the wind high in the blue sky, and listened to the Great Horned Owl pair calling to each other in the cottonwoods by Antelope Creek. She admired and learned the names of the flowers that swayed in the wind that blew constantly across the plains, from the tiny Scarlet Globemallow to the tall Showy Milkweed. Later in life she would learn the Latin names for the grasses and flowers.

Judy liked the outside ranch work, especially riding through the cattle herd with her Dad, to check for any problems with the cows or calves. His powers of observation were so well developed that he could tell each individual from all the others. If one was missing, he knew exactly which one, even when there were as many as three hundred or more. He could tell immediately if an animal was ill. Because he had a great sense of humor and liked to make people laugh, he had learned or made up several strange, but humorous sayings. Three of Judy's favorites were: "If I should return during my absence, please detain me until I get back;" "Are you up for all day if you do not fall down?" and "We will do something, even if it is wrong." Being around her Dad so much likely contributed to Judy's somewhat warped sense of humor.

Despite her status as cowhand and tomboy, Judy's horizons and expectations were consistent with those of '50's teens. She needed to get scholarships to go to college, to be a nurse, like her Mother, so she was studious and hard working. She would have liked to study paleontology, botany, or become a veterinarian, but everyone said these careers were not appropriate for a girl. Lack of money also dictated a more practical career. She dutifully went to nurses' training after two years of college. To help pay for her training, she worked at St. Luke's Hospital nursery in Denver, Colorado, for six months, changing hundreds of diapers and making baby formula. She soon found that a previous injury to her left knee made it too painful to be standing or walking for eight hours a day, as a nurse must do, so she switched to elementary education. During her stint in the nursery, she observed how surprisingly little normal babies vary. Except for amount of hair, hair color, and eye color, babies look very similar, including the genitalia on the male babies. Many years later, when she began to see serious bone and reproductive malformations in baby mammals, it was obvious to her that they were not normal variations, as biologists who lacked her experience with both human and animal babies repeatedly told her.

Judy taught for a year in a one-room country school on the Dakota prairie near her family's ranch to earn enough money to go back to college; she earned her Bachelor of Arts degree in Science and Elementary Education in 1963. Her family moved to western Montana that summer, so her first goal after they settled into their new home in Missoula, Montana, was to find a teaching position. That autumn she began teaching fourth grade at Russell Elementary School in Missoula.

After a year in Missoula, a friend who was also a teacher introduced her to her life mate, Bob Hoy. He drove an old black government surplus van and was working his way through the University of Montana Forestry School to earn a degree in Wildlife Conservation. Bob too was a prairie child, from Nebraska, where he lived on a farm and had also milked cows. Bob loved the mountains, so his goal was to work as a game warden in western Montana for the State of Montana. Prior to graduating in spring of 1965, he worked one summer for the U. S. Forest Service near Rabbit Ears Pass, Colorado; one summer in the Bob Marshall Wilderness, Montana; and another summer as a seasonal park ranger in Glacier National Park.

Judy's elementary school job was over on June 4, 1966, and they were married that evening. After their honeymoon, they left for Bob's first assignment as game warden for Phillips County in northeastern Montana. They bought a home and two acres in Malta. The mosquitoes were so thick on the Highline in summer that when she was riding her horses, Judy had to wear a coat to keep from being bitten and a bandana over her mouth so she didn't breathe them. Winters on the Highline were just as challenging, with 100 miles per hour winds and temperatures below zero for a month at a time.

The prairies near Malta were even more expansive than those of South Dakota. There were even more fossils and artifacts scattered in the gravels and sands between the bunch grasses and sagebrush, and many new species of wildlife to watch and admire. She wrote her first scientific papers when she discovered and documented several significant Native American sites for the Montana Archaeological Society. Bob shared her passion for fossils and their fossil collection grew. Judy's artistic media expanded as she experimented with Native American painting techniques, using ochre and charcoal on sandstone. She also began to care for the occasional orphan coyote, antelope, or other young animals that were brought to them because Bob was the local game warden.

And she continued to teach, this time a fifth-grade class in the Malta Elementary School. Her fifth graders loved her, as she taught them to observe and respect their natural surroundings in addition to their normal book lessons. She shared her fossils and artifacts with them, and some became her field assistants. One young man went on to become a professional paleontologist.

She also first ran afoul of the narrow minded, when some of the parents complained that she was teaching Evolution. She was reprimanded by the principal, who told her to stick to the textbooks and teach that fossils were only theories. She had to bite her tongue not to reply, "I can't walk on the ground here without stepping on a theory." And the boxes of theories in her storeroom were getting heavier by the week!

After three years in exile in what he called mosquito land, Bob was transferred back to the mountains he loved, to the Missoula District Office of the Montana Department of Fish, Wildlife and Parks. He and Judy bought a piece of property near the Clark Fork River just east of East Missoula and built a home. Judy found a teaching position Franklin Elementary School in Missoula and continued to delight youngsters by teaching the wonders of the natural world, as well as the required curriculum.

After moving back to Western Montana, Judy set up a fund to which people could donate to help pay for food and medical bills for wildlife and she began to rehabilitate wildlife year around. She received mostly birds, a few mammals, and an occasional reptile for care. Wildlife rehabbers attempt to make injured wildlife well and release them so they can continue their wild lives. They also raise orphaned or kidnapped young birds and mammals, attempt to teach them how to survive in the wild, and release them. After release, the rehabber may continue to feed the youngsters until they learn to find food by themselves. This phase of rehabilitation can take anywhere from a few days to months, depending upon what the mammal or bird has to learn in order to survive on their own.

Most young animals who needed round the clock care came in summer when Judy was free from teaching responsibilities. She learned how to take care of the various animals by consulting with veterinarians, game farmers, falconers, by reading books, or by trial and error. The most important things she learned were from the animals themselves; the critters let her know if they were not content with what she provided.

In 1975, Judy quit teaching to pursue her passion for wildlife art and be able to do wildlife rehabilitation full time. That year, she received the first fledgling Flammulated Owl, a small dark-eyed owl, ever reported in Montana. Three adult Flammulated Owls had been previously reported, but no young ones. In subsequent years several more Flammulated Owls, including nestlings were brought to Judy for care. She began what turned into a ten-year campaign to get Flammulated Owls recognized as a nesting Montana species and to get them placed on the Forest Service's Species of Special Concern list. She wanted them to be considered in forest management plans, so their specialized habitat would be preserved. Unfortunately, by the time the Forest Service office had a biologist who would listen, much of western Montana's old growth Ponderosa-Douglas Fir forests appropriate for Flammulated Owl nesting habitat had been clear-cut. Interestingly, it was a woman biologist, who quickly placed the small owls on the list of Species of Special Concern. Another woman biologist was hired to find where Flammulated Owls were nesting and several sites were identified. During the 1990s, organized trips to hear the small owls hooting became popular with birders. Best of all, the Forest Service now considers the owls' needs in their forest management plans.

In 1979, Bob was transferred by MDFWP to be the game warden for the northern half of Ravalli County, Montana, from Hamilton north to the county line at Florence. He and Judy sold their home in Missoula and purchased 52 acres along Willoughby Creek in the irrigated dry lands southeast of Stevensville on the east side of the Bitterroot Valley. The historic Bitterroot River valley is located east of the granitic peaks of the forested Idaho batholith, known as the Bitterroot Mountains, which thrust skyward to the west. The Selway-Bitterroot Wilderness incorporates these mountains and their valleys. The gentle, rounded, metamorphic Sapphire Range serves as the eastern boundary of Ravalli County. The Bitterroot River follows its course from the mountains at the south end of Ravalli County, north to its confluence with the Clark Fork of the Columbia River near Missoula.

Bob and Judy built a modest log home overlooking Willoughby Creek in the middle of what would become their 100-acre property, after purchasing several parcels of land to the north of the creek bordering the original 52 acres. The riparian area along the creek and the bluff to the north of the creek are home to an interesting diversity of native plants, mosses, amphibians, reptiles, birds, and mammals. The property was placed under Nature Conservancy protection after Judy found a globally endangered plant that had never before been found in Montana. The Hoys wanted to ensure that the rare plants and mosses would be protected and that the birds and other animals would always have a home.

A 1930's era homestead on the west end of their property had an old house and several outbuildings. The rooms of these buildings were modified to house raptors and other birds, or to serve as flight rooms where young birds could practice flying. These rooms and several wire pens provided a temporary home for hundreds of injured or orphaned animals beginning in 1980. The Hoys called their place The Bitterroot Wildlife Rehabilitation Center and Judy began training other rehabbers and coordinating wildlife rehabilitation activities in western Montana. She was given permission to use the Bitterroot Audubon Society to umbrella the fund for the western Montana rehabbers and called it the Bitterroot Audubon Wildlife Rehab Fund. Most of the western Montana rehabbers were and are sub-permittees with whom Judy has worked. Together they have cared for between 100 and 300 birds and many mammals each year for more than 35 years.

By trial and error, suggestions from friends, and observing the actions of the animals, Judy developed treatments for the variety of injuries and illnesses she and her sub-permittees confronted among the different species of birds and mammals that were brought to them. Most fledgling birds ended up at the Bitterroot Wildlife Rehab Center after being raised by other rehabbers because Judy was the only one with flight rooms. Since Bob was a Montana Department of Fish, Wildlife and Parks game warden, Judy and Bob were given special permission to care for game animals, at least temporarily, until they could be released, relocated to zoos, or taken to the Wildlife Rehab Facility in Helena, Montana.

Judy didn't just spend time with animals. She has kept several healthy birds that were flightless due to wing injuries for use in educational presentations about wild birds and wildlife ecology to schools, churches, civic clubs, and other organizations. In recognition of her contributions as both a wildlife rehabilitator and community educator, in June 1994, Patrick J. Graham, then Director of the Montana Department of Fish, Wildlife and Parks presented Judy with a framed letter of commendation that read:

"Dear Judy:

"It takes a special gift of dedication and kindness to care for orphaned and injured wildlife. Since 1968, you have shared that gift, perhaps more than anyone else in Montana, with unselfish dedication.

"Caring for and rehabilitating over 2,400 birds, mammals and reptiles is a significant contribution to the conservation of our wild resources. As important has been your work in educating families, school classes and adult groups. You have greatly magnified your impact by passing on your knowledge and dedication, training over 35 other rehabilitators to care for wildlife.

"On behalf of Montana's wildlife, its citizens, and the department, I thank you for sharing your kindness and dedication.

"Sincerely, Patrick J. Graham, Director"

Judy became increasingly involved in educating the public about wildlife and threats to the western Montana environment. She built a network of contacts in the news media, in academia, among health professionals, and in government agencies. She also kept detailed records on a variety of kinds of observations. She recorded many first records for Ravalli County of butterflies, plants, and mosses, as well as several first state records. She kept records each year of all butterflies that she and Bob saw and when they were first and last seen, reporting the data to a butterfly expert in Missoula who is writing a book on

Montana butterflies. She also photographs dragonflies and damselflies in Ravalli County to report to the Odonata database. The same type of report has been sent to the Montana Natural Heritage Program concerning birds, amphibians, and reptiles seen each year since 1980, invaluable data as some populations are declining rapidly.

Consequently, in summer of 1994, when all of the over 150 young-of-the-year Yellow-bellied Marmots on their property died suddenly, as well as most of the Western Toads, which had previously been very numerous on their land, Judy and Bob were concerned. Always curious, Judy wanted to know why. Documenting health problems and anomalous die-offs in western Montana wildlife and trying to determine the causes again changed the focus of Judy's life. In 1996, she stopped doing wildlife art and began doing wildlife research. She continued to rehabilitate wildlife, which provided much of the database on the flood of new health problems in animals brought to the rehab centers in western Montana.

The roads of western Montana are tricky to drive by day and more so at night. White-tailed deer will often suddenly leap from the road ditch into the path of on-coming vehicles, many of which are going too fast. Between 1979 and 2000, Bob, now retired from the Montana Department of Fish, Wildlife and Parks, picked up accident-killed deer in his area consisting of the northern half of Ravalli County. Judy, with permission from the MDFWP, used accident-killed deer carcasses as animal food for carnivores, both mammals and birds, in her care. Some, such as cougars and eagles, require a lot of meat. Over the past three and a half decades, Judy has butchered or necropsied roughly 2,000 dead deer.

Each summer until 2005, the Hoys cared for between three and fifteen injured, orphaned, or kidnapped white-tailed and mule deer, antelope, bighorn sheep, and moose and elk calves, preponderantly white-tailed deer fawns. Some had been hit by vehicles or hay swathers, stomped by livestock, attacked by dogs, hit fences, or were caught in fences. Many had simply been stolen from their mothers by well-meaning persons who found them where their mothers had hidden them; the Hoys call them kidnap victims.

A summer visit to the Bitterroot Wildlife Rehabilitation Center was always a delight, because numerous tiny fawns were playing among the trees in the very large deer pen or were running around in the trees and bushes in the yard or creek bottom. Wherever they were, they scampered in for their milk bottles when called. For many years in the morning or evening, older residents of the sanctuary, fostered fawns from previous years, could be seen grazing in or bouncing across the hay field or creek bottom. One doe with a crippled front leg lived to raise eleven fawns. Only the smallest fawns were confined to the deer pen to protect them from dogs; all others were completely free to roam.

As a result, Judy and Bob each have more than five decades of experience observing the growth, behavior, and anatomy of deer and other large ungulates (nearly seven decades if you count their childhood years among farm animals).

On April 11, 1996, Bob picked up a vehicle-killed yearling male (buck) white-tailed deer. When Judy lifted the hind leg to cut it off to feed the eagles, she found that the male deer had no scrotum. It would have looked like a female (doe) except that it had a short penis sheath hidden in the still long winter hair. She noted these unusual characteristics, but thought it was just a fluke. She had previously seen many hundreds of male deer both dead and alive, yet she had never seen one like that before. Between that day and the end of June, Bob picked up eight more buck deer. Only one, a three-year-old, had normal male genitalia. The rest, all yearlings, born in spring of 1995, had half a scrotum, no scrotum, or the left half of the scrotum directly in front of the right half of the scrotum.

This was very alarming to the Hoys, so on July 18, they had the MDFWP biologist come and get the two vehicle-killed yearling bucks Bob had picked up that day. One had very malformed genitalia according to all who observed it, a total of five people, including Judy, Bob, two male neighbors who were hunters, and the MDFWP biologist who picked up the two deer to take them to the MDFWP laboratory. The other buck had normal genitalia, the first normal male deer of nine observed that were born in 1995. Oddly, the laboratory report stated that "the impact with the vehicle caused the deer that five people agreed was malformed to just appear to be malformed to an inexperienced observer." The MDFWP biologist who took the deer to the lab said, "That is ridiculous! I do not know why they would say a thing like that." when he and Judy opened the report and read it together.

Throughout history, leaders, politicians, and bureaucrats, when confronted with evidence of a problem that they do not want to deal with, consistently discredit (or "shoot") the messenger. In Greek mythology, Cassandra was endowed with the gift of foresight and the curse that she and her descendants would never be believed. Ironically, in some versions, the gift involved understanding animals. Clearly Judy is a descendant of Cassandra.

The MDFWP report was the first volley in the MDFWP's now over twenty-year long battle to discredit Judy and Bob, and dismiss their evidence of obvious malformations in wildlife. Within three years of presenting Judy a commendation for her dedication and knowledge of wildlife, a top MDFWP official denied that malformations had been observed and referred to Judy as "some woman on television pointing at deer scrotums." Subsequently, Judy and Bob have repeatedly been dismissed as "inexperienced observers" or worse. Wildlife officials consistently have claimed that any abnormalities were the results of trauma associated with vehicle impact, even though many of the animals reported with birth defects were either alive or died of other causes. Their two peer-reviewed scientific papers in respected international journals have been libelously referred to as biased and unprofessional, and the credentials of their co-authors have been unfairly questioned. Judy has been a coauthor on two more peer-reviewed studies since those first two studies were published, one in 2015 and one in 2016, concerning health issues on wildlife and humans.

In 2005, the Montana Department of Fish, Wildlife and Park's policy was changed. The new policy is that all fawns that cannot be returned to their mother are to be shot, and cannot be rehabilitated, even if the mother has been killed. According to the new policy, rehabbers are no longer allowed to care for game animals of any species.

In spring of 1997, during necropsies of pregnant accident-killed white-tailed does, Judy found two female fetuses from two different does with underdeveloped skull and upper jaw, resulting in an underbite. As she was already documenting and measuring the male genitalia and teat placement on both males and females, she also began recording incidences and data on deer with underbite. In 2002, the Hoys, in collaboration with two retired scientists, a vertebrate physiologist, Ted Kerstetter, Ph.D., and an environmental chemist, Douglas Seba, Ph.D., published a paper in *The Journal of Environmental Biology* on the genital malformations and a skewed sex ratio in favor of males in the northern Ravalli County white-tailed deer population.

Even after the paper was published, Judy continued to measure accident-killed deer that Bob picked up. After Bob retired from the MDFWP, Judy continued to track prevalence of the birth defects on the white-tailed deer by examining and measuring road-killed animals on the roadside. She also measured and necropsied any dead deer found on the Hoy's property. Eventually, she and her colleagues had enough data to publish more scientific papers on the reproductive malformations and the underbite. They discovered the birth defects they had been documenting are all consistent with mineral deficiencies and consequent disruption of the fetal thyroid hormones, in addition to gene disruption during development. Zinc deficiency causes underdevelopment of the male genitalia and manganese and calcium deficiency causes the underbite and other bone malformations. Also, early in development, disruption of specific Sonic Hedgehog genes results in abnormal growth and placement of the teeth, facial bones, and various organs.

Between May 2008 and May 2011, Indiana University graduate students published three papers, the Bitterroot Valley Risk Assessment papers, concerning the malformations and the possible sources of thyroid hormone disrupting toxins. The Hoys, biologist Gary T. Haas, and I coauthored "Observations of Brachygnathia Superior on Ruminant Species in Western Montana, USA," which was published in *Wildlife Biology in Practice* in December 2011. Unfortunately, both malformations are also now being observed in many other mammal species; underdeveloped skull and facial bones have been observed in many individuals of reptile, bird, and mammal species, including human children. Because officials of the State of Montana still deny an abnormal incidence of malformations in either wild or domestic animals, the Hoys are working with independent scientists in Montana and scientists from other states.

In 2015, Judy coauthored a third study with Stephanie Seneff and Nancy Swanson, "The High Cost of Pesticides: Human and Animal Diseases" published in *Poultry, Fisheries and Wildlife Sciences*. Another study with the same authors titled "Evidence that Glyphosate is a Causative Agent in Chronic, Sub-clinical Metabolic Acidosis and Mitochondrial Dysfunction" was published in the *International Journal of Human Nutrition and Functional Medicine* in 2016. The disrupted cellular functions and developmental defects we have been observing on wild and domestic animals are identical to those experimentally induced in studies using horse foals, cattle, goats, rabbits, rodents, and quail. The proper levels of essential minerals and thyroid hormones, as well as normal gene regulation, are needed to direct the normal growth of the cells of the brain, nerves, bones, muscles, reproductive organs, eyes, ears, the internal organs, the immune system, especially the thymus and other organs of developing vertebrate young. The serious health problems in humans and most other vertebrate animals are acute deficiency of important minerals, mitochondrial disorders, metabolic acidosis, gene disruption, and hormone disruption, especially of the thyroid hormones. Birth defects as a result of those health issues are called epigenetic changes and have been shown by studies to be passed on for several generations.

Over nearly two decades of observing the increasing frequency of malformations in Montana wildlife, several suspects have emerged as likely causal agents, including many of the most used pesticides, mainly organochlorine fungicides and herbicides, relatively new insecticides containing nicotine called neonicotinoids, and especially, the most used herbicide, Roundup and its primary ingredient glyphosate.

Chlorothalonil, also called Bravo®, is a fungicide. This widely used product is chemically altered by the sun and rain or when residues are burned in wildfires to produce more toxic nitrile metabolites and free cyanide, all of which are severely thyroid hormone disrupting. Chlorothalonil exposure also damages the lungs and the liver on vertebrate species causing the exposed animals to be more susceptible to all other toxins.

Glyphosate and chlorothalonil appear to work synergistically. The correlation of effects on plant and animal cells and the timing of the sudden manifestation of previously undocumented birth defects have made these two pesticides the top suspects for causing the birth defects and other health issues, which began in spring 1995. Testing will prove or disprove this hypothesis.

Judy has written this book to help people know individual animals and to understand that an individual's life is valuable and precious. Most importantly, the main focus of this book is to inform people of a serious problem concerning the health of wildlife and domestic animals that needs immediate attention. And hopefully, because many young with birth defects will be born before the toxins causing them are banned from use, Judy's book will show that some specific birth defects can be mitigated to allow normal growth.

As Patrick Graham of the MDFWP said in his commendation letter to Judy in 1994: "It takes a special gift of dedication and kindness to care for orphaned and injured wildlife. Since 1968, you have shared that gift, perhaps more than anyone else in Montana, with unselfish dedication."

Underdeveloped upper facial bones, resulting in a short upper bill, have been documented on Golden Eagles and many other avian species. Golden Eagles have in recent years had high mortality from lead poisoning, electrocution on power lines, and hitting the turning blades at wind farms. Developmental malformations in hatchlings reduce the number of viable young who survive to replace the adults killed, resulting in an observable decline in the population.

REFERENCES

These are references for the studies concerning birth defects and health issues in animals for which Judy Hoy was a co-author. The hundreds of references in these studies collectively provide thousands of references to more studies concerning the effects of environmental toxins, especially the devastating effects pesticides have on vital cellular functions.

Hoy JA, Hoy RD, Seba D, Kerstetter TH (2002) Genital Abnormalities in White-tailed Deer (*Odocoileus virginianus*) in West-central Montana: Pesticide Exposure as a Possible Cause. *J Environ Biol* 23:189-97.
http://www.ncbi.nlm.nih.gov/pubmed/12602857

Hoy JA, Haas GT, Hoy RD, Hallock P (2011) Observations of Brachygnathia Superior in Wild Ruminants in Western Montana, USA. *Wildl Biol Pract* 7(2): 15-29.
http://dx.doi.org/10.2461/wbp.2011.7.13

Hoy J, Swanson N and Seneff S. The High Cost of Pesticides: Human and Animal Diseases. *Poult Fish Wildl Sci.* 2015; 3:132. doi:10.4172/2375-446X.1000132

Swanson N, Hoy J, Seneff S (2016) Evidence that Glyphosate is a Causative Agent in Chronic Sub-clinical Metabolic Acidosis and Mitochondrial Dysfunction. *Int J Hum Nutr Funct Med* epub in press. http://intjhumnutrfunctmed.org/journal/2016pdf/IJHNFM_2016_v4q1 p9 GlyphosateMetabolicAcidosisMitochondria.pdf

**All lives depend on
photosynthesis by plants.
Without plants, we die.**

Jenny was a member of our family for 13 years. She was very sensitive to environmental toxins throughout her life and succumbed in summer 2015 to the health issues they caused. Jenny loved to ride on our electric Club Car.

HEROES

Here I stand in my make-believe cape,
Trying to save Earth from invisible rape.
Lex Luthors have drenched her with pesticide.
Heroes, please fight on our planet's side!

Toxins released into her air by day
Drop down to where the young ones play,
Causing acidosis and cellular blight.
Pesticides are our Kryptonite.

Just one brief exposure to a potential Mom
Sets off an epigenetic time bomb.
Watching malformed young ones, dying and sick
Makes each day like living a bad horror flick.

Destroying their future. Is it fair?
Parents and grandparents, do not you care?
When all life is gone, who will be left to mind?
Will the last hero standing please push rewind?

Salute the heroes
who do their best each day to
protect our planet.

CHAPTER 1
CHANGING THE FACE OF A FAWN

My husband Bob and I run a wildlife rehabilitation center at our home in the Bitterroot Valley of western Montana. Consequently, we receive many calls concerning injured or orphaned wildlife, especially in spring. On June 10, 1998, a call came from someone who was concerned because a newborn fawn had either lost its mother or had been abandoned. I didn't know when I answered the phone that a lost fawn with a malformed face was destined to change the lives of many animals and people, especially mine.

The woman said the fawn followed her young son everywhere he went, crying frantically like a loud sheep bleat. That is the classic indication a fawn is actually in trouble and extremely hungry. Bob went immediately to check out the report. We wanted to determine whether it was possible to reunite the fawn with its mother before taking it away from the area where the doe might return to care for it. Part of Bob's job as a game warden for the Montana Department of Fish, Wildlife and Parks was to check out reports of injured or orphaned game animals.

Bob soon returned with the homeliest white-tailed deer fawn I had ever seen. Her normal-sized lower jaw was so much longer than her short, dished, underdeveloped upper face that she looked somewhat like a bulldog. This resemblance was even more pronounced because she could not close her mouth over her protruding lower incisors. Her skull was narrow with close-set eyes and a rounded, upturned muzzle. She reminded me of an insect, so I named her Firefly. The fawn appeared to be three or four days old and, as predicted by her insistent bleat for food, she was extremely hungry. Her ribs and backbone showed through her spotted skin far more than is usual on a newborn fawn. They always appear thin, but besides suffering from starvation, Firefly's hair felt dry and brittle to the touch, indicating acute dehydration.

Three years earlier in spring 1995, we began seeing several specific new birth defects in newborn wildlife, some previously unreported in the scientific literature. Those most often observed were unusual malformations of male genitalia and of skeletal structure in both sexes, with underdeveloped skull and facial bones being most prevalent. Our immediate neighbors and many other livestock owners in western Montana reported seeing the same birth defects on their newborn sheep, goats, horse and mule foals, and domestic calves. When neighborhood ranchers learned I was interested in the unusual birth defects, they often brought bodies of malformed livestock to me to examine, especially those of newborns. In addition, I was able to examine and measure different characteristics of fetus, fawn, and adult white-tailed deer, mule deer, and elk carcasses that Bob picked up as part of his job as game warden. Also, in the years after 1995, many live fawns and hatchling birds brought to us for rehabilitation had birth defects. Examining and recording measurements and other information from such a wide range of affected animals provided a huge amount of data, which I was able to organize and use later.

The facial anatomy of ruminants (grazing animals who have stomachs with four chambers such as cattle, goats, and deer) or camelids (grazing animals with three-chambered stomachs) is quite different from that of many other animals. The front part of the upper mouth contains paired premaxillary bones which are covered by a thick pad of tissue similar to the hard palate. With no upper front teeth, incisors in the lower jaw normally contact this dental pad, pinching grass and other foliage between the two surfaces and tearing it off so the animal can pull food into the mouth with its tongue. Nearly half of the deer, elk, bighorn sheep, and antelope we have examined in the last 20 years had underbite, with the normal-length lower jaw longer than the upper. This unnatural condition in a grazing animal is serious because the incisors do not contact the dental pad, greatly reducing the animal's ability to graze efficiently. Horses and other animals who do have both upper and lower incisors are also impaired when their teeth do not connect normally.

The underbite on all the animals I have had the opportunity to examine during that time was a result of upper facial bones, and occasionally the front of the skull, not being fully developed. We have been unable to determine exactly why the premaxillary bones in developing young of grazing animals are those most often affected by disrupted growth. The disruption of specific genes that dictate size and placement of the teeth and facial bones during development is suspected as a primary factor. Mineral deficiencies appear to be another factor, specifically of manganese and calcium; they have been shown by studies on cattle to cause underdeveloped facial bones and crooked legs.

The year before Firefly was found, we had received a newborn male white-tailed deer fawn who was orphaned when his mother was killed by a vehicle. He had an underbite, less severe than Firefly's, in addition to crooked bones in both front legs. I named him Skippy. We raised and released him with the other fawns we cared for that year. His slightly crooked front legs did not hinder his ability to walk or run. With only a minor underbite, Skippy was able to bite off foliage well enough to obtain adequate nutrition so he continued to do well after he was weaned.

I feared Firefly would have a much harder time getting enough food to survive after she was weaned. My first thought was to euthanize her because I didn't want her to die a slow death from starvation. I had never seen a live fawn with an underbite as severe as hers. A female fetus who died when her mother was hit by a vehicle in winter 1997 had a more severely malformed face than Firefly's. Her facial bones and muscles were so badly deformed she would likely not have lived for more than a few hours after birth.

Firefly's lower front incisors were far in front of the dental pad. Her premaxillary bones, where the dental pad is located at the front of the upper jaw, were short and narrow. Like any other wild grazing animal, Firefly would have to bite off foliage for nourishment. With her lower incisors so far in front of her dental pad, any plants she tried to bite off would slip out through the gap between them. I feared she would not have a long or happy life.

As I examined her, contemplating her bleak future, the tiny fawn looked up expectantly with her large, expressive eyes. After the pleading look she gave me, the only option I wanted to consider was to quickly get her a bottle of warm milk. I decided that raising her, severe birth defect and all, was a way to observe how much an underbite actually affects a deer's ability to obtain adequate food. Euthanizing her was always an option, especially if it became apparent that she couldn't eat well enough to thrive after she was weaned.

I was very concerned that so many herbivores were suddenly being born with debilitating birth defects, especially an underbite. This surprisingly common problem in deer and other grazing animals here in western Montana had only been previously documented in the scientific literature prior to 1995 on two white-tailed deer fawns in the eastern United States. I could find no reports for underbite in other wild grazing animals. In 1969, L. A. Ryel, a researcher who studied white-tailed deer in Michigan, examined over 36 thousand of them for facial bone and tooth malformations. He did not find a single white-tailed deer with underbite in that very extensive study.

Firefly at a week old had short upper facial bones with protruding lower teeth and lip. Photo by Alan Nelson.

The underbite phenomenon became even more concerning when I and other wildlife rehabbers began receiving several hatchling and fledgling birds with that problem each year. All my life I have had an insatiable curiosity regarding unusual conditions I observe in nature. The sudden occurrence of the same birth defect in a large number of individual newborns in multiple species of both mammals and birds was by far the most unusual phenomenon I had ever encountered, and one of the most menacing to the animals affected. To make matters worse, we were seeing an increasing number of newborn male mammals with reproductive malformations. Most alarmingly, all of the previously unreported and extremely unusual birth defects on males were also first observed in spring 1995.

Because it seemed important to document the birth defects, I began examining and recording measurements of the bite and other unusual anatomy, including the external skin of male reproductive organs on accident-killed deer. I wanted to know whether the birth defects increased or decreased each year. Tracking the prevalence of underbite

26

and other abnormalities in a common animal like white-tailed deer, especially the young ones, would hopefully help determine the cause.

The underdevelopment of upper facial bones, referred to as underbite by most people, is called brachygnathia superior by the medical profession. We were able to quantify the bite, if present on an animal, by measuring the distance between the front of the dental pad and the top of the middle incisors. We also collected comparison measurements between the width of the incisors relative to that of the dental pad on each dead white-tailed deer. Bob and I, with the help of our friend Gary T. Haas, who is a biologist, examined and measured well over 1000 white-tailed deer between 1996 and 2014. We also examined and measured smaller samples of six other species of wild and domestic grazing animals between 2005 and 2010. My brilliant and talented sister, Dr. Pamela Hallock Muller, Ph.D., another biologist, made charts and tables with our facial measurements and helped me write a paper on those malformations. In December 2011, *Wildlife Biology in Practice* published our study titled "Observations of Brachygnathia Superior in Wild Ruminants in Western Montana, USA." This paper is free on the Internet, so anyone can read it.

What I learned by caring for Firefly was responsible for my intense interest in facial malformations on vertebrate species. Because of her short premaxillary bones and consequent protruding lower jaw and lower lip, she was not able to nurse from the baby bottle nipple I usually used for newborn fawns. Her inability to completely close her mouth over her lower incisors impaired her ability to suckle. Being unable to nurse from her mother's small teats might have been the reason she was dehydrated and starving. I could find nothing else wrong with her.

I found a long, soft nipple originally designed for lambs. After I enlarged the hole in the nipple for the milk to easily flow through, she was able to drink from it because it was long enough to go clear to the back of her tongue. The milk formula, consisting of five ounces of fresh goat milk with a tablespoon of whipping cream mixed in, ran down the back of her throat when she suckled. All she had to do was swallow and she literally gulped it down. She was a hungry little deer.

After three days on the fresh goat milk formula, Firefly began showing the definitive symptoms of lactose intolerance. She would flinch, hump up, and make a grunting noise after she drank several swallows of milk. I had seen this reaction in some other fawns I had raised. It happens when the milk causes an inflammatory reaction in a fawn's first stomach. Deer have four stomach-like pouches in their digestive system and chew their cud like all ruminants. During her previous feeding, I had noticed Firefly's stool had mucous in it, which is typical of inflammation in a newborn's digestive system.

Before receiving Firefly, we had cared for other young animals with symptoms of lactose intolerance, including coyote pups, fox pups, and mountain lion kittens. Two of the fox pups were brought to me because their parents had abandoned them. That seems harsh, but when wild newborns are ill, the parents usually concentrate their efforts on the healthy siblings. When the fox pups drank milk, it caused stomach cramping and vomiting. I had learned how to alleviate both from treating them and other youngsters with lactose intolerance and immune system disorders. At each feeding until the animal is weaned, I put a tablet of the homeopathic cell salt, Hyland's Calc. Phos. 6X®, and a tablet consisting of all twelve homeopathic cell salts, Hyland's Bioplasma®, in the milk formula after warming it.

My neighbor, Jean Atthowe, had given me calc. phos. 6X to help animals with broken bones to mend faster. Jean helped many animals and people by giving me that first bottle. I now use Hyland's Calc. Phos. 30X®, because it works even better than the 6X, but without Jean's kindness, I would not have known about either. The calc. phos. 6X had worked well when I gave it to animals with broken bones, resulting in a bone taking only two thirds as long to heal than without it. At that time, I gave one tablet of calc. phos. 6X to an injured animal three or four times a day in the milk formula for mammal young and in the food for birds of all ages. Now I use calc. phos. 30X, which works even better. When I use it for birds or mammals with broken bones, the bones heal in half the time it takes when no cell salts are given. The faster wild ones get out of their splints, the better their prognosis and the less work for me.

When I was caring for Firefly, I was still using calc. phos. 6X and bioplasma combined. What happened to her after I began putting the cell salt tablets in her milk was absolutely astounding. Almost immediately, as I expected, she stopped having symptoms of lactose intolerance. She could drink her entire bottle of milk without acting like someone had stabbed her in the stomach and her stool became normal solid pellets, like small golden raisins. She was soon drinking 10 ounces of formula at a feeding, gradually increasing her consumption to a pint of milk every four hours. I continued putting cell salts in her milk each time so she could digest her food properly and grow strong bones. I didn't discover until a little over two weeks later what else the cell salts were doing.

Firefly was a sweet little fawn who quickly came to me when I called, and was exceptionally tame and affectionate for a white-tailed deer. In fact, she was too friendly, even following unfamiliar people around. When she was a little over a week old, Alan Nelson, a good friend and superb wildlife photographer, came to visit us to photograph wild birds in our yard and the fawns we had in our care that spring. Firefly followed us while Alan was photographing the pretty fawns with normal faces. Fortunately, he took two photos of her, even though he said she was so ugly that she was cute. As it turned out, those two photos were scientifically the most valuable ones he took that day.

Almost two weeks after Alan took her picture, I began teaching Firefly to eat rolled grain by holding it in the palm of my hand. It took her just a few minutes to learn to lick it into her mouth. While watching her eat, I suddenly realized she had hardly any underbite and her upper jaw was almost normal in length. She no longer had that strange bulldog look. Her rounded, upturned muzzle had become more squared, like a normal deer muzzle. It was difficult for me to believe what I could clearly see: Firefly's upper facial bones had grown to nearly normal size!

According to the information on underbite in our livestock manual, and what veterinarians had told me, an animal could not recover from being born with an underbite unless surgery was performed to shorten the lower jaw. This would be done only if an animal was very valuable, such as a thoroughbred horse foal. Other young animals born with underbite were, and often still are, euthanized. If I had given up on Firefly when she came to me, I may never have learned how to easily stimulate normal growth in underdeveloped facial bones of newborn mammals and birds with an amazing little pill.

In another week, when Firefly was three and a half weeks old, her face and bite were nearly perfect. Her lower lip still protruded slightly, but her lower incisors completely contacted the dental pad, allowing her to graze normally. The upper facial bones had not grown to normal in any of the other animals I had seen with underbite, including Skippy. Most of the other fawns, foals, calves, young goats, and lambs born with underbite drank their own mother's milk, usually much better for them than any substitute, including goat milk. But when all those untreated young grew to be adults, their underbite had neither changed nor become normal. It was quite clear the only thing I gave Firefly that could have stimulated her skull and upper face to grow to normal size and configuration was the cell salts used to mediate her lactose intolerance.

From what people in the medical community with whom I have discussed underbite have told me, that particular birth defect is assumed to be caused by the parents' genes. If both have a genetic trait for a longer-than-normal lower jaw, it can be passed to their offspring. While it appeared the veterinarians I had consulted must be wrong, they actually weren't. It is true that surgery is the only way to correct an underbite when the lower jaw is too long. However, they had not considered that the lower jaw is completely normal in length in the animals we were observing with underbite. Instead, the premaxillary bones on the upper face are abnormal, and they are too short, not too long. In a few cases, but far less prevalent, the lower jaw fails to grow to normal length and the premaxillary bones are normal, resulting in an overbite. I have since found that if an animal with a short lower jaw is given cell salts soon after birth, the lower jaw will grow to normal length.

More recently, by reading studies on cellular mineral deficiencies, I found that those of manganese, calcium, and phosphorous cause certain bones to prematurely stop growing during development. Mineral deficiencies also seriously disrupt the function of fetal thyroid hormones. Insufficient zinc causes the reproductive malformations we were finding on deer and other mammals; that of magnesium has adverse effects on the developing immune system, resulting in autoimmune disorders.

When I was caring for Firefly, I did not know what caused those adverse health effects on newborns. What I did know was that she and many other animals born with underbite (brachygnathia superior) had experienced an epigenetic change that primarily targeted the growth of the premaxillary bones. Their facial bones were actually genetically programmed to be normal, making it possible to stimulate the underdeveloped ones to grow to appropriate size. These are a completely different type of birth defect than the genetic one that results in the lower jaw being abnormally long.

The supplement (cell salt calc. phos 6X) I gave Firefly and a coyote pup named Blondie is an electrolyte that stimulates the cells that need it to actively transport calcium from the blood stream across cell membranes. It was apparent that bioplasma, which contains all twelve cell salts (also called tissue salts), stimulates cells to uptake other minerals needed for normal function. From Firefly's changes, it appeared those I gave her stimulated her cells to uptake calcium, manganese, magnesium, potassium, iron, copper, zinc, nickel, selenium, and other important minerals much more efficiently. Having them going into the cells that needed them apparently stimulated her stunted upper facial bones to grow to the size dictated by the genes inherited from her parents. At least that was my hypothesis. This hypothesis has subsequently been strengthened by causing underdeveloped bones in many other newborn mammals and birds with underbite or overbite to grow to normal by giving them the cell salt tablets.

Firefly's bite looked perfect when I checked it every few days for several weeks, turning her into a beautiful fawn, no longer strange-looking and homely. She was like the ugly duckling who became a lovely swan in the fairytale, but the change in Firefly's face was not caused by magic.

When she was about three months old, it suddenly occurred to me I should take photos to prove that her premaxillary bones had grown to normal. I wrote to Alan Nelson, asking him to send copies of the two photos he had taken of her at a week old. Thus, I was fortunate to have both before and after pictures. They made Firefly famous in the medical world when my friend Dr. Douglas Seba showed them in his presentation to the 1999 International Symposium on Man and His Environment, held each year in Dallas, Texas. The doctors, veterinarians, and other professionals were extremely interested in Firefly's complete recovery from such a serious birth defect.

We had eight other fawns in 1998 as companions for Firefly in our large deer pen, where the fawns lived until they were about six weeks old. In mid-July, we let them out of the pen during the day so they could learn what plants to eat, how to avoid predators, and many other skills they needed to survive in the wild. When I called them at midday and in the evening, the fawns came running from wherever they were on our land to drink their milk. At the evening feeding, they followed us back into the pen where they spent the night safe from wild predators and neighborhood dogs.

Four of the fawns were males (named General, Flapjack, Red, and Ghost) and four were females (Maggie, June, Julie, and Fluffy). Maggie, June, and Julie all appeared to be normal at birth. We gave Fluffy her name because her spotted fawn hair was ruffled and upright rather than lying smooth and flat like that of most fawns. The hair on the top of her head was quite long and stood straight up, something like a 1960's era rock star hair style. After reading studies on hypothyroidism, it became apparent that Fluffy's strange appearance was caused by disrupted hair growth, a common symptom of that condition. She also had an abnormally slim muzzle, with a dish face and small eyes, but she did not have an underbite like Firefly. Two of the male fawns, General and Flapjack, had short, misaligned scrotums.

Four of nine white-tailed deer fawns with birth defects strongly indicated there was a serious disruption in the normal development of these babies, and that the birth defects were occurring in numbers that were unprecedented. We reported our observations and concerns to the biologist who was head of the Montana Department of Fish, Wildlife and Parks wildlife laboratory. He came to our place to examine Firefly, General, and Flapjack, the fawns with the most serious malformations, then told Bob and me that the three youngsters did show the birth defects we had described. After a wildlife veterinarian had examined them at my request the week before, he stated in writing that the three fawns had "congenital developmental malformations." His detailed report was what prompted the MDFWP biologist to come to our place to examine the fawns himself.

Red, another male fawn, was normal in development, but redder in color than most white-tailed deer fawns. He was quite gentle and easy to handle, so I had both the wildlife veterinarian and the MDFWP biologist examine Red to compare his normal bilateral scrotum with the short, misaligned scrotums on General and Flapjack. The fourth male, Ghost, came to us two weeks after the others were examined. He was orphaned when a vehicle killed his mother. His hair was a light cream color, so light that his white spots were barely visible. Even though Ghost's hair was odd-colored (called leucism, meaning partial loss of pigmentation resulting in white, pale, or patchy coloration), his bite and genitalia were normal.

We subsequently reported the genital malformations and their prevalence in white-tailed deer (as well as a skewed sex ratio in favor of males) in a peer reviewed study published in April 2002, titled "Genital Abnormalities in White-tailed Deer (*Odocoileus virginianus*) in West-central Montana: Pesticide Exposure as a Possible Cause." My friend, Dr. Theodore H. Kerstetter (unfortunately now deceased), a retired zoology professor from Humboldt State University and a real-life hero, wrote the study, published by the *Journal of Environmental Biology*. I also wrote an extensive report to the Director of the MDFWP and to other state agencies about the increasing incidence of underdeveloped facial bones in mammals and birds.

Underbite had been increasing each year in the accident-killed white-tailed deer that Bob collected for disposal from roadsides and yards. I carefully examined and measured nearly all of them. We also inspected a number of hunter-killed big game animals for underbite each year. What we found was disturbing, as underbite was becoming more common in all species we checked, including mule deer, white-tailed deer, elk, bison, bighorn sheep, and pronghorn antelope, as well as domestic grazing animals. By spring 2001, the prevalence of underbite on white-tailed deer fawns born in Ravalli County was up to an alarming 56%. To my relief, the underbite frequency began going down in 2002 and continued decreasing each year through 2006 to a low of 33%. It was concerning when the underbite suddenly doubled to over 70% on deer fawns the next spring. After 2007, the average prevalence of underbite on 156 white-tailed deer fawns I measured during the next eight years was 67%. Only 33% had a normal bite. Mule deer and pronghorn antelope appear to have a similar extremely high incidence of underbite, based on measurements of hunter-killed heads.

It is difficult to think about the large number of animals being born with underbite now suffering long-term undernourishment because of inability to eat normally, especially in winter. Slow starvation is a sad way to die. Fortunately, after her facial bones grew to normal, Firefly was no longer likely to perish in that manner.

Filling nine bottles to feed fawns four times a day that summer and fall kept us very busy. Fortunately, they all thrived and by fall had grown winter coats. Fluffy's new hair came in soft, curly, and puffed up, similar to her fawn hair, making her easy to distinguish from other deer on our land. After the fawns were permanently released from the pen, Fluffy and Firefly remained close, browsing, resting, and coming in for grain together. All of the fawns stayed on our land most of the time during the fall hunting season, so none were killed. Each year, I breathed a big sigh of relief when hunting season ended with no casualties.

Near the end of November, the inside of the eyelids on all nine fawns began reacting to something in the air, becoming quite red and swollen with a green discharge leaking from the corners of their eyes. Firefly's were worse than the others. It was apparent she was still highly sensitive to toxic substances carried in the moist weather fronts that often passed through the Bitterroot Valley. All the fawns had been weaned, so they were no longer receiving cell salts. To counteract the effects of the chemicals in the air, I began pressing a tablet of bioplasma and one of calc. phos. 6X into the sides of nine apple slices to give to the fawns each morning and night, when they came to eat their grain. Their eyes soon cleared up and the winter passed with no more problems.

In spring, when grass and other plants began growing, the yearling fawns no longer came for grain and apple slices. Consequently, I was not able to give Firefly the cell salt tablets on a regular basis. I had a new collection of fawns and baby birds to care for, so did not have time to keep track of the yearlings. By the time they are a year old, the released white-tailed deer are usually quite wild and completely on their own.

Two of the orphaned fawns brought to us for rehab in spring 1999 had underbite, but not as severe as Firefly's. I put one of each of the two cell salt tablets in the milk formula for all fawns that year, from their first bottle to the last. All of them grew up with no problems and the premaxillary bones of the two with underbite grew to normal in a little less than two weeks, so all their incisors contacted the dental pad as ruminants' incisors are supposed to do. I had begun to expect that outcome, but each time it happened, it was almost as thrilling as the first time with Firefly's recovery.

Most importantly, by spring 1999, I had seen between 20 and 30 accident-killed deer with underbite, some fawns and some adults. Most of the wild deer born with underbite, including those who managed to survive to adulthood, had a milder defect than Firefly's. Obviously, a fawn born with a severe underbite seldom survives to grow up. Out of over a thousand deer I have since examined, hundreds have had this condition, but I have seen fewer than a dozen adults with as severe an underbite as Firefly's.

Several of the hatchling birds I received for care in spring 1999 had underdeveloped skulls and short upper bills, resulting in the normal lower bill being longer than the abnormally short upper one. I gave a small piece of the two cell salt tablets to the little birds every three hours to see whether their facial bones would grow like those of newborn mammals. Amazingly, they became normal in just two days. Hatchling birds grow a lot faster than young mammals, so their underdeveloped bones grow to normal much more quickly.

Since spring 1997, hatchlings, especially crows, jays, and robins, sometimes have rubbery leg bones as fledglings because the cartilage does not ossify into solid bone when it should. This is also typical of mineral deficiencies and the resultant thyroid hormone disruption. When most birds first hatch, their bones are primarily cartilage, except for those species that can walk and run soon after hatching. As the young bird grows, the cartilage becomes solid, hollow bones. However, leg bones that do not completely ossify cannot support the bird's weight as it becomes heavier, often spontaneously breaking in multiple places. When I give cell salts to the birds who come in with weak legs, their bones become solid in two or three days. If they have developed stress fractures, I splint them to keep the bones immobile and straight. The fractures heal in five or six days and the birds can stand, walk, and perch normally.

In July, when Firefly was just over a year old, I realized I had not seen her for more than a week. This concerned me because she was usually around our yard every day. While looking for her in the brush along the creek, where deer often bed down, I found evidence that a deer was experiencing severe diarrhea. I suspected it was Firefly, because she was extremely sensitive to pesticides that were heavily sprayed during summer, here and in states upwind. Several friends and relatives had called me the week before, complaining of symptoms related to chemical sensitivity, and my lungs had been quite congested, indicating something toxic was in the air. Where we live in western Montana, large amounts of herbicides, fungicides, and insecticides (pesticide is the umbrella term for all of those) are sprayed on pastures, fields, golf courses, and lawns. Sensitive animals like Firefly often get diarrhea and inflamed eyelids when exposed to the mixtures of pesticides.

After a quick trip back to the house for some apple slices, including one with the two cell salt tablets stuck into the side, I went deer hunting. It took nearly an hour of searching the half-mile of creek bottom on both sides of the creek before I finally found Firefly in a thick patch of snowberry bushes on the east side of our property. When I held out the apple slices in my hand, she walked right up to me and hungrily ate them. She looked thin, with patches of hair falling out all over her back and sides like a patient being treated with chemotherapy. She also had watery diarrhea. The conjunctiva of both eyes was red and swollen. And, possibly most concerning, she was walking on the back of her hooves, rather than on the tips of her toes, as is normal. The tendons in the pastern, the joint just above her hooves had become weak, likely due to mineral deficiencies caused by toxins in the air. Roundup®, one of the most used herbicides in our area, causes multiple mineral deficiencies; apparently poor Firefly was not Roundup Ready®. It was difficult for her to walk or run, making her vulnerable to being caught by dogs or coyotes.

It was disturbing that something in the air, and thus likely in water and on foliage here in western Montana, could have such a serious effect on a wild animal's health. After 20 years of reporting symptoms consistent with pesticide exposure in wild and domestic animals to the authorities, it has become quite clear that very few people are willing to address the possibility that our so-called clean air and water are in fact quite toxic.

It seems important to identify which toxins are causing these serious problems and discontinue their use. The result would be cleaner air and water and far fewer health problems for humans as well as wildlife and livestock. Unfortunately, clean air and clean water are two primary selling points for land developers promoting businesses and encouraging people to move here to Ravalli County. Thus, money appears to be the primary motivation for State and County Health Departments' adamant refusal to admit there is a problem with air-borne toxins, as well as their stated reluctance to ask the EPA to do testing to determine which toxins are causing symptoms of mineral deficiency and hormone disruption. The state and local officials do not want anyone to know about birth defects in western Montana because people would not want to come here to live and spend money. However, these problems in wildlife and human newborns are increasing each year throughout the United States, so it really doesn't matter where people live. We are being exposed everywhere to pesticides in the air, water, and most of the food we eat.

The next morning, after I had fed all the fawns and young birds, I again went searching for Firefly, who had remained in the same area as the day before. She gratefully ate all the apple slices I took for her. Late that afternoon, she came to our yard, where I offered apple slices, cell salts, and some grain. After that, she began coming each morning and evening for her treats and cell salts. The diarrhea cleared up, she started gaining weight, and hair began growing in the bald spots on her back and sides.

Because she was still walking on the back of her rear hooves, her dewclaws (the two little hoof-like projections on the back of a deer's foot) touched the ground with each step. I have learned that weakness in the first joint above the foot or hooves is a common symptom of chemical exposure and the resulting disruption of mineral uptake by cells in young mammals. By mid-August, walking on the back of her hooves had allowed the hoof tips to grow long and begin to curl up, making it impossible for her to walk normally. I carefully trimmed the extra growth with hoof clippers, returning her hooves to their previous length and shape. She could then walk and run like a normal deer, wearing down her hooves naturally. By late fall, Firefly's winter hair had completely grown in, covering the unsightly bare spots. She had finally become a beautiful, healthy doe.

Beginning in spring 1998, I sent photos of animals with birth defects and data about their prevalence to my friend, Dr. Douglas Seba, an independent research biologist who lives in Florida. Dr. Seba studies the atmospheric transport of dust, which carries heavy metals, bacteria, viruses, fungi, and chemicals, including pesticides and other toxins. As long ago as the 1970s, research by Dr. Seba and his colleagues showed that dust, and everything it contains, travels thousands of miles in fast-moving weather fronts.

He presented my photos and data along with his at the International Symposium on Man and His Environment in 1998 and continued presenting new photos and updated data each year thereafter for several years. For the 1999 presentation, my photos included the before and after ones of Firefly's face. Dr. Seba told between three and four hundred researchers and medical doctors from all over the world about Firefly's unprecedented recovery from severe brachygnathia superior to a normal bite after being given homeopathic cell salts. They were as amazed as I had been when I first saw Firefly's face grow to normal configuration. Many of the scientists who attended subsequent symposiums asked Dr. Seba about Firefly and how she was doing. It was evident her story had made an impression on many of them.

I found little real information on how homeopathic cell salts work, and none on how or why they stimulate underdeveloped bones in young vertebrates to grow to normal. Many doctors and veterinarians here in our area say that any apparent results from using homeopathic cell salts are simply placebo effects, even after I show them before and after photos, including those of Firefly and newborn foals. A placebo effect is defined as a perceived beneficial result from taking a supposed medicine that does not actually contain properties which can cause the result. In other words, nothing in the medication, in this case homeopathic cell salts, can account for positive results, so "it's all in your head." Interestingly, most doctors and veterinarians I know were taught that non-human animals are incapable of the abstract thinking a placebo effect requires. Also, there is the important consideration that Firefly and all the other newborn animals successfully treated did not know they were being given the cell salt tablets in their food. Therefore, a placebo effect is virtually impossible and, as Star Trek's Dr. Spock would say, is completely illogical.

After attending Dr. Seba's presentations, veterinary pathologist Dr. William Croft called me at the end of November 1999 to ask if he could come here to examine any animals we had available, especially those with birth defects. I told him I would be thrilled to have him stay with us, making it much easier for him to examine any dead deer Bob was called to pick up. Dr. Croft arrived in mid-December from his home in Wisconsin and stayed four days. While he was here, he examined our live goats, several wild birds in my care, and some cleaned skulls of animals with underbite I had saved. He was especially interested in the malformed fetus specimens I had preserved in formalin. He also looked at many photos I had taken of animal deformities.

Bob found 10 dead white-tailed deer for us to necropsy, eight of which had birth defects. Some had underbite, several males had reproductive malformations, and one male had both problems. Two of the adult females with underbite had died with no apparent trauma, such as being shot or hit by a car. Dr. Croft's necropsy showed that a large blood vessel in one lung of each animal had ruptured, drowning them in their own blood.

Finding that two adult does had died of lung hemorrhage made me even more concerned about Firefly's strange health problems in the summer months. I showed Dr. Croft photos of her pathetic appearance when she had hair loss and walked on her dewclaws. He agreed that she appeared to be reacting to a chemical exposure, but said several toxins could have that effect, so he was unable to help determine which chemical(s) might be responsible. I also introduced him to Firefly. He could easily see she no longer had an underbite and had grown a beautiful coat of winter hair.

Dr. Croft wrote a report describing the malformations and other health problems he had observed in the necropsied deer and the live animals he examined. His report was sent to the County Commissioners and Boards of Health of Missoula and Ravalli counties, the Montana

Department of Fish, Wildlife and Parks (MDFWP), the Montana State Health Department, and the Governor of Montana.

Firefly, looking beautiful the winter she was 1½ years old, with her hair all grown back and her facial bones normal.

After the head of the MDFWP Wildlife Laboratory had examined Firefly when she was nine days old, he told Bob and me she had underdeveloped facial bones and that it was a congenital malformation. Consequently, it was unexpected and concerning when the same official immediately wrote a rebuttal to Dr. Croft's letter (sent to the same county and state agencies) stating that Dr. Croft most likely didn't know deer anatomy. He also implied that I paid Dr. Croft to come from Wisconsin to examine the animals, calling Dr. Croft's trip "a paid junket." Both of these statements were totally untrue and extremely unfortunate.

As a result, the Montana Department of Fish, Wildlife and Parks, the Boards of Health in Missoula and Ravalli Counties, and the State Board of Health completely ignored Dr. Croft's findings. They adamantly refused to ask the EPA to conduct tests to determine what was then, and still is, causing the mineral deficiencies, fetal thyroid hormone disruption, and the consequent birth defects. The prevalence of underbite and reproductive malformations in mammals continued to increase after 1999, going up to nearly 70% for both birth defects.

It was very encouraging to have a world-renowned veterinary pathologist come all the way to the Bitterroot Valley to examine health problems in local animals and, most importantly, confirm as correct what we had observed regarding the birth defects. Unfortunately, everyone who could have done something to initiate testing to find the cause of the debilitating developmental malformations ignored Dr. Croft's report.

Due to underbite and other birth defects, the survival rate of young game animals consistently declined for many years. Of course, humans can always find a scapegoat other than themselves to blame. Wolves, a frequent target, were introduced into Yellowstone National Park in winter 1995, about eight months *after* we began observing serious birth defects on many species of wild and domestic mammals. How is that for timing?

The airborne toxins do not appear to affect carnivores as severely as they do grazing animals, rodents, and birds. Not surprisingly, wolf populations increased faster than biologists predicted. This was most likely because the predators found high numbers of weakened, malformed, or dead grazing animals to eat in their new homes. If wolves had lived here on our land when Firefly couldn't run because of her weak pasterns, she would have been an easy lunch for a wolf pack.

Besides hair loss, another serious symptom of mineral deficiency and hypothyroidism is the inability to maintain body heat and energy, making it difficult for an affected animal to survive harsh conditions such as long, cold winters with deep snow. In addition, this inability results in the death of many newborns, especially if there is inclement weather when they are born. Also, it isn't at all difficult for a carnivore to kill and eat young animals weakened by birth defects. Interestingly, the biologists do not even consider the fact that wolves and other predators can walk right up to and easily dine on animals, including adults, who die of hypothermia, bleeding lungs, or any of the other adverse health problems that result in the death of prey animals continuously exposed to deadly pesticides.

In 2013, a friend sent me a study done by the U. S. Fish and Wildlife Service ("Neonatal Mortality of Elk in Wyoming: Environmental, Population, and Predator Effects," *Biological Technical Publication BTP-R6007-2006*) concerning elk calf survival in Wyoming during two extremely important time periods. The first study period was from 1990 through 1992. The second was from 1997 through 1999, three years after several millions of pounds of fungicides, most commonly the nitrile, chlorothalonil, also called Daconil® or Bravo®, began being sprayed each growing season beginning in 1994 to combat potato blight on fields directly upwind of the study area. In addition, beginning in spring 1996, many millions of pounds of Roundup® were applied on the newly-released, genetically-modified Roundup Ready® grain and soy crops, also located directly upwind of the study area. Glyphosate, the main ingredient in Roundup®, and chlorothalonil have similar and synergistic debilitating effects on multiple cellular functions. To add insult to injury, because glyphosate chelates (binds up) multiple trace minerals required by the cells of animals, the resultant mineral deficiencies and thyroid hormone disruption cause serious birth defects and other deadly adverse health symptoms in developing young.

Glyphosate has been found in human mothers' milk in the United States at levels from 760 to 1600 times higher than Europe allows in drinking water. Testing of milk from dairy cows found glyphosate contamination at higher levels than what was found in human milk; therefore, it is also very likely in the milk of wild grazing animals like elk and deer. Ruminants eat a large amount of foliage, much of which has glyphosate, chlorothalonil, and other pesticides in and on the leaves. The pesticides are also in the air and surface water. Obviously, elk calves born after 1996 in the study area would have been simultaneously exposed to biologically significant levels of both chlorothalonil and glyphosate during fetal development. Constant post-natal exposure from drinking contaminated mother's milk after they were born likely continued to adversely affect the development of those who were strong enough to stand up and suckle.

During the first part of the elk calf study in 1990-1992, there was low birth mortality and predators caught very few calves after they reached 12 days of age. The calves were mature and strong enough less than two weeks after birth in each year of the three-year study period to join the nurse herd, where they were protected by many adult females.

In the second time-period of the study, between 1997-1999, after the cows and calves were exposed to new, much higher levels of chlorothalonil and Roundup®, calves were significantly slower to mature, taking an astounding 49 days to begin following their mother and join the protective herd. The calves had high mortality beginning at birth. Because predators were able to easily kill elk calves four times longer than prior to the excessive fungicide and glyphosate pre- and postnatal exposures, the mortality rate remained high, leaving few surviving young by fall. The difference between 12 days before joining the protection of the herd and 49 days is of major significance.

Based on recent studies of the effects of glyphosate and chlorothalonil on developing young, being exposed to biologically significant levels of those toxins in the air, water, and foliage ingested by the mothers was what caused the newborn elk calves in the second study period to have serious birth defects and health problems. Those who managed to survive for more than two or three days after being born were less healthy and had slower growth. Even the calves who did not have serious birth defects would still be continuously exposed to the thyroid hormone disrupting and mineral chelating chemicals in their mother's milk and in the air, resulting in the much slower growth and maturity rate in the second time-period of the study.

When I brought this study to the attention of my colleagues, mainly independent biologists, they could not understand why such a significant discrepancy in the health of elk calves in the two study periods did not raise all manner of red flags. The severe winter of 1996-97 was suggested as a cause by the study authors, as was less nutrition in the foliage the elk ingested. Why the foliage might have contained less essential nutrients was not stated. It is now known that chlorothalonil damages the liver and glyphosate chelates essential minerals, both in plants and in the animals who eat them. With both toxins also causing serious thyroid hormone disruption, symptoms of malnutrition and failure to thrive would be inevitable. Interestingly, those were the exact symptoms in wild young like Firefly and newborns of domestic livestock here in Ravalli County during the same time period as the second part of the elk study. Although the elk study was done in Wyoming, several hundred miles away, both the Yellowstone ecosystem and the Bitterroot Valley are directly downwind of fields in states where chlorothalonil and Roundup® began being excessively applied.

After Dr. Croft went back to his home in Wisconsin, life here returned to normal. All during the winter, Firefly came for her grain and apple slices with cell salts every morning and evening, always appearing healthy. Possibly she was exposed to fewer pesticides in winter, with almost none applied here and far less sprayed upwind during those months.

In fall 1999, Firefly began to mentor our three rehab fawns, a female and two males. When we turned the fawns out of the pen, they returned for their bottle each morning, noon, and night like other fawns we had raised. During fall and winter, they came to our yard twice a day for grain. After Firefly became their surrogate mother, they followed her around throughout the winter and she helped them learn survival skills. The little doe remained with Firefly the next summer, too. Female fawns usually stay in close contact with their mother for at least two years, often even longer. The 1999 male fawns, like most yearlings, spent their second summer with other yearling males.

Firefly lived to be four and one-half years old. Each year for three years, she adopted and mentored the new group of fawns we released. She was caring and motherly toward them, helping them learn what to eat and how to avoid dogs, coyotes, and other predators. Unfortunately, she did not survive the fall 2002 hunting season. She usually remained somewhere on our land, but would occasionally go onto neighboring properties. Many of our neighbors shoot deer on their properties during hunting season and some when it isn't hunting season. Oddly, she never appeared to be pregnant nor did she ever have a fawn of her own.

Since Firefly's amazing recovery, rehabbers and livestock owners have helped many newborn animals with underdeveloped bones grow to normal by giving them Hyland's Calc. Phos. 6X® or 30X, or both Hyland's Calc. Phos. 30X® and Hyland's Bioplasma®. The list includes: elk calves, mule deer fawns, white-tailed deer fawns, calves, foals, lambs, young goats, newborn llama, and hatchling birds, in many states. Studies need to be done to determine whether homeopathic cell salts might help children born with underdeveloped bones, especially facial and limb bones. Also, it is possible that giving cell salts might help children born with other symptoms caused by fetal thyroid hormone disruption and mineral deficiencies. It seems important to learn whether it helps with brain disorders such as autism, bipolar disorder, attention deficit disorder, or other health issues connected to disruption of proper mineral levels in the affected parts of a developing child's brain.

What I learned from the astounding growth to normal of Firefly's premaxillary bones was extremely important. By sharing that information with other rehabbers, livestock owners, and mothers of children, many other mammals and birds have had their underdeveloped bones stimulated to grow to normal, changing faces one at a time. Firefly's continuing legacy will be for newborn babies and other young animals to be helped to develop more like their genes program them to be, rather than what is dictated by epigenetic changes caused by toxic chemicals in the environment.

With the help of our wild friends and human colleagues, Bob and I have made many new and important discoveries. We have observed and reported previously unreported birth defects in young of mammals and birds. We have learned how to help interrupted growth of bones, bills, feathers, and hair resume growth and become normal. This is important, as those developmental malformations have serious effects on wild animals, often causing death. With the help of caring scientists and researchers like my sister Pamela Hallock Muller, Douglas Seba, Ted Kerstetter, Gary Haas, Stephanie Seneff, Nancy Swanson, Don Huber, Anthony Samsel, Tony Mitra, Josh Leavitt, and many others, we are tracking some of the factors responsible for underbite and other developmental birth defects. Hopefully, by sharing what we have learned, we can help prevent the extinction of numerous vertebrate species, and help pass on a planet that remains livable.

**Genetics loads gun,
environment pulls trigger,
causing deformed young.**

CHAPTER 2
A COYOTE SHOWS THE WAY

Many native cultures in North America revere the coyote for its intelligence. Stories of how Coyote instructed the People in ways to improve their lives have been passed down through many generations. Consequently, it was appropriate that a coyote led me to discover how to use homeopathic cell salts to help return animals to good health. On some animals, including myself, the results were unexpected and remarkable.

Our home in the Bitterroot Valley (Ravalli County) of western Montana has the tall, craggy Bitterroot Mountains to the west and the lower, more rounded Sapphire Mountains to the east. The rugged peaks and forest-covered slopes change with the seasons, but are always breathtaking in their beauty. The mountains have in recent years been breathtaking in another way. The tall peaks of the Bitterroot Mountains are instrumental in slowing weather fronts coming across the states upwind to the west and southwest. Those storms initially pass over large agricultural areas where many pesticides are sprayed. Strong winds pick up pesticide-laden dust from the fields, carrying it for hundreds or even thousands of miles. Winds are slowed and the chemical-covered dust is condensed when fronts come up against the west side of the mountains. Consequently, the dust and chemicals are first deposited in snow and rain on the mountaintops, and then they drop into valleys between the mountain ranges, where most of the animals live.

In 2010, the USGS conducted scientific studies of toxin levels in snow, high mountain lake water, plants, and animals on mountaintops in several national parks (Landers DH, et. al., "The Western Airborne Contaminant Assessment Project (WACAP): An Interdisciplinary Evaluation of the Impacts of Airborne Contaminants in Western US National Parks," published in *Environmental Science & Technology*). Glacier National Park is the closest one to us that was examined. Test results showed snow, lake water, foliage, and animal tissue contain many pesticides, PCB's, heavy metals, bacteria, and viruses. Male fish in mountain lakes there were found to have both male and female sex organs. Very low-level exposures to the mixtures of such toxins cause changes in nutrient levels in plants and debilitating birth defects in embryos and fetuses.

In another important study, researchers looking for the causes of malformations on frogs took water samples from 77 different sites in several western states, including the Bitterroot River in Hamilton, Montana, in July 1999. (Biek, R., Funk, W.C., Maxell, B.A. & Mills, L.S. "What is Missing in Amphibian Decline Research: Insights from Ecological Sensitivity Analysis" published in *Conservation Biology*). Soon after publication in 2002, a copy of the study was sent to me by a friend. The researchers had not informed officials in Montana that biologically significant amounts of the highly estrogenic chemical, alachlor, was present in the Bitterroot River. Consequently, I sent copies of their study to the Governor of Montana, State Health and Agriculture Departments, and our county officials. None of them seemed concerned that the amount of alachlor in snow falling on the Bitterroot Mountains was high enough to cause an average of 0.53 ppb in snowmelt running into the river in mid-summer.

In fact, when I sent Governor Judy Martz a copy of the study, her reply in a letter to me was, "0.53 ppb is not very much pesticide in that Ravalli County pond." I respectfully wrote back to her, suggesting that 0.53 ppb of alachlor in a major river running through an area where alachlor is not even used is far more environmentally significant than finding the same amount in a pond. It would take much more alachlor to contaminate the amount of water in a river the size of the Bitterroot River than it would to contaminate a pond, even a fairly large pond. I also suggested to her that the Bitterroot River has not been a pond since the last time glacial Lake Missoula drained over 13,000 years ago. I doubt she appreciated my attempt at humor.

I was concerned about 0.53 ppb of alachlor in our surface water because atrazine, a similar "sister" chemical to alachlor, was reported by amphibian researcher Tyrone Hayes to cause reproductive anomalies in frogs at concentrations as low as 0.1 part per billion, one fifth the amount of alachlor found in the Bitterroot River. When exposed to water containing atrazine, immature male frogs develop female as well as male sex organs and have less testosterone than most female frogs. Atrazine is and was used here in Ravalli County. Both alachlor and atrazine have been shown to be dangerous hormone disrupters. Those two herbicides have also been strongly implicated in damage to immune systems in amphibians (making them more susceptible to parasites and infections) and to resultant declines in amphibian populations. Also, if that amount of alachlor was being deposited in the high mountain snow pack, with the spring melt contaminating the entire Bitterroot River, it would seem obvious that other pesticides were likely doing the same.

As early as summer 1994, I began noticing that, when fast moving weather fronts passed through our area, animals became ill, sometimes even becoming paralyzed. Many died. Several of my friends and I developed a severe chronic cough. We also found we had become more sensitive to locally sprayed pesticides, especially herbicides, and other chemicals, such as household cleaners, to which we were exposed. In addition, people appeared much more sensitive to side effects of prescription drugs. Lawyers have made considerable money suing pharmaceutical companies for what their "bad drugs" did to people, when the health problems appear to be caused by synergistic effects of chemicals in the air in combination with the prescription drugs.

In June 1996, I became very ill after being exposed to a mixture of fresh lawn herbicides containing 2,4-D and other organochlorine herbicides. I experienced severe lung damage, extreme fatigue, memory loss, and other symptoms, including the sudden, significant depletion of bone mass commonly known as osteoporosis. I subsequently found several studies that showed organochlorine pesticides disrupt the ability of our cells to take in and use calcium in a normal manner. Consequent disruption of calcium going to muscle, brain, and bone cells that need it result in a number of disorders, including osteoporosis, osteoarthritis, fibromyalgia, and short-term memory loss. What few doctors tell their patients is that lawn sprays to which they are often exposed can cause those symptoms.

After exposure to the lawn spray mixture, my joints and muscles hurt nearly all of the time. When moist weather fronts passed through our area, the pain became worse. I have an observable adverse reaction to exposure to nearly all pesticides, especially the herbicide 2,4-D. Shortly after inhaling it, my lungs fill with fluid so I become very short of breath. I also have trouble remembering numbers, doing mathematical computations, remembering people's names, or spelling simple words, all serious neurological symptoms.

By summer 1997, three doctors told me I was going to die within six months because of the inflammation and fluid in my lungs. My condition became much worse whenever I was exposed to combinations of pesticides, which are impossible to avoid. The doctors insisted it was because I took care of birds, but I am not allergic to birds or anything else, except cigarette smoke, some kinds of vehicle exhaust (especially diesel and snowmobile), and pesticides. I also had many other health problems at that time, but thanks to what I learned from a little coyote, my six months were up 20 years ago and so far, I am still alive.

Not only was my health worse that summer, I was having a much harder time successfully raising the baby mammals and birds brought to me for care. Whenever it rained, young animals who were eating well and appeared healthy would suddenly become lethargic, stop eating, develop diarrhea, and quickly die. It was significant that my symptoms became much worse at the same time hatchling birds and baby mammals became ill.

Young mammals living on our land, especially the Columbian ground squirrel and yellow-bellied marmot babies, died by the hundreds. I sent bodies of a young marmot I caught and euthanized and a baby raccoon to the Montana State Agricultural Laboratory for testing. The little raccoon suddenly began vomiting, developed severe diarrhea, and died so quickly that normal treatment had no chance to work. The lungs of the marmot were damaged so badly the tissue was actually bleeding. With every breath, blood dripped from its nostrils, further impairing its ability to breathe, the reason I was able to catch and euthanize it. The results from the Agriculture Laboratory stated both animals had severely damaged lungs, congested liver, and consequent damage to their digestive system. They tested for bacteria and viruses, but could not find a cause for the symptoms. However, it was not particularly comforting to find out that something in the air was so toxic it killed over 150 young marmots in a matter of days.

Hemorrhaging lungs in the young marmot was especially concerning, as I had never before seen that particular problem. Since 1997, I have necropsied many animals who died from drowning in their own blood when it filled their lungs and thoracic cavity. In February 2011, my next-door neighbor called to report her pet donkey had just died. It had bloody froth coming out of its nostrils and had died of hemorrhaging blood vessels in its lungs. After 17 years of seeing animals die in this way, it no longer surprised me.

In the late 1990s, many birds and some mammals were dying immediately after rainstorms. In March 1999, I collected snow water in glass pans in our yard and sent it to a laboratory for testing. They found nearly half a part per billion of a combination of the fungicide chlorothalonil (Bravo® or Daconil®) and two similar chemicals, likely the two metabolites of chlorothalonil. Metabolites are the chemicals a pesticide becomes when exposure to water and sunshine change it or break it down into different but similar, and often more toxic, chemicals. Chlorothalonil is composed of a hexachlorobenzene ring with two molecules of cyanide attached. The metabolites also contain molecules of cyanide which are often released into the air as free cyanide.

The snow water I had tested contained 0.43 ppb of chlorothalonil and its metabolites. In a study, it took only 0.1 ppb to kill all aquatic life, including amphibians, in the study tanks. All grazing animals and other plant eaters were then and still are being exposed to cyanide when they eat foliage. Chlorothalonil is now the most used fungicide in the world. When snow melts, chemical-laden water runs into streams, so the animals have to drink water containing cyanide, in addition to the many highly used herbicides, like Roundup®, 2,4-D, and other toxins.

Cyanide in any form is a deadly poison to most mammals, especially canines. According to studies, it is highly damaging to thyroid glands and can severely disrupt thyroid hormones during fetal development. The cyanide and nicotine combination in cigarette smoke has been shown to cause the malformations and health problems collectively called Fetal Tobacco Syndrome in babies born to mothers who smoke while pregnant.

Amazingly, in total disregard for the health of most animals on the planet, chemical companies developed new insecticides out of nicotine, called neonicotinoids. Farmers began using large amounts of those toxins and now neonics, as most people call them, are the most used insecticides in the world. They are strongly implicated by multiple studies to be a primary cause of honeybee and wild bee die-offs, in addition to their exposure to glyphosate and chlorothalonil. In one study, when honeybees were exposed to chlorothalonil and a neonicotinoid at the same time, the bees died a thousand times faster than with exposure to just the neonic alone. Also, not surprisingly, the bees become addicted to nicotine in the pollen and seek it out, resulting in certain death, similar to humans and cigarettes. The increasing declines in insect pollinators is of great concern, since without them, we will lose up to one third of the plant products we depend on for food, particularly fruits and berries.

With the herbicide Roundup® almost constantly in the air, weather fronts are even more dangerous. Besides chelating many important minerals in the plants and animals exposed to it, Roundup's® main component, glyphosate, also disrupts thyroid hormone functions as well as those of certain genes, Vitamin A, and several vital enzymes.

By 2006, the combination of neonics, glyphosate, and chlorothalonil on and in plants visited by bees was so lethal to honey bees they began dying by the millions. Also, many of the wild bee populations have nearly disappeared, especially our big, beautiful bumblebees. In spring 2007, the year after honeybees began dying, underbite in newborn mammals was documented to be twice the prevalence it was in 2006. Also, the autism rate in human newborns has doubled since 2006. The effect on children's brains is not surprising since scientists have found the neonicotinoid pesticides kill bees' brain cells, preventing them from learning, feeding, and reproducing. If neonics kill bees' brain cells, what horrific damage are they doing to the even more sensitive brains of developing human fetuses and newborns?

Toxins in the air have also visibly affected adult females in our Columbian ground squirrel colony nearly every summer since 2006. Many of them become uncoordinated and frequently tip over on their backs or sides when they attempt to sit upright on their haunches. Running is even more difficult. The affected squirrels often tumble over on their sides with their feet and legs thrashing the air as if they were still running. This might be humorous to watch if it was not so alarming. Most people to whom I reported our observations claimed the animals likely had a disease. But the female ground squirrels and other animals, including mountain cottontails and porcupines who fell over when they tried to run or walk, did not die unless they were killed by a predator. Also, having a disease did not explain why baby birds in my care became ill on the same days the tipping problem became worse. Because so many young mammals and birds brought to me for care in spring and summer 1997 suddenly died, I seriously considered giving up wildlife rehabilitation for good. Fortunately, I didn't or I wouldn't have met Blondie.

In April 1998, two teenage boys brought us five adorable baby coyotes, orphaned when their mother was shot. For as long as I can remember, I have loved and admired coyotes and the five little pups were at their cutest. There were three females and two males. I named the smallest one Blondie because she was lighter in color than her siblings. I called her brothers Smoky and Grey and her sisters Lady and Wolfie.

At first, I kept all of them inside our house in a large cardboard box. Being very small, they needed extra warmth at night and required feeding every three hours. When they were old enough to eat by themselves, I placed them in a 13 by 26-foot, covered, chain link pen, built on a cement pad so they couldn't dig out. It had a warm doghouse with thick, soft, grass hay for bedding.

Unfortunately, all four of the larger pups bullied little Blondie unmercifully. They were quite rough and I was afraid they would injure her, so I put her by herself in a six by 13-foot covered pen. Because she had no siblings with whom to play, I took her out for play sessions or walks several times a day. In the hay field, she could explore all the delightful smells of field mice and other animals. I encouraged her to find mice, voles, and grasshoppers, but told her no when she looked with interest at our domestic ducks, baby goats, or other animals I did not want her to chase.

Blondie was afraid of other people and the other coyote pups, but seemed to accept me unconditionally. Whenever I came to play with her, she wagged her tail so hard, her whole rear end wriggled with it. She was always ecstatic to see me, greeting me in proper coyote fashion by licking all over my hands and face. When we went out walking, she stayed nearby; if she ventured too far away, I just called her name and she came right back.

I have to admit I completely broke the cardinal rule of rehabilitating wildlife, becoming very attached to Blondie. We did not have a dog at the time and she was better behaved and much more affectionate than most dogs I had been around. The other four coyotes played together in their large kennel. They all let me handle them if I needed to, but as is usual with most coyote pups, they remained quite shy, especially Wolfie. All of them ate as much food as they wanted each day, including mice, puppy food, and fresh goat milk. When it was available, I gave them road-killed deer meat and bones to chew.

One morning I found an unpleasant surprise when I went to feed the six-week-old pups. Blondie was anxiously trying to walk with quivering front legs that could barely hold her up. They were bowed out sideways in an odd way at the joint that corresponds to our wrist. She was also holding her right hind leg completely off the ground, refusing to walk on it. If her foot touched the ground she cried out in pain. I couldn't find anything wrong with the leg or the foot. The other four pups appeared to be unaffected by whatever had happened to Blondie. Since she was alone in a predator-proof kennel, there was no way she could have been injured by another animal.

That morning was bright and sunny after two days of misting rain. Since it was Sunday, I waited until the next morning to call our veterinarian. After I described Blondie's symptoms, telling him they appeared to be getting worse, he said Blondie had rickets, resulting from a lack of calcium. This was quite puzzling because each day Blondie was eating from six to eight whole mice, with all their bones, plus drinking nearly a quart of goat milk. Her diet was very high in calcium. She also ate a small amount of commercial puppy food each day.

I called another veterinarian, described the symptoms, and received the same diagnosis. Both suggested I give her more calcium, telling me recovery from rickets was a long process, taking from weeks to months before seeing any improvement. They said it was unlikely Blondie would ever recover from such a severe case as I described. That was *not* what I wanted to hear. I wanted my little furry friend to be healthy as soon as possible.

Planning to follow the veterinarians' advice, I went to the medicine cabinet for calcium tablets. When I opened the door, the first thing I saw was the bottle of Hyland's Calc. Phos. 6X® my friend Jean Atthowe had given me to help birds and animals with broken bones. As soon as I saw the calc. phos. bottle, I had an "aha moment." If it has an observable positive effect on healing broken bones, it must somehow stimulate calcium uptake. I hoped it might help alleviate Blondie's condition, especially if something had interfered with the cellular uptake of the more-than-sufficient amount of calcium in her diet. I decided to give her two tablets of calc. phos. several times a day and watch her closely for any change. I didn't know this would turn out to be a life-changing decision for hundreds of animals, including myself.

It was 9:00 in the morning when I placed the first two tablets of calc. phos. in Blondie's mouth. For breakfast, I gave her a dish of milk and several mice to eat. After milking the goats and feeding the other four coyote pups and the birds I kept in small flight rooms, I went back to the house to feed the hatchling birds and cook our noon meal. Immediately after lunch, I fed the fawns and at 12:30, went to give Blondie two more tablets. She seemed to be in less pain and was not shaking as hard when she tried to walk. I made her comfortable on her bed of straw, putting her remaining two mice right in front of her so she could eat them without moving. I also left her water pan close after offering her a drink.

At 3:00, I checked on Blondie and fed her and the other pups their afternoon meal. Amazingly, she was walking on all four legs without limping or whining. I was thrilled to see her front legs were straighter, though not yet completely normal. I gave her two more tablets, all the while telling her what a good puppy she was. I was elated at her progress, and rewarded her with a nice brushing and a short playtime. Later in the evening, when I went to milk goats and feed the coyote pups, Blondie had improved even more. I gave her two more tablets and a good night hug.

The thought briefly occurred to me that calc. phos. 6X tablets were almost magical, but I do not believe in magic. I did some research and found that homeopathic cell salts are simply electrolytes that stimulate transport of important minerals like calcium, zinc, manganese, magnesium, selenium, and others across cell membranes. Thus calc. phos. stimulates the uptake of calcium by cells that need it. This is not magic at all, but it is extremely helpful science.

By the next morning, except for a very slight outward bend in her front leg joints, Blondie's rickets-like symptoms were gone. I gave her two tablets then and two more just before noon. After our noon meal, I went down to feed the hawks and eagles and play with Blondie, letting her out of her kennel for a run. Her front legs were completely straight and apparently pain-free. She dashed around and around, obviously happy to be healthy and able to run and play after three days of being cooped up, a long time to a little pup.

While Blondie was dashing happily around and around, I could only stand and watch. I had been experiencing severe joint pain in both arms and legs since an herbicide exposure in 1996 had caused serious health problems, and the pain was far worse that week. Wondering if calc. phos. 6X could make joint pain go away on an old critter like me, I popped two tablets into my mouth. I continued to take two tablets every four hours except at night, similar to what I had given Blondie. In about 36 hours, the same amount of time it took Blondie to recover completely, I had no joint pain at all. I do not know which of us was happier. I was absolutely elated because I could run nearly as fast as Blondie without experiencing excruciating pain. She was excited to have me run with her, instead of just watching her play. We both celebrated by having a race halfway across the hay field and back. Blondie won, but not by much. I did fairly well considering just two days before I could barely walk and could hardly move my left arm.

I called our veterinarian and thanked him for his help, telling him the coyote pup had completely recovered. He said she did not have rickets if she recovered in just three days and asked what I had given her. I told him about the calc. phos. 6X, a homeopathic cell salt. He would not believe anything homeopathic could possibly be responsible for her recovery, so I told him about my recovery to substantiate the amazing effects of the cell salt on Blondie. He also refused to believe my equally fast recovery from chronic joint and muscle pain, which I had had for several years. In reflection, it did sound like an extremely tall tale. But those two astounding incidents were nothing compared to what was to come. Blondie had helped me acquire a basic understanding of how a homeopathic cell salt works as an electrolyte, providing a rapid-acting antidote for many of the health problems caused by mineral-deprived cells.

A week later, I celebrated my newly acquired mobility by hiking with Bob up the four-and-a half-mile trail to the top of a mountain named Saint Mary's Peak in the Bitterroot Mountains. We like going there in summer because the mountain-top flowers are spectacular. The trail up to a Forest Service fire watch lookout on the top is not very difficult, but I had thought I would never be able to hike up any mountain again. Before taking the calc. phos., I could hardly make it up our basement stairs. I was thrilled to have no pain and no problem hiking up or down. We left the parking area at 9:30, arrived at the top at 11:30, ate lunch, looked at flowers for an hour, and arrived back at the parking lot by 2:00. We had to be home in time to feed the fawns at 3:00. All the young birds were eating by themselves by then.

A few weeks after Blondie and I recovered from our ailments, I received a severely emaciated and dehydrated bobcat kitten. Kitcat had somehow been separated from her mother, apparently surviving for several days without food or water. She was found unconscious and nearly dead. From this kitten, I learned that giving a combination of one tablet of calc. phos. 6X or 30X and one of the cell salt combination called bioplasma (containing all twelve homeopathic cell salts) mixed into an electrolytes solution produces recoveries so remarkable a fiction writer could not make them up. And, according to some people, the results I've seen defy logic.

As soon as Kitcat arrived, I placed a tablet each of calc. phos. and bioplasma under her dry tongue, putting several drops of liquid electrolytes on the tablets to dissolve them and more on her tongue to moisten it. Realizing it was not possible for me to get enough liquid into an unconscious kitten to hydrate her, I rushed her to our veterinarian to have electrolytes administered by syringe directly under her skin. After about 45 minutes of receiving subcutaneous electrolytes, Kitcat awakened and began walking around in the recovery kennel. The veterinarian continued to inject sterile electrolytes under her skin, but without more cell salts, her cells and blood vessels gradually ceased their uptake of the fluids. The electrolyte solution remained under Kitcat's skin rather than going into the cells. She relapsed at 12:30 that afternoon and became completely unconscious by 1:00, about 4 hours after I had first given her the two cell salt tablets.

The veterinarian called at 1:30 p.m. to tell me the kitten was not doing well, but he didn't want me to come to get her until 5:00, just before the clinic closed. He continued administering the subcutaneous electrolytes for the rest of the afternoon without noticeable change. When I went to the clinic to get Kitcat, the unconscious kitten looked like a small bag of water. She actually appeared to be dead. Her eyes were extremely sunken, the normally moist and shiny corneas dull and dry-looking. Her little heart was barely beating, her breathing was shallow, and her mouth was completely dry. The veterinarian said she was dying. He thought she likely had kidney or liver failure or both, because her cells were no longer assimilating the electrolytes like they had in the morning.

I carefully placed Kitcat on a soft blanket in a box I had brought for her. As soon as I arrived home, I placed calc. phos. and bioplasma under her tongue, dissolving them with drops of liquid electrolytes, which also helped moisten her dry mouth. I continued to occasionally put a few drops of the liquid electrolytes into her mouth to keep it moist. Quickly and visibly, all the fluid that had been collecting under her skin was absorbed directly into her blood and cells. I watched in wonder as the unnatural roundness caused by subcutaneous fluid disappeared and Kitcat began regaining her normal kitten shape. Her sunken eyes and dry corneas were becoming rounded and normal-looking.

In about 45 minutes, Kitcat blinked her eyes open and shakily stood up. She soon began walking around, crying for food. After drinking a small amount of milk with vitamin supplements, she curled up and went to sleep. Every half hour until I went to bed at 11:00, I gave her small amounts of milk. And every three hours, all night and every day until she was weaned, I gave her one each of the two cell salt tablets with her milk formula.

The bobcat kitten's quick recovery from severe dehydration, then the relapse and repeat recovery, had provided unequivocal evidence for homeopathic cell salts' positive effects on stimulating mineral and consequent fluid uptake by the cells. Most importantly, the positive effects of the cell salts appeared to cease approximately four hours after receiving the tablets. The inability of the kitten's cells to uptake minerals and fluids in liquid electrolytes injected under her skin after the effects of the cell salts stopped was painfully obvious. I have found what animals show us is always true and extremely important, if we can correctly interpret what their behavior indicates.

This was another stunning lesson from a young animal on how to use homeopathic cell salts. By combining them with ordinary liquid electrolytes, what might be called a super-electrolyte results. I had previously used liquid electrolytes, both oral and subcutaneous, on many animals and birds. I had not previously used cell salts in combination with them, so was amazed at the difference. After receiving both, Kitcat initially recovered in less than an hour. She relapsed into unconsciousness after four hours without more cell salts, even though she was given copious amounts of subcutaneous liquid electrolytes. Then she literally came back from the brink of death about 45 minutes after again receiving the two cell salts.

Kitcat's amazing recovery was just one of many I have been privileged to witness when I or other people used bioplasma or both bioplasma and calc. phos. 6X or 30X, in combination with liquid electrolytes. It was fortunate for Blondie's brothers and sisters that the bobcat kitten taught me how cell salts and electrolytes work together. Not long after the incident with Kitcat, a weather front came through our area during the night from the southwest, after passing directly over the Idaho potato field area. Blondie was still receiving both calc. phos. and bioplasma three times a day, possibly the reason she showed no ill effects from the toxins in the weather front, especially the cyanide. Her siblings were not so fortunate. By 9:00 the next morning, all of the other pups had started vomiting, and by noon had severe bloody mucous diarrhea, typical of cyanide poisoning in canines.

I caught each pup and put the two cell salt tablets directly on their tongue, adding my electrolyte formula and both of the cell salt tablets to their water and Blondie's. Wolfie and Smoke had recovered by the end of the day, but Lady and Grey were still vomiting. I took those two pups to our intensive care kennel in our basement, so I could squirt cell salts and electrolytes slowly into their mouths with a syringe at regular intervals during the night. The pups finally stopped vomiting and by noon the next day both appeared fully recovered. I returned them to their outside kennel with Wolfie and Smoke. The four pups were happy to see each other and had a greeting romp to celebrate.

I had been so busy with her sick siblings I had not given Blondie her usual playtime the previous day. Before taking her out for a run in the hayfield, I examined Blondie to make certain she was still healthy. She was delighted to finally get out to play, showing no visible effects from what made the other pups ill.

After that episode, the pups grew fast on all they could eat of mice, goat milk, and puppy food. Every morning and night, I gave each of them a tablet of calc. phos. and one of bioplasma and there were no more bouts of vomiting or diarrhea. When Smoke, Grey, and Wolfie were nearly full grown, we released them at a friend's place. He owns over 300 acres where they could hunt and explore. His land connects directly to Forest Service land on the west, giving the young coyotes an extensive area in which to live and hunt without crossing paths with humans. Because she had a urinary tract infection, Lady had to stay with Blondie until she was healthy enough to be released.

Blondie was still quite small. As I had taught her not to chase anything but mice and voles, I felt it was safe to let her out to explore and practice her hunting skills. During one of her forays out into the world, some animal, likely a neighbor's dog, had bitten off over half of her beautiful, fluffy, blond tail, leaving it very short. One day in October, I let Lady out to play with Blondie while I cleaned their pens. I had not taught Lady to leave other animals alone, as the plan had been to release her with the other three pups. Unfortunately, she decided to chase a cat belonging to a neighbor who lived a short distance up the road to the south, about 200 feet from our barn and other old buildings. The neighbor called us and complained, so I put the pups back into the two, big side-by-side pens where we usually kept deer fawns. Lady still picked on Blondie, so they could not stay together in the same enclosure.

The day before Thanksgiving, I let Blondie out to hunt for voles while we cleaned her pen. That evening, after we had finished cleaning, I couldn't find Blondie. She must have been out exploring, because she didn't come when I called. I wasn't too worried, since she never bothered anything.

The next day, before going to my brother's house for dinner, I had to feed all the animals and birds and milk the goats. I still had not located Blondie. Thinking we could come home early so I could look for her, we went to dinner. As soon as we arrived home, I set off on my four-wheeler to find the little coyote. I was almost to the barn area where my goats live when I heard a loud crack, obviously a rifle shot. I drove past the barn at top speed toward the neighbor's place, where Lady had chased the cat. The neighbor was running for his house as fast as his legs could propel his overweight body, and he was carrying a rifle. He obviously had shot something and didn't want me to know he had done it. I felt a sick feeling in my stomach the second I saw him.

About 10 feet past our land, Blondie was lying dead beside the road, bleeding from a bullet hole through her side. She was not breathing so I drove up the road to the neighbor's house to ask why he had shot her. He said it was because a coyote chased his cat. I told him the coyote that had chased his cat was penned up and the coyote he shot was trained not to chase or eat anything except mice. He said he could not tell one coyote from another. I pointed out that the one he shot had only half a tail and was a different color, emphasizing that it didn't look anything like the one that chased his cat. I also suggested he had no right to kill the coyote as it was only a few steps off of our property on another neighbors' land and not even on the land he was renting. Not too surprisingly, he angrily threatened to shoot me when I reminded him I had not shot either of his cats, even though they were often on our land killing wildlife. Fortunately, his wife stepped in front of him, suggesting he cool down and put away the gun.

Seeing no point in arguing with a trigger-happy, obviously insane man, I left. I picked up Blondie's small, limp body, took her home, and buried her. That Thanksgiving still ranks as the worst of my life. I have never forgiven myself for not finding Blondie and putting her in the pen before I went to dinner.

A few days later, we took Lady to the release site at our friend's place, where they still occasionally saw the other pups. I do not know how long they survived or if any of them lived long enough to reproduce. Our friend lost track of them after about six weeks. Hopefully at least some of the young coyotes survived to find a home territory and have pups of their own.

What I learned by helping Blondie recover from her joint problem may have saved my life. Being completely pain free has definitely made life much more pleasant. The cell salt and electrolyte combination helped several other members of my family who, like me, are very chemically sensitive. It also helped many friends and their children make amazing recoveries from adverse health problems, especially those related to chemical exposure. The cell salts and the combination of cell salts and liquid electrolytes have helped save the lives of hundreds of birds and mammals in the care of rehabbers and livestock owners.

It was not fair for Blondie to have such a sad fate. I would think that in such a big place as western Montana, there would have been room for my one small coyote friend. Unfortunately, there are just too many people.

**For showing humans
how better to live, reward
for coyote is death.**

Blondie, the coyote, helped me and consequently many others learn how to live a much healthier life when she was just a puppy handful.

CHAPTER 3
JUMPSTARTING CELLS

While treating small animals in spring 1998, a series of fortunate discoveries made it possible for me to devise a formula that has worked well to help birds and animals recover from injuries, broken bones, chemical exposures, and even certain birth defects. The same simple combination of two kinds of electrolytes has helped keep me feeling healthy and pain free. I have shared this information with other wildlife rehabbers and livestock owners, many of whom have also used it successfully.

After treating both birds and mammals with the homeopathic product Hyland's Bioplasma®, I discovered its 12 cell salts significantly increased the cell stimulating effect of the commonly used Lactated Ringer's Solution®, Pedialyte®, or other liquid electrolytes. The cell salts appear to increase the negative charge inside an animal's cells, so are electrolytes in pill form that help restore the body's bioelectricity. This enables the cells of animals to uptake the positively charged minerals needed for normal cellular processes. Since discovering this advantageous synergy, I always give a tablet of bioplasma, and usually a tablet of Hyland's Calc. Phos. 30X® at the same time I give any electrolyte solution.

Several brands of liquid electrolytes are available in pharmacies, grocery stores, or health food stores, but I make my own. Most liquid electrolytes contain water, sodium chloride, sodium bicarbonate, potassium chloride, and sugar. Fortunately, Bob found a recipe used by the United Nations for the dry ingredients added to water to make electrolytes for dehydrated children. I modified their formula by leaving out sugar and adding one tablet each of bioplasma and calc. phos. 30X. Sugar is added to the commercially made electrolyte solutions like Lactated Ringer's Solution® and Pedialyte® to stimulate cells to uptake minerals and water more quickly. Bioplasma does what sugar is supposed to do and, most importantly, appears to stimulate cells to transport minerals and water across cell membranes much more quickly and effectively than sugar, especially if the sugar fails to do that as happened in Kitcat's case.

To make the modified UN electrolyte formula, I thoroughly mix the following dry ingredients in a bowl and store them in a closed container: one part regular salt (sodium chloride), two parts baking soda (sodium bicarbonate), and one part potassium chloride, which can be purchased at health food stores. I use the salt substitute Morton's No Salt®, which is mostly potassium chloride and is easy to find near table salt in grocery stores. I dissolve one eighth teaspoon of this dry mixture in eight ounces of water whenever I need liquid electrolytes for animals in my care, or for me. I always add one tablet each of bioplasma and calc. phos. 30X in place of sugar in what I call my electrolyte combination. Sugar is not particularly good for some birds, such as owls. If the bird or mammal needs carbohydrates, I give it a drop of a commercial supplement called Nutrical® the second time I give them my electrolytes, about 15 to 20 minutes after the first administration. This ensures they are hydrated enough to be able to digest the carbohydrate supplement.

One of the 12 cell salts in bioplasma is calc. phos. 3X, which stimulates cells needing calcium to more efficiently access that available in the blood stream. Some important cells that must have adequate amounts of calcium to function optimally are brain, muscle, digestive system, and bone cells. Hyland's Calc. Phos.® (calcarea phosphorica) is sold in several strengths: 3X, 6X, and 30X being the most common. I have found that the cell stimulating effects of calc. phos. 30X last longer and are more effective than the calc. phos. 3X that is in bioplasma or calc. phos. 6X. For example, a broken bone on an injured animal which has been given the two homeopathic cell salts, bioplasma, and calc. phos. 30X, will heal in half the time the bone heals without the cell salts. If the animal is given 6X instead, the bone heals in two-thirds of the normal healing time, a measurable difference of several days.

My electrolyte combination also promotes faster recovery from illnesses and digestive problems because having adequate mineral levels, and consequent normal bioelectricity in the cells, helps the immune and digestive systems to function much better. Symptoms related to improper calcium utilization in animals of all ages include short-term memory difficulties, digestion problems, improper calcium deposits, bone loss or broken bones, joint pain, muscle pain, acid reflux, lactose intolerance, and in newborns, underdeveloped bones, contracted tendons, weak ankles, and disrupted bone growth. All of those symptoms have been mitigated on many animals by giving just the two cell salts. Even underdeveloped feathers on fledgling birds can be stimulated to grow to normal with oral administration of bioplasma and calc. phos. 30X in my electrolyte solution. After recovery, I continue to give the two cell salts twice daily with regular food and plain water to maintain good health in the animal until it is released.

Many new studies have shown the herbicide glyphosate (found in Roundup®) causes facial and other malformations in vertebrates, including fish, amphibians, birds, and mammals. Most important, developmental malformations in human newborns, especially of the head and face, were shown to occur in areas which had high glyphosate use. Excessive amounts are sprayed on crops genetically modified to be resistant to glyphosate (Roundup Ready®), killing weeds, but not the genetically modified food crop plants. It is also often sprayed on ripe wheat, corn, oats, and other grain that is not genetically modified to make the crop die immediately prior to harvest*. This results in a high level of glyphosate on harvested seeds used for human and animal food; 80% of tested processed food sold for human or pet consumption that includes grain products contain biologically significant levels of glyphosate. Grain products in livestock, poultry, and rodent feed have also been found to contain various amounts of glyphosate.

*(Grains are considered ripe when their plants are dead and dry. Different areas of huge grain fields do not necessarily ripen at the same time so some plants are still at least partly green when the rest are ready. Entire fields are sprayed with herbicides to ensure all plants are dead, making harvesting them more efficient. When plants have been genetically modified to be resistant to glyphosate, they not only have been sprayed with more glyphosate initially, but in the dry-down or desiccation stage just before harvest, they must be sprayed with a different herbicide to kill them.)

Many health problems wildlife rehabbers have remedied in newborns with the two cell salt tablets alone or in combination with an electrolyte solution appear to be caused by adverse epigenetic changes during development. The new patterns of gene expression are regulated by cellular material called the epigenome. (The prefix, epi-, means above.) The epigenome sits on top of the genome and just outside of it. These epigenetic "marks" or "switches" on the genome tell the genes when to turn on or off and dictate the strength of gene expression.

Environmental factors, such as nutrition, radiation, and chemical exposure, influence gene expression during the development of a young animal. Exposures to radiation and hormone-disrupting, mineral-chelating chemicals have increased significantly in the last 20 years. A combination of mineral deficiencies and thyroid hormone disruption appear to be seriously altering important hormonal functions on developing vertebrate young. Epigenetic changes can be passed to the next generation, and then passed on again by those young who survive to reproduce. Even though these changes can be passed on for several generations, the actual DNA of the genes is not affected. In other words, they are changes in gene activity that do not involve alterations to the genetic code. Adverse epigenetic changes to individual organisms represent a biological response to an environmental factor or factors. An example of a relatively new epigenetic change in animal young that has become increasingly common over the last 20 years is disruption of the development of facial bones in newborns of many mammal and bird species.

All cell types (e.g. brain, muscle, organs) in one animal contain the exact same DNA. Epigenetic switches silence certain gene sequences and activate others so new cells can differentiate. If the switches do not work correctly, the cells may begin to continuously reproduce, resulting in cancer. Or premature cell death may occur, resulting in the failure of certain organs to develop normally or function correctly. It takes only the addition of a methyl group, consisting of one carbon atom attached to three hydrogen atoms, to change an epigenome. When a methyl group attaches to a specific spot on a gene, it can change that gene's expression, turning it off or on, lessening its expression or increasing it.

Underdeveloped premaxillary bones in grazing animals (upper jaw in other mammals and reptiles or the bone of the upper mandible on birds) and underdeveloped lower jaw are examples of gene/s for the specific affected facial bone/s either being turned off too quickly or having too little expression, resulting in under- or overbite. Giving the homeopathic cell salt calc. phos. 30X appears to cause the gene to switch back on, or at least somehow stimulate the affected facial bone or bones to begin growing again and grow to what is dictated to be normal by the individual's DNA. Unfortunately, many medical professionals consider this to be impossible, even with substantial photographic proof.

Disrupted development of the lower jaw caused Magic, one of my goats born in 2002, to have a severe overbite. I began giving her a tablet each of calc. phos. 6X and bioplasma as soon as she was born and her underdeveloped lower jawbone grew to appropriate length, resulting in a normal bite and an attractive face. I hadn't yet found that calc. phos. 30X was significantly more effective, so was still using 6X. The growth of the lower jawbone to normal size occurred because her short jawbone was actually genetically programmed to be normal in length. If it had been genetically programmed to be short, it would have been impossible for it to grow to normal length.

I had Magic and her two sisters until November 2015, when a neighbor's three large dogs killed all of them in one night. Five years after the triplets were born, their mother, a black Alpine milk goat, had to be euthanized because of cancer. Most common cancers are now known to be the result of inflammation. Epigenetic changes in the affected cells of inflamed tissue during cell division cause cancer to develop. It has become quite common in domestic goats and other animals, including humans.

Several goat owners have told me that Nubian goats have a genetic defect which often causes them to be born with an underbite. I gave calc. phos. 6X and bioplasma to my Nubian goats who were born with underbite and to Magic, who was half Nubian. The cell salts successfully stimulated the underdeveloped bones to grow to normal size in all the affected goat kids. If an underdeveloped bone can be stimulated to grow to normal with an electrolyte, the disrupted bone development would have to have been caused by an epigenetic change, not a genetic defect. The bone is clearly genetically programmed to be normal in length for the breed and sex of the animal or it would be completely impossible to stimulate it to grow to normal with electrolytes.

Many studies and reviews describe how environmental factors, especially pesticides and other toxins, disrupt the function of hormones and enzymes that guide the proper development of a fetus. The majority of newborn mammals and birds with disrupted facial bone development have an underbite. This epigenetic change is prevalent on between 40% and 60% of the newborns in several species of grazing animal in Montana and surrounding states, including white-tailed deer, mule deer, pronghorn antelope, and domestic goats.

An underdeveloped lower jaw, overbite, is far less common in mammals, and is extremely rare in birds. However, human newborns are reported to have an increasing prevalence of underdeveloped lower jaw and chin. Both types of birth defects have been connected to exposure

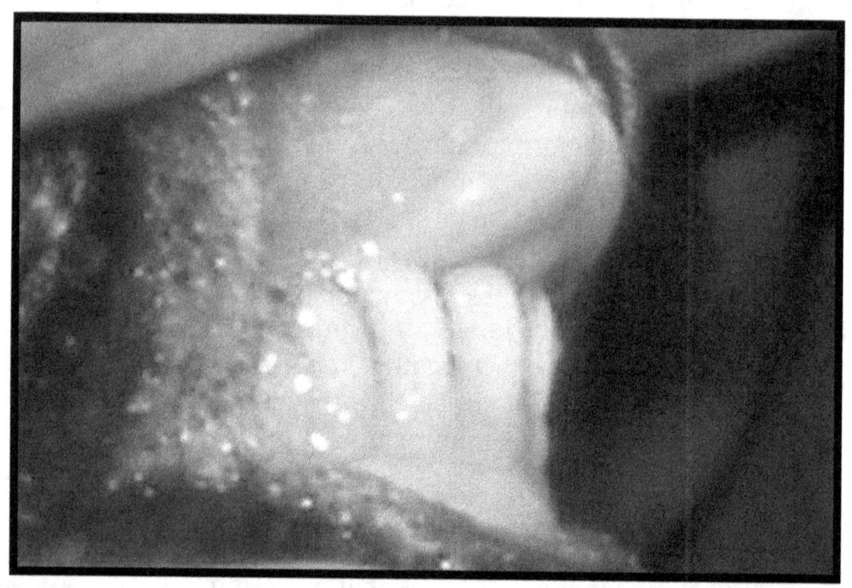

Magic had a severe overbite at birth because of a short lower jaw.

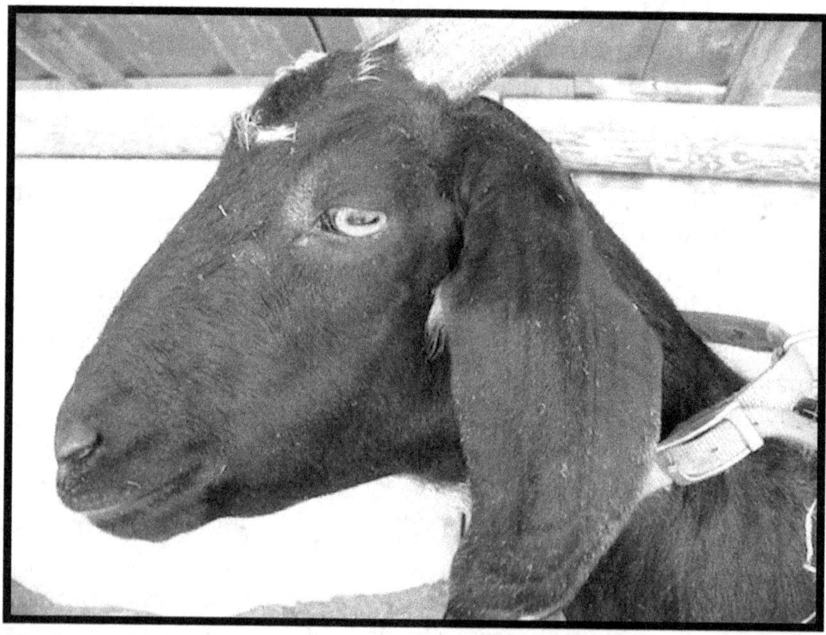

Magic had a normal bite after successful treatment with the cell salts.

to certain toxins, particularly herbicides known to cause mineral deficiencies. These deficits, especially of manganese, can disrupt fetal thyroid hormone functions, resulting in fetal hypothyroidism. In addition, sufficient manganese is absolutely essential for normal calcium metabolism and bone growth. Consequently, mineral deficiencies and the resulting fetal hypothyroidism can cause a wide range of birth defects in developing young.

When normal signals by epigenetic switches are disrupted, it causes changes in developing mammals and birds that can range from devastatingly ugly to strikingly beautiful. Melanin gives developing feathers or hair their normal colors. Birds or mammals born with disruption of melanin production or distribution, have areas of white or, less often, black where colored feathers or hair normally grow. In recent years, people have taken photos of many mammals and birds with unique and unusual coloring.

The developing cells of a number of birds in a wide variety of species produce white coloration where dark feathers should be. This abnormal feather color is called leucism and affected birds are particularly striking in appearance. Because leucistic birds are more easily seen, they often attract the attention of bird watchers (and, unfortunately, predators). I nicknamed the mostly white ones "Ghost Birds."

Many health problems in young animals that wildlife rehabbers have been able to remedy with my electrolyte combination are the result of far more devastating epigenetic changes than disrupted coloration. We have successfully caused a range of developmental problems to grow to be normal or close to normal, including underbite and overbite, crooked legs and toes, contracted tendons, disrupted feather or hair development, disrupted digestion, and others.

The affected young animals are given my electrolyte solution or commercial liquid electrolytes in combination with one tablet each of bioplasma and calc. phos. 30X, administered three or four times a day by the rehabber. Sometimes the animal's cells do not respond to this treatment because it does not work on every individual. Fortunately those who have used this method to help themselves or animals in their care have had far more successes than failures.

My hypothesis as to why cell salts significantly expedite cell hydration is that liquid electrolytes hydrate cells faster when the twelve cell salts are present to stimulate the cells, promoting faster transport of minerals into them. Stimulating cells to utilize calcium is very important for proper cellular function by the digestive organs. Thus, administering calc. phos. 30X and bioplasma appears to observably benefit digestive processes and other cellular functions dependent on calcium being readily available to all cells that need it. The two cell salt tablets may be mixed with any electrolyte solution, put into a milk formula after warming it, mixed in food, or placed directly in the mouth.

It is not surprising that I have found animals with broken bones heal faster when they are given both homeopathic tablets every three or four hours. This is likely because bioplasma stimulates uptake of other important minerals necessary for bone growth. Recovery has been fastest when both are taken or given three or four times daily, but if given at least morning and night, faster recovery than what is suggested by medical professionals has been consistently achieved in most animals. For example, broken bones in three women were completely healed in three weeks when they took calc. phos 30X during recovery. All three doctors told his patient she would be on crutches for six weeks and were astounded when the broken bone was completely healed in half that time. Broken bones in wildlife given calc. phos. 30X consistently heal in half the time it took prior to my using cell salts.

In a test done by scientists with homeopathic cell salts, a tablet was dissolved in distilled water and the mixture examined with an electron microscope. Those scientists found microscopic crystalline structures with a negative electrical charge had formed in the water. The negative charge in cells of animals given cell salts appears to enhance active transport of positively charged minerals from the bloodstream into cells that require those minerals (including calcium, selenium, magnesium, copper, manganese, zinc, nickel, iron, and others) to function properly. Mineral deficiencies usually result in adverse health issues.

A carbohydrate and vitamin combination such as Nutrical® can be mixed with liquid electrolytes for treatment of emaciated wild or domestic mammals or birds after cellular hydration has occurred, which usually takes 35 to 45 minutes. Most veterinary clinics and drug stores carry this or similar products. Nutrical® is designed to stimulate the digestive system of the animal to begin working and provides the vitamins and energy necessary for digestion; it can also stimulate appetite in those refusing to eat.

The bird or mammal can be offered food appropriate for its age and species as soon as it is hydrated enough to digest it. For birds, my electrolyte combination may be added to the food at each feeding until the bird has completely recovered and is eating normally. The electrolyte solution may be given to mammal young between milk formula feedings, but there must be at least an hour between the liquid electrolytes and a milk feeding. Giving milk and liquid electrolytes at the same time to a young mammal, thus diluting milk, can cause it to form a toxin in a newborn's stomach and make it ill or even kill it. **Never dilute milk with water when used for feeding.** Usually after a baby mammal is drinking and digesting milk, it no longer needs liquid electrolytes, but the two cell salt tablets should be dissolved in the warmed milk formula just prior to feeding.

I have also found, for young mammals who are vomiting or have diarrhea, that giving one tablet each of calc. phos. 30X (6X works well also) and bioplasma every two hours, while frequently giving small amounts of liquid electrolytes, will usually alleviate symptoms in six hours or less. It is best to continue giving both tablets every three hours until a dehydrated animal has completely recovered from symptoms including starvation, vomiting, or diarrhea. Milk should not be fed to mammal young who are vomiting. They can be fed milk when the vomiting stops, beginning with a small amount every two or three hours. I give both cell salts to young animals at least three times a day until birds have fledged or mammals are weaned, promoting strong bones and normal keratin development in the feathers or hair.

To help an adult mammal recover from illness, diarrhea, or vomiting, I give as much as the animal will drink of the electrolyte solution every three hours, with one tablet each of bioplasma and calc. phos. 30X dissolved in it. The cell salt tablets can also be placed directly into the animal's mouth. This usually alleviates vomiting and diarrhea within a few hours. If it doesn't, the animal should be seen by a veterinarian to determine the cause of the symptoms.

Properly hydrated cells work much better than dehydrated ones. When I am ill, I drink a glass of water containing 1/8 teaspoon of my dry electrolyte mixture, and take one tablet each of bioplasma and calc. phos. 30X first thing in the morning and several times daily. I have found no greater effect on animals or myself by administering two or more tablets of the cell salts at a time than with just one of each. Personally, I take the two kinds of cell salt tablets four times every day, and drink plenty of water or other fluids. Younger people have reported that taking cell salts twice a day, morning and evening, is enough to keep them feeling healthy and energetic. I have found the electrolyte combination helps me feel well and pain free, but it may not work as effectively on others. It depends on the ability of a person's body to alleviate what is causing their adverse health issues. The cell salts themselves do not cure anything. However, properly functioning cells can cure illnesses and other health issues. Cell salts are electrolytes which appear to help cells function more efficiently. Cell salts are not drugs.

When working or playing strenuously, drinking my electrolyte combination every three hours the day before and then during the high activity period appears to result in less soreness and a higher and longer-lasting energy level. It is important to drink adequate water in addition to the electrolytes. People who are hiking have reported an observable positive effect when drinking my electrolyte combination two or three times a day. Show horses given the electrolyte combination to drink, before, during, and for at least a day after a show, have had the same positive results, with high energy levels and less muscle soreness.

Several companies produce homeopathic cell salts, but I use Hyland's brand. Bioplasma and calc. phos. 6X or 30X can be obtained at very reasonable prices by shopping on the Internet. I've found calc. phos. 30X more effective than 6X because the positive bioelectrical effects on the cells last twice as long.

Giving the cell salt tablets in the formula to bottle fed young ones three or more times a day is easily accomplished because newborn mammals should be fed every three or four hours anyway. Birds heal quickly and sleep at night; therefore, giving the two cell salt tablets every three hours during the day seems to work well for any bird with a broken bone or for young birds with digestive problems or underdeveloped bones. Hatchlings of fast-growing, large domestic birds like grouse, chickens, turkeys, or waterfowl should be fed a high protein game bird starter with at least 30% protein to provide essential nutrients. If they are also given one tablet each of calc. phos. 30X and bioplasma in their drinking water morning and night to help their cells utilize minerals and other nutrients, young birds usually have no joint or digestive problems.

When I use my electrolyte combination on dehydrated birds and mammals, the synergistic effect between the bioplasma, calc. phos. 30X, and modified United Nations electrolyte solution is often amazing. Owls, hawks, and small mammals have gone from lying unconscious and appearing dead to being able to stand, walk, and digest food in slightly less than an hour. Carnivorous birds like hawks, eagles, and owls can then be fed small amounts of rodent meat right away, as long as the electrolytes continue to be tubed into their crop every 20 to 30 minutes. Feeding dehydrated or starved individuals, mammals and birds, too soon can cause them to die. When my electrolyte combination is administered, they are able to eat and digest food much more quickly than when the cell salts are not included.

I know of several people who have taken the electrolyte combination four times a day for several days prior to and right after having surgery. They recovered more rapidly from surgery, had little to no pain, and healed more quickly than people who had the same surgery but didn't take the electrolyte combination. This even occurred for elderly patients. Such fast recovery from injuries suggests that, besides promoting rapid hydration of the cells, the electrolyte combination containing the two cell salt tablets likely helps stimulate the immune system to work at optimum levels. Animals with injuries recover much more quickly and antibiotics appear to work more effectively when the combination is given to the injured individual. Adult humans can drink my electrolyte combination at least twice a day and plain water the rest of the time. For adult mammals, the homemade electrolytes (or commercial liquid electrolytes) can be dissolved in their drinking water with cell salt tablets added or directly placed in the animal's mouth.

The reason certain symptoms tend to recur on some individuals is often their greater sensitivity to toxic chemical combinations in the air, which is now literally an airborne chemical soup. All life is continuously exposed by ingestion, inhalation, and skin contact, but some individuals are much more sensitive to it than others. According to studies, approximately 37% of the adult human population in the U.S. experiences Multiple Chemical Sensitivity. The majority of chemically sensitive people (about 70%) are female. Taking the electrolyte combination has also worked well for people who have hypersensitive reactions to perfumes or pesticides, with symptoms being alleviated in a short time. Exposure to such toxins can cause coughing, headache, and swelling and reddening of the face and eyes. Exposed individuals may also experience a red rash, burning eyes, nausea, and disorientation.

Before and after they are born, young animals, including children, can be much more seriously impacted by far lower toxin concentrations than those affecting adults. In developing young, very low-level chemical exposures result in energy depletion in the cells, which causes their proteins to be degraded. The proteins have to produce enough energy to provide growth, and to simultaneously challenge the effects of bacteria, viruses, and toxins. Often this is impossible for cells of developing young because exposure to toxins causes mineral imbalances and oxygen depletion. These issues result in severe energy depletion, which can cause a developing embryo or fetus to have improper growth of one or more organs or systems, including heart, lungs, skeletal, and immune systems.

Most concerning, birds and mammals hatched or born with normally developed facial bones were observed to suddenly develop quite a severe underbite within 36 to 48 hours after exposure to a known application of commonly used herbicides, especially 2,4-D. I could find no report in scientific studies of this happening prior to our observations of this phenomenon. An interesting incident involved a hatchling Bank Swallow rescued from a collapsed bank containing the nest burrow. A man working nearby saw the bank fall and hurriedly dug into the debris to search for hatchlings. After finding three dead babies and one alive, he called to ask if he could bring me the little swallow for care. I asked him to bring all the hatchlings so I could examine the dead ones.

All of the swallows had a shorter upper bill than lower and smaller than normal eyes. The man told me he had been working in the same area for several days so I asked whether he had observed any spraying of pesticides nearby. He had seen the county weed truck spray both sides of the road with herbicides two days prior to the collapse of the bank, confirming why all the hatchlings had an underbite.

My friend Wayne Tree came to visit the day the swallow arrived for care. Wayne always had his camera with him, so I asked him to photograph the underbite on the little swallow. Every three hours during the day, until I released it, I gave it calc. phos. 30X and bioplasma in its food. After two days, its upper face had grown to look completely normal. I released the fledgling swallow when it was old enough to fly well. They learn to catch flying insects fairly quickly if released where other swallows are feeding. Unfortunately, I did not have anyone take a photo of the swallow after its upper bill had grown to normal length; my camera was not working at the time.

To my knowledge, overbite has not been observed to suddenly occur after an animal is hatched or born, like the underbite, but it has been seen in newborn and adult mammals, especially wild and domestic grazing animals, and is reported to be increasing in newborn children. It is important to stress that giving calc. phos. 6X or 30X and bioplasma two or three times daily to domestic animals born with underbite or overbite has caused the underdeveloped bones to grow to normal length, resulting in a normal bite. With either underbite or overbite, prognosis is best in both mammals and birds if cell salts are given at least twice daily beginning immediately after the animal is born or hatched, or immediately after the disrupted bone development occurs on previously normal young after being affected by toxin exposure.

The hatchling Bank Swallow with underdevelopment of the upper face, showing the short upper bill and small eye. Photo by Wayne Tree.

Positive effects like improved bone density or improvement in cellular or organ function can only be determined by before-and-after medical tests. Scientific studies of the beneficial effects of homeopathic cell salts alone and in combination with liquid electrolyte solutions would seem to be warranted, since most men, women, and children, as well as domestic animals and wildlife, have observable positive effects when the electrolyte combination I discovered was taken or given, and for some issues, when just one or both homeopathic cell salts were administered. A few individuals appear to have no effects, likely because each animal is different or their cells are not able to mitigate the problem. Many of the positive effects of the two cell salts and amazing hydrating effects of my electrolyte combination were first observed on newborns or young animals I raised, as described in the stories in this book about Firefly and other deer fawns, Blondie, Kitcat, Magic, an elk calf, bear cubs, birds, and many other animals. They have continued to produce similar excellent results on hundreds of animals received by rehabbers in the years since.

**You are seldom so
broken that you can't be fixed
by a loving lick.**

CHAPTER 4
HUNGRY BEARS AND BARE BEARS

Orphaned triplet black bear cubs are shown in a photo taken by Kathleen Meyer. Honey is being licked by her brother, Smokey, while Blackie keeps close watch on the photographer.

In spring 1998, the same spring Firefly was born with severe under-bite, nearly all of the bushes and trees throughout western Montana that usually produce abundant berries produced almost none. Only a few blossoms had been pollinated, with all species of fruiting bushes being affected. The experts never determined if this phenomenon was caused by a failure of the bushes to produce blossoms or due to a lack of pollinators. Whether plants were high on the mountains, at medium elevations, or at lower elevations made no difference. Berries were few and far between. The huckleberry crop did not materialize; serviceberries were hard to find, as were chokecherries, elderberries, and all other wild fruit. Dr. Charles Jonkel, a wildlife biologist specializing in bears, stated in a news interview that such a failure of fruit production in so many species of plants was a phenomenon that would likely happen only once in 500 years. Unfortunately, with fewer and fewer bees and other wild pollinators, this may become common.

Identical failed berry production also occurred that spring in Ontario, Canada, resulting in the same effects on female bears and cubs as in western Montana. To find enough alternative food to gain sufficient fat for surviving hibernation, large numbers of mothers brought their cubs down to low elevations where most of the people live. Many females were killed or frightened away from their cubs, orphaning dozens of starving babies. Some people said the mothers were so desperate they abandoned their cubs, but bears seldom do that for any reason. A number of them were shot by people protecting beehives and chickens. Many were killed during the fall hunting season and others were hit by cars. As a result of inadequate fat reserves, some adult bears and many cubs likely died of starvation during the winter. Far fewer black bears were seen the next two or three years, indicating a decline in the population.

In western Montana, game wardens captured at least 70 orphaned cubs, who were taken to the three rehabilitation facilities with large, covered pens strong enough to contain young bears. Any kennel or pen used for bear cubs has to be strong and on cement, so they can't dig under the chain link panel sides. Being a wild animal, they do not take kindly to being handled, so many cubs are captured by tranquilizing them. Healthy black bear cubs weigh only four to six pounds when they come out of the den with their mother, but by fall, when female bears are most often killed for getting into chicken houses, honeybee hives, or other trouble with people, the cubs can weigh from 20 to 30 pounds. How heavy they are by denning time in September depends on how much food is available in the habitat where they live. If their mother is killed and they are on their own for an extended period, they lose weight, often weighing only around 15 pounds by the time they are captured.

The high black bear population in the Flathead Valley, with little to no fruit on which to fatten, resulted in many mothers getting into trouble in that part of western Montana. Consequently, 35 bear cubs were captured and taken to the wildlife rehab center in Kalispell. Beth Watne, who ran that facility, had to build several new kennels in order to hold all the bears brought to her. Fortunately, she was able to put several similar-sized cubs in each large kennel. MDFWP personnel took 20 or more to their Helena rehabilitation facility.

Bob, as game warden for MDFWP, had the job of catching orphaned cubs in our area. He brought them home, putting them in chain link kennels we had built for young bears in previous years. We had installed all of the kennels on a large concrete slab that was on our land when we bought it. Hungry cubs caught by other wardens soon joined those Bob captured, so we eventually had 13 young bears to feed and house. It was necessary to borrow and install more kennels, and build additional plywood shelters to put in them. Most shelters were designed to hold two young bears. Single cubs of similar size were placed in the same enclosure; some were siblings who were housed together. Bear cubs prefer to have a friend or sibling with whom to wrestle and play. They cuddle up together to keep each other warm during cold winter days and nights. We put the only set of triplets in a 13 by 13-foot kennel, complete with an insulated doghouse large enough to hold all three growing cubs.

Except for one bear, who managed to escape after he had become quite fat, and a two-year-old female, who was released alone, all the bears were released in pairs. Experts say younger cubs have a much better chance of survival when they are not alone, because there are two pairs of eyes and ears, and two noses to detect danger in the form of predators or large male bears. Also by watching each other, the bears learn what to eat, where to find food, and which large animals to avoid. Such information, usually taught to them by their mothers, is vitally important for a young bear's survival.

Success in locating food may be especially helpful with pairs who are not siblings, since each may have learned from its mother where to find special foods that the other might not know. How to catch fish, dig out and catch ground squirrels and other small rodents, where to find moths, beetles, and other insects, how to rob a wild beehive of its honey, which plant tops, roots, or fruits are good to eat, and where to find the most nutritious, edible plants are just a few of the many survival skills mother bears pass on to their cubs. The type of habitat in her territory determines which foods each bear utilizes. Some would be available in isolated ecosystems that are not found in other areas. The habitat where cubs are released after spending the winter in captivity may differ from the one where the cubs were born and lived during the summer with their mothers. Thus, the combined knowledge of two cubs greatly enhances the likelihood of survival for both.

Morning and evening, Bob fed each cub a bowl of puppy food, a day-old donut (donated by a friend who ran a local bakery), and a cup of sliced apples. The cubs always ate the donut first, then the dog food and apples. We hoped the apples would clean their teeth after they ate the donut. Whenever we could, we gave them various pieces of fruits and vegetables donated by local grocery stores.

With the help of Kathleen Meyer, an author, photographer, and good friend, we set up an adopt-a-cub program so people could adopt one and donate some money to help buy dog food. At that time, it cost over $100 per bear for puppy food to feed it through the winter. Kathleen took photos of the cubs, made copies, and mailed them to all the generous people who adopted one. A class at Lone Rock School, a Bitterroot Valley elementary school, adopted Black Velvet, a small female. The class raised money to help pay for her food by selling T-shirts with her photo on them.

One of the first cubs Bob caught in fall 1998 was Yogi, a one-year-old male, also black in color. Yogi came from south of Victor, Montana, where a vehicle hit him, stunning him and badly bruising his right shoulder. We placed him in a smaller pen by himself. Being a year and a half old, he was larger than the eight- and nine-month-old cubs who came to us later. When he first arrived, we gave Yogi a dose of homeopathic cell salts and electrolytes twice a day to help him recover from his injuries. He ate well, but was not putting on much weight. One day, the grocery store owner gave us a box of over-ripe peaches. After removing the pits, which contain cyanide, Bob gave Yogi some to eat along with his large dish of dog food. The next day, Yogi began passing hundreds of white roundworms. Every stool he produced for two days was full of dead worms. It was kind of disconcerting to us that a few peaches had enough insecticide on them to completely deworm a bear cub, but fortunately, eliminating the parasites was good for Yogi. He began gaining weight much faster and remained healthy.

His shoulder recovered completely, so he could walk and run unimpeded. By late fall, he was fat enough to hibernate, so Bob released him. Yogi was never tranquilized. He was placed in a carrying cage while still stunned by the vehicle impact, and at the time of release he was sufficiently manageable without it. We put a wooden carrying box in his kennel, blocked the door to his house, and Yogi dashed right into the carrying box. We quickly closed the door and put the box into the back of Bob's pickup. Bob drove to the release site he had chosen for Yogi, high up in the Bitterroot Mountains. At the site, Bob slid the carrying box out of the pickup with a ramp and pulley. When it was on the ground, he opened the door. Yogi ran out of the box straight to the nearest tree, scrambling up the rough trunk as fast as his legs would go. From his vantage point high in the tree, he watched as Bob returned the carrying box to his truck and drove away. Hopefully, Yogi was able to find a good den site where he could hibernate through the winter.

This type of release avoids any adverse reactions to a tranquilizer. The chemicals in them can cause sensitive bear cubs, especially females, to be ill for a long period of time. If these bears are released immediately after being tranquilized, the long-lasting effects can impede their ability to find food or avoid predators. Wolves and adult male bears will kill cubs if they can catch them. Young bears have to be vigilant at all times and adept at climbing trees to avoid being eaten by large predators.

Another bear who did not remain with us all winter was fairly hefty for his age. By fall, a yearling is actually a year and a half old. We named him Griz because he was a beautiful golden brown, like a Grizzly Bear. A warden from Missoula County brought Griz to us after being tranquilized because he was running around in people's yards in the town of Superior, Montana. With the help of electrolytes and cell salts, he quickly recovered from the effects of the drugs. Griz arrived in the middle of September, ate well, and gained weight quickly. By the end of October, he was fat, healthy, and appeared ready to hibernate. Bears usually do not hibernate while we have them in captivity, but we were not destined to find out if Griz would have.

One evening near the first of November, I left the padlock off the top U-shaped latch on Griz's kennel door so Bob wouldn't have to unlock it when he arrived in a few minutes to feed the bears. I went back to the house to feed fawns and a phone call caused a 15-minute delay in Bob's arrival to the bear pens, an unfortunate chain of events.

There are two U-shaped latches holding the doors closed, one about waist high, the other near the bottom. Having two latches is supposed to prevent animals in the kennel from opening the door. Griz, however, was able to quickly raise and unlatch both, then push open the door. He was gone by the time Bob arrived at the pens. Griz must have run straight to the closest mountains, about four miles away, because we never had any reports of bears in the neighborhood. It doesn't take long for a bear to run that far, so he was likely well into the mountains by morning. All we could do is hope he was able to find a warm, protected den in which to hibernate. Being well-fed, intelligent, resourceful, and independent was definitely in his favor.

A few days before Halloween, a set of triplet cubs was captured in Superior, Montana, the same town where Griz was caught. All the cubs, two females and a male, were black. We named the girls Honey and Blackie; their slightly larger brother was Smokey. The tissue inside the upper and lower eyelids is normally pinkish-white on a healthy animal. Both Honey and Blackie had severely inflamed conjunctiva, with the tissue so red and swollen it protruded up over part of the eye. This condition is called blepharitis and indicates their immune systems were reacting quite severely to an irritant. The triplets had all been tranquilized, the drug appearing to affect the two females more than any other cubs we received for care. Both had severe mucous diarrhea and didn't eat much for the first 10 days after they came to us. Smokey, the male, only required a couple days to recover from the effects of the tranquilizer. Unlike his sensitive sisters, he began eating well and gaining weight right away.

I gave all three the homeopathic cell salt tablets three times a day by poking them into the side of an apple slice. It was a bit tricky to throw it just right so the bear I wanted to eat it actually did. They all liked apples, so tried to get the slice when I threw it. To distract the bear or bears who had already eaten a treated slice, I threw untreated ones to them. Then I was able to throw a treated slice directly in front of the bear who still needed one, so eventually they all received their cell salt tablets.

By mid-November, all three cubs were eating like bears and gaining weight. They played and wrestled, often licking each other, and were always affectionate towards one another. They were fun to watch, but were not like human children. They hardly ever quarreled, not even over food. All went well with all the bears in our care until January 1999. At that time, for reasons that remain unknown, many species of animal, including humans, began experiencing symptoms consistent with an acute chemical exposure. Both Honey and Blackie again began having severe mucous diarrhea, similar to what they experienced when they were tranquilized. This time though, they alarmingly had bright red blood in their feces. Even worse, since it was winter and outside temperatures were cold, both began losing their winter coat, with beautiful black hair falling off in bunches. By the end of January, they had lost all of their hair except for that on their head and neck. They were very strange-looking bears, with bare gray bodies and black furry heads. There was no sign of any parasite or other explanation for their strange hair loss. Both cubs had smooth whitish-grey skin with no sore spots or crawly things anywhere. It was more like a chemotherapy-type of hair loss. Smokey, the male, did not have any symptoms at all, even though he slept with his sisters. This is also not consistent with a parasite infestation or other type of infection. Parasites do not care whether their lunch is male or female. Many environmental toxins are estrogenic, causing an estrogen-dominance hormone imbalance in females. Males seem to be protected, at least somewhat, by their male hormones.

Blackie's mental state was more affected by whatever was in the air than any other bear we had ever cared for during winter. She would get startled or became frightened easily. Then she would pace rapidly back and forth on one side of the kennel. When the first bears began showing adverse symptoms, I gave all of the cubs both of the cell salt tablets in apple slices to stimulate their cells to work properly. I also began putting electrolytes in their water once a day, similar to what we did for those who had been tranquilized. By mid-February, Honey and Blackie acted more normal and their hair began growing back. At the end of April, the two females were covered with beautiful, black, shiny hair, showing no new symptoms of chemical poisoning, although Blackie still occasionally paced the side of the kennel. The three steadily grew bigger and they and the other bears still in our care at the end of May appeared completely healthy. The MDFWP wardens had scheduled five of the cubs for release around the first week of June.

Not long after we received the triplets, several more cubs were captured and brought to us for care. Yogette was a little black female who had required tranquilization for capture at the school playground in Frenchtown, Montana. While she was unconscious, a red tag was placed in one ear, saving her from being tranquilized on release day. When she arrived, Yogette had the same chemical poisoning symptoms as Honey and Blackie had after being tranquilized. The inside of both of her eyelids were so red and swollen the conjunctiva could be seen protruding out from under both lower lids. It took nearly two weeks for the inflammation to diminish and the mucous in her stool to clear up. After that she was healthy until she again had some symptoms as a result of the air pollution in January. Fortunately, she didn't suffer severe hair loss like some of the other cubs.

Soon after Yogette arrived, we gave her a roommate. Elkie, a small black male from Elk Ridge, near Hamilton, Montana, was captured in a barrel trap, so was not subjected to a tranquilizer. He was very healthy and ate well, seeming not at all sensitive to the air pollution. Not having to recover from a tranquilizer, he began eating well immediately. He was a real chowhound and was soon as big as Yogette, who had been somewhat larger when the two first arrived. They ate, slept, and played together through the winter and were fat and healthy by spring.

We put Elkie and Yogette in carrying boxes and Bob released them together in late May. Yogette's ear tag was never turned in by a hunter nor was she ever recaptured by the MDFWP. That usually means either the cubs do not survive after release, or they live and never get into trouble. There is always the possibility that a predator kills the bear, or it may be killed illegally; in either case, the ear tag would not be turned in. The best we could do was provide a chance at survival by fattening them up and releasing them far from human habitation. Elkie was not ear-tagged, so we did not expect any post-release information about him. In fact, we never received reports about even the ear-tagged or tattooed bears that Bob had released from our care during his years as a warden.

We received several more bear cubs in November and December. At that time, we had so many arriving each week, we had to borrow a large kennel from our neighbor, who didn't plan to use it that winter. We returned it after the bears were released. We also built another 26 by 13-foot kennel, which we divided into two 13 by 13-foot sections, which held two bears each.

In mid-November, we received a small brown male I called Lolo because he came from three miles west of Lolo, Montana. He was smaller than the others we received in November and December so we originally put him in a kennel by himself. We didn't know whether Lolo had been tranquilized when he was captured; he was awake when he arrived. He ate well and had only slightly inflamed conjunctiva. Lolo had just a little mucous in his stool in January when many other animals, including several of the other bears, had more severe symptoms of exposure to environmental toxins.

In February, another small brown male was brought to us. I called him Lewie after Meriwether Lewis because he was captured at Traveler's Rest near Lolo. Lewie was the final bear we received that winter, and amazingly, was Lolo's twin. As soon as we put them together, they acted like long lost brothers, showing obvious pleasure in seeing each other again. Instead of standing apart and checking each other out like cubs usually do when first placed together, Lolo and Lewie immediately rushed toward each other, each wrapping the other in long front legs, just like two children hugging. They sat there for a long time in each other's arms, both making low moaning noises. I could imagine them saying "Where have you been? I have missed you so much!" They reminded me of human siblings I had seen reunited on television after being separated for many years, hugging while sobbing for joy.

The two cubs played and wrestled together for a long time after their touching reunion and lengthy hug. Lolo had been eating well since November. Lewie also ate well from the beginning of his captivity, and soon caught up with Lolo's rotund shape. They looked like furry brown balls. Until his brother joined him, Lolo had been shy and brooding, seldom coming out of his house. Having his twin with him changed his whole personality.

The two played outside much of the day, seeming happy and content the rest of the winter. When spring came, Bob released them together in a remote mountain area, as far from civilization as possible. We had them run into the transport boxes, so they didn't have to be tranquilized. Like the other bears Bob had freed, they ran right out of the box and up the nearest tree. Hopefully this was the beginning of a long life in the wild where they belonged. As it turned out, the bears Bob returned to the mountains were far luckier than the five bears fated to be released by other MDFWP wardens, because they were not subjected to the stress of being shot with a tranquilizer gun, nor did they have to recover from effects of the drug after being released.

During the first part of November, several other bear cubs had been captured and brought to us for care. Black Velvet, a beautiful female, and Blueberry, a brown male, came in just days apart, so were placed in kennels next to each other. They seemed to like each other, but Black Velvet was only nine months old and much smaller than Blueberry, who was nearly two years old. We were afraid to put them both in the small kennel, but they were released together. We hoped they would remain together so Black Velvet could learn survival skills from Blueberry. Having been with his mother for over a year and a half, Blueberry should have learned many skills that Black Velvet would not have had time to learn from hers, being separated just nine months after birth. Normally, cubs remain with the mother until they are old enough to be on their own as yearlings. They hibernate together and, after the family comes out of hibernation, the year-old cubs remain with her until late spring or early summer. Then she permanently leaves them to find a male bear, mate, and subsequently produce another family of cubs.

We received two more small cubs a few days after Blueberry and Black Velvet had settled in. Both were females I named Huckleberry and Raspberry. Huckleberry was very black with a bluish tinge in bright sunlight; Raspberry was a pretty reddish-brown. Though the species name is Black Bear, each has its own individual color and color patterns, possibilities including white, light blond, golden brown, grayish brown, reddish brown, dark brown, brownish black, dusky black, and blue black, with varying amounts of white on the chest or no white markings. Over the years, we cared for Black Bears of every color except completely white.

Huckleberry and Raspberry came from two different areas, so were unrelated but, because they were the same size, we put them together. Just in case they didn't like sharing, we provided separate sleeping boxes. They immediately bonded, acting like best friends. After they chose one of the boxes for their home, we removed the second one for another bear in a different kennel.

The conjunctiva on Huckleberry's right eye was so red and swollen it partially covered the bottom inside corner of her eye. Huckleberry, Raspberry, Black Velvet, and Blueberry were all very sensitive to pollution in the weather fronts. After the incident in January, both Huckleberry and Raspberry lost the hair on their rumps and part way up their sides, but did not lose as much as Honey and Blackie. We had been caring for bear cubs for more than 25 years without ever before having any bear lose its hair, ruling out stress from captivity or change in diet as likely causes for this strange occurrence. However, hair loss is quite common with chemical poisoning. The question was, what was in the air in mid-January that was so incredibly toxic?

Through most of that January (1999), we gave all of the bears homeopathic cell salts four times a day in a slice of apple. We added a pinch of the dry electrolyte mixture to their water twice daily to prevent dehydration from diarrhea. During the second week of January, all the female bears and Blueberry, the little brown male, began having an even more serious reaction. I know the cause had to be airborne because many other animals in the valley, including humans, all began having health problems at exactly the same time. The symptoms were similar in all, except for the hair loss, which apparently only affected some bears. Many people had diarrhea, abdominal pain, serious respiratory problems, burning eyes, and extremely red, swollen conjunctiva. Other animals, especially our always-sensitive milk goats and many of the wild deer who live in our area, had diarrhea. Most also had red, swollen conjunctiva, with green discharge running out of the corners of their eyes and down their faces. Several of the bear cubs would not eat anything right after a new weather front came through and some had bloody, runny stools after the most seriously toxic ones flowed through the Bitterroot Valley from the west. Fortunately, the electrolyte combination cleared up the bloody diarrhea fairly quickly, as that condition can be deadly if it continues too long.

I gave Blueberry his name because of his blue ear tag, which allowed him to avoid tranquilization on release day. Black Velvet did not have one so regrettably she did have to be tranquilized. Blueberry had taken a long time to recover from the drug when he was captured, and was nearly as sensitive to the contaminants in weather fronts as Huckleberry and Raspberry.

By mid-February all of the bears were finally healthy again. Their conjunctiva was no longer red and swollen, they were eating well with no digestive problems, and by March, all those with hair loss had completely regrown their coat.

During the last of April and the first part of May, the bears would often climb up the side of the kennel and stare out toward the green forested mountains in the distance. They were unequivocally indicating they were anxious to get out of their jail-like kennels and return to the wild where they were born. In mid-May, we loaded Huckleberry and Raspberry into carrying boxes and Bob took them far back into the mountains. They were finally free.

The first week of June, the day the Montana Department of Fish, Wildlife and Parks had scheduled release of the remaining cubs, began as a beautiful spring morning. At about 9:00 a.m. several game wardens arrived. Two of their pickups were pulling culvert-like bear traps on wheels, which they planned to use for transporting the animals to release sites. We still had five: the triplets, Black Velvet, and Blueberry. The triplets were going to be released together in one area. Black Velvet and Blueberry were to be hard released in another area. A hard release is when the bears are chased by bear dogs as soon as they run out of the culvert traps, with people yelling and shooting bean bags at them. The purpose is to instill fear of people and dogs, teaching the bears to avoid areas populated by humans and their domestic animals.

Because the wardens had forgotten to ear tag Black Velvet at the time of capture, the sergeant insisted she had to be tranquilized again. They had also forgotten to ear tag the triplets when they were originally caught. The first of May, I had asked them do the tranquilizing and ear tagging at least a month before the bears were to be released. That way, the sensitive ones would have time to recover from the drug in a safe place. They said that was too much trouble, indicating they did not believe there was such a thing as a chemically sensitive bear. As it turned out, doing as I suggested would have been far less trouble. More importantly, the bears would have had a much better chance to survive.

The drug used was Telazol, fairly new at that time and considered safer than the older types of tranquilizer. The warden sergeant also wanted to try a new gun that fired darts with a twenty-two blank. That gun contributed in large part to what ended up being a disastrous day. He shot a dart at Blackie first. Frightened by the commotion and all the strangers, she was pacing rapidly back and forth on the far side of the pen. The dart hit her in the rump but, after fifteen minutes, she had not missed a step, still pacing as fast as before. I had warned the sergeant more than once that tranquilizing Blackie or Honey would make them very ill at best and could even kill them because they both had adverse reactions to chemicals. The Telazol did not seem to be working properly on Blackie, either because she was severely stressed or because the dart had failed to deliver the entire dose into her muscle.

After backing off to wait for Blackie to get drowsy, the warden fired a dart at Smokey, but it bounced out, releasing most of the tranquilizer into his fur. Then he went to Black Velvet's pen and fired a dart at her. Again, the dart popped right out, releasing at least some of the Telazol into her fur. The problem was they couldn't tell how much had gone into the three cubs' muscles. Poor little Black Velvet seemed totally stunned that someone would shoot at her or for that matter hurt her. Apparently, having good interactions with Bob when he fed and watered her had made her forget she had been shot with a tranquilizer dart before. At least the new dart gun was useful for something. It was proving to be quite proficient at training bears to be afraid of people.

While the wardens loaded darts for an older type of tranquilizer gun, Bob and I peacefully caught Blueberry in our carrying box. Bob tipped the plywood sleeping box to make Blueberry run out. I placed the carrying box, with a sliding door at one end, where his sleeping box had been. Blueberry watched the whole procedure, and then ran right into the carrying box. I just stepped over and slid the door down, trapping him inside. The men carried him to a cart attached to my four-wheeler, which I drove to the culvert trap. When they placed the end of the box into the culvert and opened the sliding door, Blueberry ran into the culvert trap in which he would be transported to the release site.

I asked again that we forget about tranquilizing the other four bears and just load them in the same way. It would have been so much less stressful for the bears, but the wardens would not even consider it, insisting they had to have ear tags. We checked the already-darted cubs, Blackie, Smokey, and Black Velvet. Except for Blackie, they were not showing any visible effects of the Telazol that had been shot into them with the first darts. Blackie's eyes were twitching, but she was pacing even faster than before she was shot. The wardens had a conference to determine how much more tranquilizer to give them and what to use to inject it.

Bob drove to our house on the four-wheeler to get the homemade jab pole he had used successfully for many years. It was a steel pole with a place in one end to put a drug-filled dart. You just poke the dart into the bear's rump and the pressure on the pole pushes the contents into the bear, similar to giving it an injection with a syringe. As soon as Bob returned, the wardens decided I should have each bear go into the carrying box so they could inject the drug with the jab pole.

I told them I could easily get the bears to go into the carrying box, repeating that if they gave Blackie more of the tranquilizer, she might die. They could see she was already severely stressed. I tried one final time to convince them she was extremely sensitive to chemicals. I was also worried about Honey, because she and Blackie both had had a severe reaction to the tranquilizer when they were captured the previous fall. I might as well have been talking to the cement we were standing on. My concerns were completely ignored.

I entered the triplets' pen and, while the three were all out of their house, I nailed the door closed so they could no longer go inside. The men brought the carrying box into the pen. I told them to go somewhere out of sight, while I calmed the triplets. Blackie went into the box, which she likely considered a safe place to hide. I slid the door shut and the men carried her to the back of the warden sergeant's pickup. I kept

Blackie's attention at the wire end of the box, while Bob lifted the sliding door, exposing her rump. By using a flashlight to get a good view of her, the sergeant was able to inject her with the dart on the jab pole. It took two tries, as he did not push hard enough to empty the dart the first time. Bob explained to him how the jab pole works. By giving a good push, the dart stops once it is in the bear, with the end of the pole sliding forward to push the plunger to inject the drug. They moved the truck into the shade and waited for Blackie to become unconscious. Telazol dehydrates the animal and causes rapid breathing. Blackie was already breathing very fast before being injected with more of the drug.

The wardens all left the area where Blackie was sitting, saying we had to stay away so she would not be bothered by our presence while she lost consciousness. They went over to the pen where Smokey and Honey had been observing our activities with what appeared to be keen interest, but was more likely trepidation. One of the wardens decided to try the new gun again, shooting Smokey in the lower part of the hind leg. That made me angry, because the needle on a dart shot from a gun can cause impact damage to the bone, with the possibility of developing an infection later.

Suddenly, I had an overwhelming feeling that something was terribly wrong with Blackie. It had been less than three minutes since she was injected. I went to check on her in spite of the warden's instructions to stay away. Her tongue was hanging far out the side of her mouth; it and the inside of her mouth were a horrible shade of purple. She was not breathing. I yelled loud enough for the entire county to hear, "You've got a dead bear here." All the wardens ran to the pickup where Blackie's motionless body lay in the carrying box. Working together, they dragged her out and laid her on the pickup bed. One began CPR; another checked her mouth and trachea to see if there was an obstruction. It was obvious to me when I first saw her that it was far too late to help her. Her bright, intelligent eyes were completely dull and lifeless.

Then overwhelming anger took over my good sense and I said, "I told you that you would kill her if you tranquilized her. I do not know why you couldn't listen." That was it. I had done the unforgivable. I, a woman, had essentially said "I told you so" to a whole group of men. Fish, Wildlife and Parks never again let us care for bears. Bob and I weren't the ones who killed the cub, but we were to be forever punished for my indiscretion. Bob was the primary caregiver to the bears. It was completely unfair to punish him for my crime.

In my defense, after caring for them for so long and nursing them back to health through bouts of bloody diarrhea, hair loss, blepharitis, and other immune dysfunctions, only someone with a stone heart would not feel affection and concern for every one of those cubs. They can't learn to talk in human language like birds do, but they communicate in many other ways. They are affectionate and caring toward their sibling or kennel mate, interacting in ways similar to young children. To Bob and me, Blackie and all the other cubs were intelligent, sentient individuals, each with his or her own unique personality. It was very difficult to watch a bear we had known and cared for die because of an ear tag.

The wardens worked on Blackie's lifeless body for several more minutes before placing her into one of their trucks. I asked them to take her body to the Fish, Wildlife and Parks lab for a necropsy, saying I would like a copy of the lab report. I never received one, so assume no necropsy was performed. The cause of death was obvious to the wardens. More of the tranquilizer had apparently been injected than they realized the first time they shot Blackie. Receiving an additional full dose was more than her chemically-sensitive system could handle, with a tragic result.

We soon turned our attention to the other cubs. I coaxed Black Velvet into the carrying box, where they were able to easily inject Telazol into her rump with the jab pole. She quickly became completely unconscious, her breathing shallow. They pushed their ear tag through the tender skin and locked it into place with tagging pliers. Black Velvet was going to be released with Blueberry, but they did not want to put the unconscious cub into the same culvert trap with him. The carrying box containing Black Velvet was loaded into the back of the pickup that was hooked to the culvert trap, ensuring the bears would arrive at their release site together. The vehicle was parked in the shade of a large elm while the remaining two cubs were tranquilized and loaded.

The wardens decided they needed a third culvert trap, so a call was made and it was soon on the way. Meanwhile, Honey was shot with the older tranquilizer gun, which they had finally gotten to work. She went down so quickly, I was concerned for her life. I watched her closely to make certain she continued to breathe. She did, although rather rapidly, her rib cage visibly rising and falling. The ear tag was pushed through her ear and locked. They put her into the culvert trap to take her to the release site chosen for her and Smokey. Rather than three bears released together, we would be lucky if there were two live ones remaining.

Smokey had not gone down from the drug that went into his leg, but he was woozy. He sat down presenting his rump for a third dart from the gun. The accumulation of the drug from three darts began to take effect, but he seemed determined to remain conscious. He sat there weaving from side to side, hitting the ground in front of him repeatedly with his right paw. The third culvert trap arrived and was backed up to the door of the pen with only Smokey, looking quite dizzy, remaining. Four wardens put on gloves, picked him up, carried him like a sack of potatoes to the trap, and held him down while they put in the ear tag. After pushing Smokey into the trap, they lowered the door, finally ready to head for the two release sites.

Tranquilizing the four bears had taken three and a half hours, so it was late afternoon by the time the release sites were reached. If it weren't for the ear tags, which bears often catch on tree branches and pull out anyway, they would all have been alive, healthy, and released much earlier in the day. Bob and I did not go. I did not want anything more to do with that release. I felt like a traitor and a murderer, as I was the one who had cajoled Blackie into the carrying box. And I had distracted her while the warden pushed the killing drug into her flesh. We had worked so hard to make her well, all for naught. She would never again get to run free in the mountains, play with her siblings, bathe and drink from mountain streams, eat succulent grasses, roots, and berries or hibernate, sleeping through long, cold winters. She would never get to be a mother; she would never get to be a bear. Because of an ear tag, she had spent eight months in a cage for nothing.

A friend of mine did go to the release sites and told me everything that happened. Fortunately, Honey and Smokey, the first ones released, were not scheduled to be given adverse conditioning. Honey tumbled out of the culvert trap and just sat there because her hind legs were not functional. She could not run from bear dogs, beanbags, or anything else. Bears recover from the effects of Telazol front end first. Honey tried to drag herself away from the trucks, traps, and terrifying people with her front legs. She soon gave up after making hardly any progress. Smokey was released soon after Honey. In slightly better condition, he had recovered enough to run out of the trap, with his hindquarters flopping almost comically. Weaving drunkenly, he loped over to Honey, paying no attention to the people or the trucks. After sniffing Honey all over, he wobbled off a short distance with his hind legs still not coordinated, sat down, and began eating grass. One of the wardens volunteered to remain with the cubs until they recovered from the drug. Hopefully there were no grizzlies or large male black bears in the area, because Honey had not fully recovered her coordination when the warden left the vulnerable youngsters with no protection and went home.

My friend reported to me that by the time they released the second pair, Black Velvet had recovered her ability to control her legs enough to run and climb a tree. A good thing if she was going to run from the Karelian bear dogs with which the bears were to be chased as soon as they left their respective cages. These dogs are excellent at providing adverse conditioning on bears, but it works best if the bears are actually able to run away.

They backed up the culvert trap so the exit was facing the way they wanted Blueberry to run when the heavy door was raised. Then dogs on leashes were told to bark. Blueberry was released with dogs barking, beanbags being shot at him, cracker shells going off, and people yelling and whooping loudly. He quickly reached the base of a tall pine, going up to near the top as fast as he could climb. There he remained, clinging tightly to the narrow tree trunk, looking down fearfully at the commotion below.

Then it was Black Velvet's turn. First, they placed her transport box on the ground with the door facing the direction Blueberry had gone. While she was still in the box, they had the dogs bark to scare her. When they raised the door, she scrambled out, running as fast as her wobbly legs would carry her, straight for the nearest tree. She climbed to about 50 feet above the dogs and people. With all four legs wrapped firmly around the tree trunk, she remained there glaring down at her tormenters. All the people stood around visiting for about a half hour, prolonging the time of terror for the little bears, before they pronounced the release a success and went home. We hope the two frightened bears were able to safely climb down their respective trees and find each other. We never heard of them being seen or reported by anyone after their release.

Unfortunately, Honey and Smokey were released too close to human houses. Within a week, they were reportedly seen in someone's yard in an urban area. At least that gave us confirmation that Honey had recovered from the tranquilizer and was still alive. On the negative side, such behavior is not at all conducive to their long-term survival. Adverse conditioning with the Karelian bear dogs would have been extremely helpful at that point. We have not had a bear cub to care for since that winter. Hardly any bears were seen the next two winters, let alone a cub. Bob retired from Fish, Wildlife and Parks in 2000, so he no longer catches orphaned bear cubs. Game wardens now take all of them to the state wildlife rehab facility in Helena, Montana. We called the winter of 1998-1999 the "Year of the Bears" because here in western Montana there were so many hungry bears and bare bears.

**A bear's survival
highly depends on berries
and pollinators.**

Hunt's Bumblebee (*Bombus huntii*) nectaring on a petunia. Many species of wild pollinators are going extinct. Without bees and other pollinators, many species of plants and the animals who depend upon them for food and shelter could also become extinct.

CHAPTER 5
THE CHANGING FACES OF ANIMALS

In 1991, seven years before Firefly was born, Mt. Pinatubo (a volcano in the Philippines) erupted, throwing massive amounts of gases and dust into the atmosphere. Scientists believed that by spring 1992, those gases would cause significant damage to the ozone layer protecting life on Earth from the sun's ultraviolet radiation. The expected damage did occur, but not until winter 1993. By March, in addition to a thinning of the ozone layer over the south polar region, there was a large area of thinning directly over the Northern Hemisphere, extending from 60 degrees to 30 degrees north latitude. Ravalli County, Montana, where we live, is directly in the center.

Unfortunately, thinning of the protective ozone layer allowed ultraviolet radiation to reach Earth's surface at rates not previously recorded. This proved particularly damaging to many plants and animals from early spring 1993 through 1994. Damage was intensified when the ultra-high radiation initiated certain human actions which, when combined with the consequences of new genetic modification to plants, resulted in changing the appearance of plants, animals, and the entire face of the planet.

The higher than normal ultraviolet radiation caused potato blight to mutate and become resistant to commonly used fungicides. Consequently, millions of pounds of the more toxic ones, particularly chlorothalonil (containing cyanide), were applied on many thousands of acres of potato fields in the United States, Canada, and other countries. The effects on plants and animals here were compounded by previously discussed massive increases of Roundup® use in the Bitterroot Valley and in all states upwind, as well as throughout the United States, on the new, genetically modified crops. The 1996 increase in Roundup® use continued each year on those crops and successive others genetically modified to be resistant.

Besides causing multiple mineral deficiencies and disruption of thyroid hormone functions during vertebrate development, Roundup® has been shown to disrupt specific genes with a cute-sounding name.

Unfortunately, the results of disrupted Sonic Hedgehog genes on baby animals are definitely not cute. Fear and politics have kept people from reporting and addressing the function-disrupting effects on those genes, as well as on thyroid hormones, retinoic acid, enzymes, and proteins in the young, even their own children.

By 1997, the consequent widespread impact on fetal development caused by the synergistic effects of herbicides and fungicides resulted in unprecedented changes in faces, reproductive organs, heart, lungs, thymus, and other organs in uncountable numbers of individual animals throughout Montana and over all of North America. Several of the birth defects have not been sufficiently studied to determine the actual mechanisms in play to cause a specific malformation. The most puzzling birth defect relative to cause is the strange misalignment of the testes and corresponding hemiscrota* during fetal formation of the scrotal sac on male mammals. More males of several ruminant species are now born with misaligned hemiscrota than are born with a normal bilateral* scrotum.

*(Hemiscrota refers to the two sides of a scrotum, each containing one testis. In misaligned hemiscrota, one is in front of the other instead of the normal side-by-side configuration technically referred to as bilateral.)

Another birth defect that was basically ignored and so received little study is misplacement of the teats forward of the normal groin area early in fetal development in both sexes of ruminants. Fortunately, since spring 2002, that malformation, which also began in 1995, is no longer present in white-tailed deer or other ruminants I have examined. It was likely caused by something used on the mint fields in Ravalli County, since quite a few female dairy calves born here in the same time period reportedly had teats and udder forward of the normal groin area. The last of the mint fields were plowed under in spring 2001. After the chemicals specifically sprayed on that crop were no longer used, teats on wild and domestic ruminants were again formed in the normal groin area. This may not constitute a smoking gun but it certainly suggests one or more of the chemicals used on mint should be highly suspect with regard to causing misplacement of teats on ruminants.

In addition to local farmers no longer using the seriously toxic chemicals common in mint farming, use of fungicides for blight, particularly chlorothalonil, on potato fields in states upwind of Ravalli County decreased significantly in 2001. Adverse symptoms in newborns immediately began to decrease as well, and continued to do so each year through 2006. The more serious birth defects that cause mortality were far less prevalent in wild young, so many more began to survive to adulthood. By spring of 2006, incidence of facial malformations in examined white-tailed deer fawns had decreased from 56% in 2001 to 33%. In addition, according to statistics provided by MDFWP to the media, big game populations increased significantly between 2002 and 2006.

Unfortunately for recovering ruminant populations and many other life forms, in summer 2006 there was a massive increase in use of glyphosate by many millions of pounds. Large amounts began being used on the new Roundup Ready® alfalfa, in addition to other genetically modified crops on which it was already used. Also, in 2006, many extensively used herbicides produced with new formulations (including Roundup®, 2,4-D, dicamba, and others) began being used. The next spring, symptoms of fetal hypothyroidism, gene disruption, and multiple mineral deficiencies increased significantly. Most alarming, the incidence of underbite, enlarged right heart ventricle, inflammation of lungs, and damaged thymus more than doubled; at least one of those health issues was present on nearly every examined newborn of our study animal, white-tailed deer. Underbite prevalence in fawns averaged over 65% each year from 2007 through 2013. Another concern was that hearts of birds and mammals of all ages that I necropsied in summer of 2006, and in subsequent years through 2010, had dilated lymphatic vessels on the surface. No one I consulted in the medical profession could tell me what causes it because it had seldom been documented by the medical community.

In addition to pesticides coming here by atmospheric transport, there was extensive application of the new salt formulation Roundup® used on newly planted Roundup Ready® alfalfa fields in Ravalli County during the 2006 growing season. This practice exposed animals in western Montana to even higher levels of glyphosate. Not surprising, poor fawn survival was reported for 2007 and for several years after, corresponding with the alarming increase in disrupted development of hearts, blood vessels, and other organs, in addition to doubled prevalence of underdeveloped facial bones.

To add to the assault on developing young of animal species, increased use of relatively new insecticides also took place in summer 2006. These compounds, created from synthetic nicotine to kill insects on crops and to coat seeds prior to planting, are called neonicotinoids (often shortened to neonics). The result of this addition to the toxic mixture was more disruption of thyroid hormone functions and greater adverse effects on embryonic and fetal development. Neonics soon became the most used insecticides in the world. Adding even more to the adverse effects on world health, the use of glyphosate experienced a huge, planet-wide increase when Roundup Ready® seeds for many food crops began being sold in other countries during the same time period.

Ruminants with short lower jaws (overbite) are easily discerned because they are so odd looking. Prior to 2007, that particular birth defect was seldom observed on white-tailed deer in western Montana. Beginning then, prevalence of overbite on wild ruminants, especially moose, white-tailed deer, mule deer, and pronghorn antelope increased; it continues to remain between 8% and 15% which, according to biology books, is high enough to "raise red flags." Interestingly, I haven't seen any indication of concern from the game departments in any of many states that appear to have an alarming prevalence of overbite in their game animal populations, based on photos posted on the Internet by hunters. In eastern United States, white-tailed deer with severe overbite are deridingly nicknamed "Dork Deer."

Being a patented mineral chelator, Roundup® (glyphosate) binds up minerals, making them unavailable to cells. When taken up by plants, glyphosate chelates many minerals, most importantly for normal bone growth in herbivores, calcium, manganese, and potassium, greatly decreasing the mineral content of the foliage. For example, in a comparison test, calcium was over 6000 ppm (parts per million) in unmodified corn, compared to less than 15 ppm in genetically modified, glyphosate-resistant corn that had been sprayed with Roundup®. Nitrogen, phosphorus, potassium, sulfur, magnesium, manganese, iron, and other minerals were also decreased, but calcium levels were by far the most affected. Other genetically modified food crops sprayed with glyphosate, including alfalfa eaten by domestic grazing animals and some wild ruminants, likely have similar mineral depletion.

Thus, Roundup® exposure affects mineral levels in foliage the animals eat and in the animals themselves, resulting in biologically relevant mineral deficiencies. Pregnant females and especially their developing young experience the greatest adverse effects. The drastic simultaneous deficiencies in multiple minerals have been directly connected to a number of severe birth defects by hundreds of studies and reviews. The chelation effect on minerals in plants provides excellent insight as to why so many individuals of all wild and domestic ungulate species were so severely affected simultaneously. All ungulates are vegetarians.

Most concerning is, if the highly-used organochlorine compounds had been properly tested, chlorothalonil, 2,4-D, dicamba, and others likely would also have been found to affect calcium and other mineral availability to the cells, or to disrupt normal uptake of minerals, or both. DDT significantly disrupted cellular calcium, especially in female birds. Many organochlorine compounds appear to have a detrimental effect on cellular uptake of calcium, particularly in cells of developing young. Exposure to 2,4-D, dicamba, and other organochlorine herbicides has been observed to cause an immediate and easily observable disruption of bone growth in upper bills and facial bones of hatchling birds. Chicks who had normal facial bone structure as new hatchlings have been found to have an underdeveloped upper bill within two days after exposure to 2,4-D or mixtures of herbicides that include it. This same phenomenon was also observed on a total of 12 newborn goats in three separate incidents. Obviously, an animal who develops an underbite after it is born does not technically have a birth defect. What should be evident is that such herbicides are seriously unhealthy for developing young before *and* after they are born, and exposure to any of them can cause immediate deleterious effects.

Mineral chelation by highly-used glyphosate, chlorothalonil, neonics, 2,4-D, and other pesticides would also explain the underdeveloped bones, hair, feathers, and other birth defects related to calcium disruption in the many individuals of various species being affected. For example, rodents, birds, and insects whose diets are composed mainly of plant material have health problems and birth defects very similar to those of ungulate species. Plants are obviously being greatly changed nutritionally by toxins in soil in which they grow, rain and snow that water them, and in the plants themselves. Consequently, they appear to no longer serve the nutritional needs of animals who depend on them to survive. This is especially true in growing young, who require specific nutrients for development. The deadly damage to plants and disruption of the minerals they provide to all animals in the food chain are likely affecting normal development of young over the entire planet.

In addition to all the other cellular mechanisms impacted by glyphosate, it also disrupts retinoic acid levels, which are extremely important to normal embryonic development of vertebrates. High levels of retinoic acid produced by glyphosate exposure in study animals (frogs, chicks, and rats) caused neural tubal defects and craniofacial malformations in their young. Those particular studies of glyphosate exposure were done because human fetuses and newborns of parents who lived in South America near fields sprayed with glyphosate-based herbicides experienced a four-fold increase in neural tubal defects, craniofacial malformations, and cancer. Thus, the extensive worldwide use of Roundup® appears to be causing major changes in the bodies and faces of animals everywhere, including, most alarmingly, to those of children.

Developmental malformations of reproductive organs as a result of exposure to endocrine or hormone disruptors have been highly studied in fish, amphibians, and a few species of birds and mammals. However, failure of facial bones to grow properly, especially in mammal species, had rarely been reported in scientific literature prior to the late 1990s. One highly relevant study, done on beef cattle in Australia by Dr. Peter White, revealed that a certain level of manganese had to be available to developing domestic calf fetuses or the calf would be born with an underbite and often crooked limbs. Manganese deficiency is known to disrupt cellular calcium metabolism, as well as thyroid hormone levels; both are imperative for normal fetal development.

If a fetus or newborn suffers from low thyroid hormone levels or disrupted thyroid hormone functions, medical professionals refer to the resulting condition as Congenital Fetal Hypothyroidism (CFH). A major cause specified for this condition is malnutrition, which of course results in mineral deficiencies. A second cause is exposure to higher than normal radiation, which affects iodine levels. However, since 1994, exposure to extremely low levels of certain hormone disrupting toxins, particularly pesticide combinations that have been shown to work synergistically, appears to be the main cause of the increasing prevalence of CFH.

Growing fetuses have been exposed to malnutrition, radiation, and occasional natural toxins for as long as vertebrates have been on Earth. Vertebrate species evolved defenses to protect their young from most naturally occurring thyroid hormone disrupters. When many man-made chemicals began being spread throughout the environment, the fetuses' natural defenses were no longer able to protect them. Most concerning, many of those manmade chemicals actually take the place of vital hormones in fetal cells without performing the functions of natural hormones. Proper levels of minerals, thyroid hormones, glutathione, retinoic acid, Vitamin D, and other vitamins have been shown to be crucial for normal development of an embryo or fetus. Decreases or increases in the essential levels of any or all of those or other hormones, such as steroids and aromatase, result in serious developmental problems and lifelong adverse health issues.

It is disturbing that developmental malformations are not being widely recognized as a major cause of significant declines in populations of our once-common birds. Habitat loss and global climate change are the reasons most often stated. Few consider that year-round resident birds are in decline even where habitat or climate has not changed significantly. Also, no mention was made in 1993 and 1994 of the possible effects of high ultraviolet radiation on birds, especially hatchlings. Amazingly, these easily observed abnormalities are largely ignored even by avid bird watchers, as are the obvious adverse effects on adult birds. Occasionally after a rainstorm in our area, many adult birds act ill, with fluffed up feathers and drooping wings, and some have trouble landing when flying from branch to branch. This condition in individual birds receives little notice and no investigation unless the event results in a large number of visible bird deaths.

Bird populations are reported to be declining in remote areas relatively unchanged by human actions except, of course, for deadly toxins in the air, rain, and snow. We should consider that insects eat foliage contaminated by the toxins and birds then eat the insects. Many birds feed on seeds and berries coated with the pollutants. The toxins also kill insects the birds need for food and those that are pollinators, as well as damaging leaves and roots of fruit-bearing bushes and trees. This limits the availability of food for large numbers of birds. Also, while hormone, vitamin, gene, and mineral disruption often cause adverse health problems for adult birds, it is deadly for developing embryos and hatchlings.

Jack Kirkley, a friend and biologist who teaches ornithology, made a statement concerning facial malformations found in birds. His astute observation, also applicable to other vertebrate species, was, "If a substantial number of live birds are being found that are somehow coping with variously deformed beaks, then how many more birds may actually be rapidly dying from their deformities and are not being found or accounted for? In other words, the tough survivors that are being counted may only represent a tiny fraction, the tip of the iceberg, so to speak, of the actual number of deformed individuals that either fail to fledge from their nests or fail to survive very long after fledging. Likely, most are never seen by a human observer. Only those deformed birds that somehow manage to live long enough to be trapped by a scientist, or turned in to a rehabilitator, will end up being counted." Jack forgot to include the many birds documented with malformed bills by bird photographers.

Interestingly, a study of grassland birds, published early in 2013 by Canadian scientists Dr. Pierre Mineau and Melanie Whiteside, showed that lethal pesticide risk was close to four times more responsible for grassland bird declines than a change in the birds' habitat. Also, the American Bird Conservancy released an important review, authored by Dr. Pierre Mineau with Cynthia Palmer as coauthor, in spring 2013. Their conclusion was that the insecticides called neonics are extremely deadly to birds. Just one or two seeds treated with it can kill a bird and one tenth of the amount found on one treated seed coated with a neonic will adversely affect the birds' ability to reproduce. In addition, neonics are thought to be a major contributor to the death of billions of honeybees since 2006, and a significant factor in the drastic decline of wild insect pollinators. Even more alarming, neonics have been shown to work synergistically with chlorothalonil to kill bees and other pollinators up to 1000 times faster than neonics alone. Glyphosate also kills bees, especially with simultaneous exposure to other pesticides.

Blaming only climate change and habitat loss for declines in mammal populations completely ignores strong evidence that a high prevalence of both wild and domestic mammals is being born with serious birth defects. Many of those abnormalities cause mortality before or soon after birth. Scientists and government officials either have not recognized or won't admit the extent of the damage to mammals, especially grazing animals. This is likely because many of them are used for human food.

However, a search of the Internet indicates that people are observing underbite in many of their newborn domestic animals. Some also have small eye openings, a narrow face and skull, and malformed lower incisors. This is a serious change in structure of the craniofacial bones. Because it impacts a grazing animal's ability to obtain adequate nutrition, affected adult females are often unable to produce viable young as a result of being undernourished. As malnutrition has also been found to cause both fetal thyroid hormone disruption and mineral deficiencies, there is likely a compounding effect, especially during winter months when food is less readily available to wildlife. These combined factors exacerbate disruption of normal fetal growth, resulting in the next generation having even more serious health problems, including multiple birth defects. Similar effects can occur even in well-fed animals, especially if the food provided for them is lacking in vitamins and minerals or has been contaminated with mineral-chelating toxins.

Some people blame bad genes for the malformations. Such changes during development, called epigenetic changes, are shown by studies to be passed on for several generations, but the DNA is not altered. Many young animals affected with a variety of epigenetic changes survive to produce another generation. Unfortunately, those young are even more likely to have malformed young. This escalation of epigenetic changes will probably continue until the causation factors are mitigated or until all newborns have the epigenetic change. The worst-case scenario is that affected populations will decline to the point of extinction. If the responsible toxins are no longer used, the epigenetic changes will hopefully dissipate so most vertebrate young will again have normal development and survive to replace adults killed by accident, harsh weather, or predators. But with nature, it is hard to predict anything with certainty.

Equines, ruminants, and camelids appear to be highly susceptible to mineral, gene, and thyroid disrupting toxins on or in the foliage they consume. Equines eat a large amount of plant material and, with ruminants and camelids, the toxins remain in their digestive system for a longer period because of their multi-chambered stomach.

On cattle or other ruminant with a normal bite, all of the lower incisors contact the dental pad, a thick, tough tissue covering the front of the paired premaxillary bones, the flat, wide bones at the front of the upper jaw on ruminants. The muzzle and upper lip make up the other soft tissue at the front of the premaxillary bones. When normal, the front of the lower lip should be immediately behind the rear of the upper lip.

White-tailed deer, mule deer, elk, moose, pronghorn antelope, bighorn sheep, mountain goat, caribou, and bison are wild ruminants who have lived in Montana and other parts of the northern hemisphere for millions of years. Fossils have shown almost no incidence of facial malformations, nor have there been reports in most of recorded history. In studies of over 36,000 white-tailed deer done in Michigan in the

1960s by L. A. Ryel and colleagues, who specifically examined the animals for tooth and facial malformations, not one was found with an underbite.

Closer to where Bob and I live in Ravalli County, Montana, prominent wildlife biologist Dr. Bart O'Gara examined 100 adult white-tailed deer and 32 fetuses collected on Lee Metcalf National Wildlife Refuge in winter 1991-92. He was looking for lung disease, any type of birth defect, and other physical problems in the deer population on the refuge. Because deer numbers were much higher than optimum for the amount of forage on the refuge, it was assumed there would be health problems. However, Dr. O'Gara found no malformations of any kind and only one older doe with pneumonia. He found an even sex ratio of 16 males and 16 females in the 32 fetuses he examined, and no diseases or defects. His study clearly showed the malformations and sex ratios skewed in favor of males consistent with metabolic acidosis, mitochondrial dysfunction, mineral deficiencies, and the resulting fetal hypothyroidism, were not present in the Ravalli County white-tailed deer population immediately prior to 1995.

In addition to causing big game animal populations to decline precipitously, inability to graze normally because of an underbite results in less weight gain in domestic livestock, whose owners are paid a price per pound for animals they sell. Because those with underbite usually weigh less than individuals with a normal bite, owners receive less money than from normal animals. Livestock owners seldom report underbite or other malformations caused by fetal hypothyroidism because they do not want people who consume meat and dairy products to know that domestic livestock have multiple birth defects. Interestingly, toxins an animal is exposed to while in the womb would not necessarily be present in the meat at the age of butchering.

In fall 2009, I examined the heads of 16 one-and-a-half-year-old steers from 12 ranches scattered throughout the northern portion of Ravalli County in western Montana. The purpose was to get an estimate of the prevalence of underbite on cattle in our area. Of those 16 steers, only four had a normal bite and the rest, three-fourths of the sample, had underbite. This should have been of great concern to livestock owners. Some just ignored the problem; other ranchers began spending large amounts on mineral testing by veterinarians and to provide mineral supplements for their pregnant cows. Fortunately, the specialized

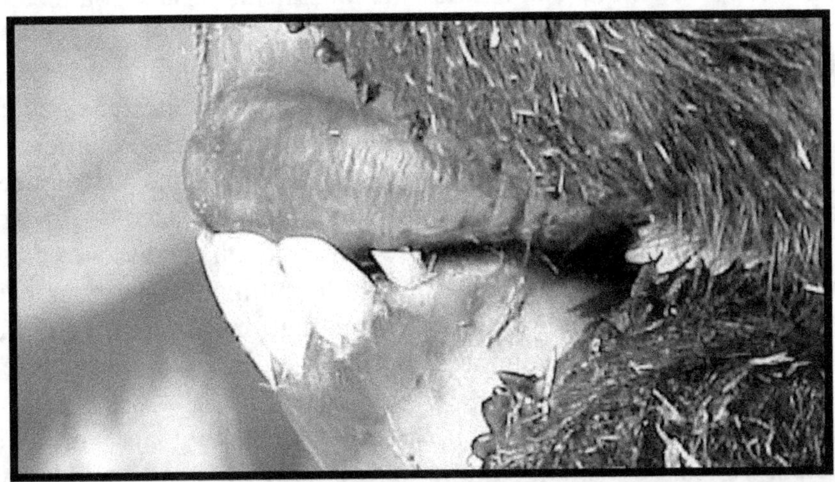

A normal bite on a beef calf has all of the lower incisors contacting the thick-skinned premaxillary pad.

This is a female mix-breed milk goat with a severe underbite and an easily observed underdeveloped premaxillary pad, much narrower than the incisors. Nearly all newborn goats of multiple breeds examined in spring 2008, 2009, and 2010 had this malformation, but some were not this severe.

mineral supplements appear to alleviate most health issues connected to mineral deficiencies in newborn calves.

In 1996, after determining that many species of animal were being born with a variety of birth defects, we began using white-tailed deer as our primary study animal to examine, measure, and document the various malformations. Our purpose was to determine the prevalence of measurable defects each year, especially in fawns. We used white-tailed deer for the study animal because there were enough carcasses available to provide a large sample. Several other wild ruminant species appear to have an even higher incidence of the same malformations we found in the deer, but only small numbers of those species were available to examine.

Because I was curious as to how badly domestic goats were being affected, I checked a small sample of young-of-the-year goats born in Ravalli County each spring from 2008 to 2010. Most of the 40 individuals I examined had a very narrow premaxillary pad and a moderate to severe underbite. In fall 2010, Samantha Croft, an enthusiastic high school freshman in Missoula, Montana, began studying underbite in domestic goat herds in western Montana as a science fair project. She found the prevalence of underbite to be 56% in a variety of breeds, ages, and both sexes. For her sophomore year project, she compared the incidence of facial bone malformations in goats in western Montana to those in other states and found it even higher here than in most of the other states where underbite was reported. Only Tennessee, with 61%, had a higher percentage. Interestingly, four goats from one herd were photographed for a local newspaper article in summer 2017, with two of the four having an obvious underbite.

For a birth defect to be present in so many individual goats of various breeds, it would have to be caused by severe mineral deficiencies or exposure to some type of hormone disrupting chemical or chemicals, high radiation, or a combination of those factors simultaneously. Multiple pesticides carried in air and moist weather fronts, falling on foliage and into surface water throughout western Montana, would expose all goats to the same chemicals. Malnutrition is seldom a factor in well-cared-for herds.

In some individuals of newborn ruminant species, there appears to be abnormal growth of the lower front teeth (incisors). That, in addition to unnaturally short, narrow premaxillary bones, causes a major discrepancy between width of the dental pad on the upper jaw and that

Front view of a dead white-tailed deer fawn with normal facial development.

Front view of a dead white-tailed deer fawn with a severe underbite, crooked lower incisors, rounded skull top, and small eyes.

Side view of the lower incisors contacting the dental pad on the same normal fawn.

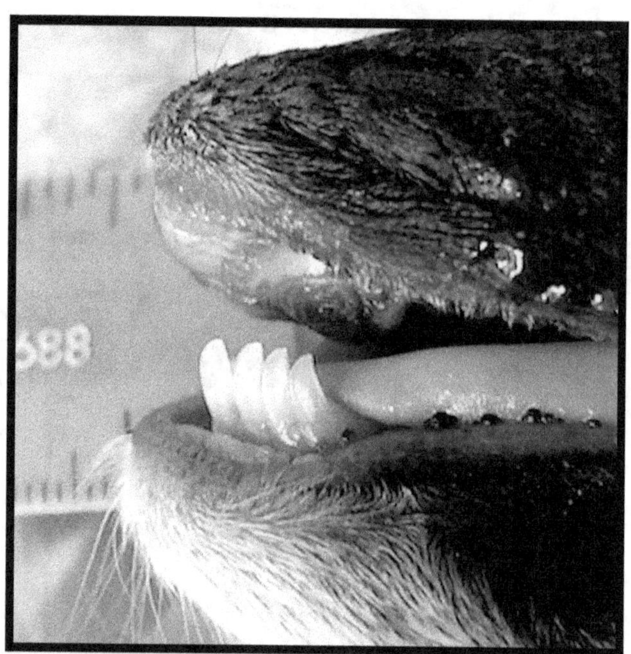

Side view of the fawn with underbite, showing the lower incisors far forward of the dental pad.

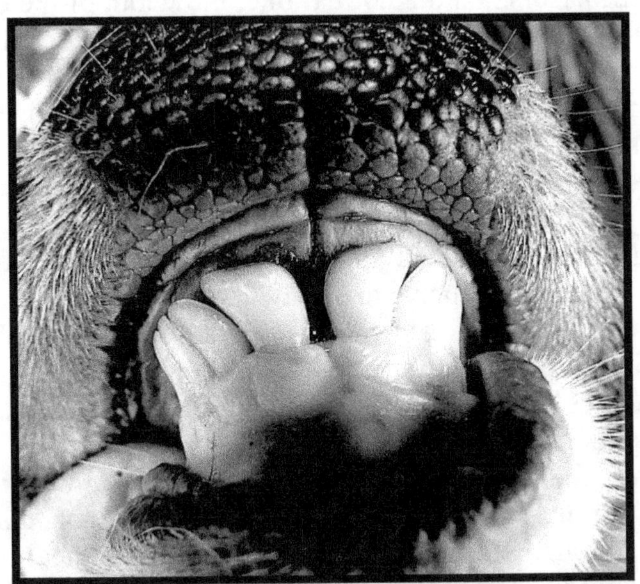

**Front view of the same fawn with normal bite
showing all incisors contact the dental pad.**

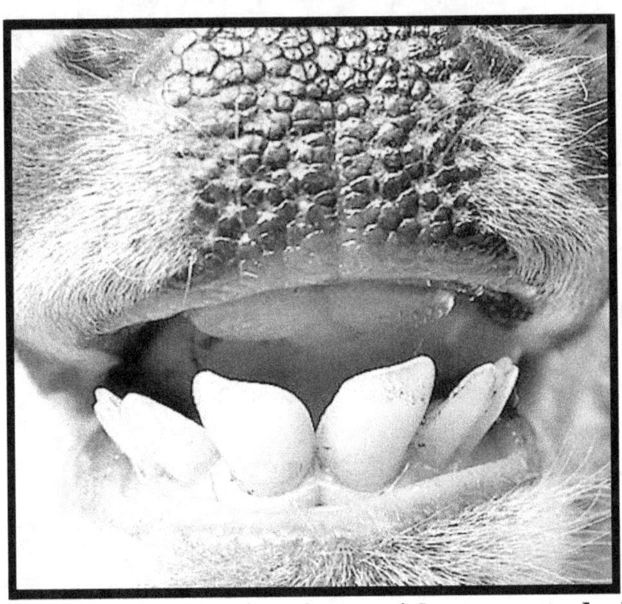

**A different, slightly older fawn with severe underbite,
showing widely spaced, tipped out lower incisors and
much narrower dental pad than lower incisors.**

of the lower incisors. With a normal bite, the width of the eight lower incisors combined is narrower than the dental pad, so all contact the pad when the mouth is closed. In animals with wide, over-sized lower incisors, only the middle incisors contact the dental pad even when the premaxillary bones are normal in length and width. The three smaller teeth on each side consequently do not receive normal use and become overgrown due to lack of wear.

If grazing animals are evolving new facial and tooth configurations, the changes are not conducive to survival. My colleagues and I did not find these unusual dental features in wild or domestic ruminants prior to 1995, and until 2007 they remained rare. These previously unreported tooth anomalies now appear quite common in newborn ruminants, another way the faces of grazing animals are changing.

Many pathological conditions are the result of exposure to endocrine disrupting chemicals, including many of the common diseases and syndromes now afflicting humans. Also, something medical doctors tend to ignore is that a person's body can have a synergistically adverse reaction to a prescribed drug when constantly and simultaneously exposed to endocrine disrupting chemicals in their environment. I am often told there is an epidemic of thyroid problems, including hypothyroidism and thyroid cancer, in addition to diabetes and observable obesity in children and adults living in our area. Doctors are now saying that up to 80% of people in the United States suffer from thyroid problems, especially hypothyroidism. Most people I see in stores or on the streets do not appear at all undernourished, so malnutrition is not likely the cause of these health issues. That leaves exposure to hormone disrupting toxins, especially in air and food, as the most likely cause of so many humans having these problems. Interestingly, the various disruptions in normal cellular function as a result of exposure to glyphosate and other pesticides often results in obesity, which is another change in the faces of affected humans.

For example, increasing childhood obesity is resulting in changes to the appearance of millions of children. Eating too much and not exercising enough has been stated as reasons for the massive increase in obesity and diabetes in newborn babies. This is obviously very wrong, because babies less than a year old mostly drink their mother's milk or a formula, and prior to learning to walk, have never gotten much exercise. Even the drastic effects of obesity and diabetes are minor compared to premature birth and its lifelong health issues, childhood cancers, heart defects, autism, microcephaly, and the related but worse anencephaly. All those health issues are increasing at rates that threaten normal childhood and many actually change a child's face to be different from what it was genetically programmed to be.

In the years between 1995 and 2013, we documented hundreds of individual animals of many species with underdeveloped facial bones. Those in which I personally have examined skulls and found underbite and narrow palate include bison, cattle, bighorn sheep, Dall sheep, domestic sheep, domestic yak, domestic goats, mountain goats, elk, moose, mule deer, white-tailed deer, pronghorn antelope, horse foals, llamas, alpacas, dogs, wolves, domestic cats, domestic pigs, multiple individuals of many bird species, and even pet iguanas. Iguanas with underbite indicate a similar change in facial features of at least one reptile species. I did not see, but had reported to me, several individuals of other mammal species with underbite in other states and countries, including guar, roe deer, red deer, Columbia black-tailed deer, and Sitka black-tailed deer. Underdevelopment of facial bones appears to affect newborns of both sexes equally.

Since the three primary causes of fetal hypothyroidism are reported to be exposure to toxins, radiation, and malnutrition with resultant mineral deficiencies, I tried to determine the origin of those factors in western Montana. Our primary sources of radiation exposure are power lines, cell towers, and higher than normal ultraviolet radiation because of ozone depletion. A major cause of malnutrition in female wild grazing animals, especially during pregnancy, is being unable to obtain enough food in winter. This is especially true of those with underbite and mineral deficiencies, which often cause them to be undernourished year around.

Severe mineral deficiencies are likely caused by exposure to Roundup®, which chelates multiple minerals in plants exposed by direct application or by falling in rain and snow on the plants and the soil in which they grow. This capacity to efficiently kill plants is why glyphosate began being used as an herbicide. When unsuspecting animals (including humans) eat the plants, they also ingest high levels of Roundup® along with the foliage, root, or seed head eaten. Exposed plants provide low levels of the chelated minerals. Ingested glyphosate then chelates affected minerals in the bodies of the animals, compounding their deficiencies.

Besides causing major mineral deficiencies, glyphosate and other herbicides disrupt the normal functions of various hormones, important enzymes, and beneficial gut bacteria. Because of exposure to chemicals, especially those which affect the digestive processes, animals often suffer from inability to properly digest and metabolize whatever food they are able to find and eat. The combination of mineral deficiencies, inability to digest food, and disrupted ability to maintain heat and energy in a normal manner makes it more difficult for animals to survive cold temperatures, especially in winter.

Officials at the MDFWP have adamantly refused to admit that wild grazing animals are being born with the high prevalence of underbite we found in our studies. Nor will they admit the presence of other serious malformations, including underdeveloped and malformed male genitalia, the subject of our first prevalence study on white-tailed deer. Their claim is that people will not buy hunting licenses or visit Montana to see wildlife if they find out wild birds and mammals here have birth defects. However, there has been no decline in tourism because of changes in wild animals. Even people with livestock or pets often do not really look at their animals. Most of those living in towns and cities seem quite disconnected from the natural world, so do not notice such changes at all. When they do notice and photograph malformed animals, they often post them with captions making fun of the animal's birth defect, rather than expressing any concern for it.

For years now, hunters have been shooting deer, elk, and other big game animals who have disturbingly abnormal faces and obvious malformations of the male genitalia. There has been no public outcry concerning the easily seen deformities on harvested animals. Hunters' families have been eating meat from big game animals with these abnormalities for over 20 years and hunters are still buying licenses.

Unfortunately, a sad result of continuing to ignore the epidemic of developmental malformations is that eventually there might be no individuals of some species left for tourists to observe and photograph, or for hunters to harvest. We are already in a world-wide mass extinction event, according to researchers. Public outcry will not likely occur until wildlife numbers decline to the point where repercussions from losses in businesses related to hunting and outdoor activities, and consequent jobs lost, will reverberate throughout the United States. The question is, will we simply continue to blame wild predators for the declines? Or will we face up to the adverse changes in anatomical features of wildlife in time to save them and the jobs that depend on them?

Bone malformations we have observed in both birds and mammals since 1995, include underdeveloped facial bones and skull, crooked limbs, limbs partially or completely unformed, abnormal or unformed toes or feet, and malformation of the keel bone in birds (analogous to the mammalian sternum). Mandibular brachygnathia, commonly called overbite, has been observed on a large number of individuals of ruminant species, but on only one bird, a hatchling House Sparrow. For some reason I haven't been able to determine, overbite is not nearly as prevalent as underbite, especially on birds. The overbite we are observing in mammals is the result of underdevelopment of the front of the lower jaw, called the diastema on ruminants, causing an easily observable change in the face of affected individuals. One severe example I examined was a vehicle-killed male pronghorn antelope in Nevada. It was very strange-looking, with an extremely short lower jaw, and it also had malformed genitalia. To see what white-tailed deer with a short lower jaw look like, search for "Dork Deer images" on the Internet.

In birds, both under-developed upper bill and disrupted feather development often result in mortality soon after affected fledglings leave the nest. Without normal-length flight feathers, the young birds can't fly and are soon eaten by predators. If they can fly and their underbite is not too severe, they can learn to find and pick up food. Some survive to be observed as adults, like the male Evening Grosbeak with obvious underbite, photographed by Eugene Beckes in the Flathead Valley north of Missoula, Montana. The bird had a short upper bill, but was able to eat. Eugene has photographed many adult wild birds of a variety of species with short upper bills and one Black-capped Chickadee with overgrown bills near where he lives in St. Ignatius, Montana.

Most of the affected species are birds who remain in or near the area where they fledged, overwintering and nesting in the same region each year as long as food is available. Birds who migrate long distances must go through many areas sprayed with multiple chemicals or fly over regions with pollution spewing from factories, refineries, and other major sources of toxins. We would expect migrators to be more affected than residents, but actually more of the latter have been observed with overgrown bills. It is possible that the majority of affected migrants die of starvation during their journey.

A male Evening Grosbeak with an underdeveloped upper bill was photographed near St. Ignatius, MT by Eugene Beckes.

The hard material covering the upper and lower bills of most birds is called the rhamphotheca. It is similar in composition to our fingernails and, like fingernails, it normally grows slowly but continuously. This replaces keratin on bill tips as it wears down with use. Another serious change in the faces of birds is overgrowth of the rhamphotheca on adults. I called the phenomenon sudden rhamphotheca growth. Alaska USGS researchers Colleen Handel and Caroline Van Hemert have named it Avian Keratin Disorder, to include abnormalities of all the keratin parts of a bird, including rhamphotheca, feathers, and leg scales. Similar to western Montana birds, some in Alaska have been observed with abnormal or disrupted feather growth in addition to bill malformations. Abnormal growth of leg scales has been found on birds in Alaska, but not often on birds in our area of Montana.

With overgrown rhamphotheca, the tips of one or both bills begin to grow much faster than normal. The fast growth can continue from several days up to two or more weeks. Incidence of this phenomenon appears to be increasing in a number of bird species in Alaska. Over 2000 Black-capped Chickadees and lesser numbers of other resident Alaskan birds with overgrown bills have been reported to USGS researchers. In 2010, Northwestern Crows had a 36% prevalence of overgrown bills. This is being called an epidemic by researchers.

It is interesting that a 36% rate of overgrown bills on crows is considered an alarming epidemic by ornithologists. However, most government biologists refused to recognize the nearly 70% prevalence of brachygnathia superior we found in white-tailed deer fawns from 2007 through 2013, as reported in two peer reviewed studies. Montana State Fish, Wildlife and Parks biologists have repeatedly stated that underbite in deer and other big game animals is a normal variation, completely contrary to information found on veterinary websites. Those authors describe both underbite and overbite as serious congenital defects in all species of domestic livestock and suggest that animals with those conditions should be culled, which emphasizes that medical professionals consider underbite and overbite to be very serious birth defects.

The intention for such culling is to improve the gene pool by preventing affected animals from living long enough to reproduce. However, this would have no effect on the prevalence of the problem because it is not due to DNA mutations. It is, in fact, epigenetic in nature, meaning the actual genes remain the same but are switched on or off abnormally as a result of exposure to toxins.

Disrupted hormones and/or bacterial infection, according to recent findings, appear to be closely connected to fast rhamphotheca growth on adult birds in Alaskan studies. However, sudden mineral deficiencies, especially abrupt, severe disruption of the uptake of manganese and calcium by growing facial bone cells, is the likely cause of the upper bill being underdeveloped on hatchlings with underbite. Many adult birds most prone to experiencing fast rhamphotheca growth also have a short upper bill. An example of this multiple effect was observed on Piney, a Clark's Nutcracker I received for care as a fledgling.

Piney was found on the ground by two girls who noticed a cat stalking him. He had disrupted feather development in both wings, which prevented him from flying when he left the nest. Several primary flight feathers had grown in upside down, while some were short and not fully developed. I pulled out the malformed feathers, stimulating regrowth, and gave him calc. phos. 6X and bioplasma with his food, and diluted liquid electrolytes instead of plain water for about a week. My electrolyte combination apparently stimulated normal mineral uptake by the cells because, when Piney's new flight feathers grew in, they were normal in shape and placement. I was pleased when he began to fly quite well. Besides his feather problems, Piney had a slightly underdeveloped upper bill as a fledgling. I trimmed the lower bill so it was slightly shorter than the upper, as it would be with normal facial bone development, and thought he was nearly ready for release.

Early one morning, after an overnight rainstorm, I went to the flight room to give Piney food and fresh water. To my dismay, I found he had become paralyzed during the night. He was sitting on the floor with his head hanging nearly upside down and sideways to the right. He couldn't stand up or walk and of course he could no longer fly. He was a very pathetic-looking little bird.

After two days of treatment with my electrolyte combination plus a natural sulfur compound, methylsulfonylmethane (MSM), which sometimes helps animals recover from neurological problems, Piney was able to stand and walk normally and hold his head upright. Unfortunately, he was never again able to fly well enough to be released.

About two weeks after he recovered from the paralysis, both of his bill tips suddenly and visibly began growing rapidly. When the overgrowth stopped after about 10 days, the lower bill was nearly half an inch longer than normal with a downward curve in it. The much shorter upper bill was slightly over a quarter inch too long and also curved downward near the tip. I had been observing Piney several times a day before, during, and after the fast growth of his rhamphotheca and also his debilitating reaction to whatever was in the rainstorm. All the evidence indicated that something toxic in the rain caused Piney to experience the serious health symptoms suggestive of hormone disruption, as well as extreme neurological damage. An estrogenic toxin would likely affect his pituitary gland, stimulating excess production of growth hormone, which in turn would have stimulated Piney's rhamphotheca cells to grow much faster than normal.

Sadly, because he was never again able to fly well enough to be released, Piney had to be euthanized. Having to euthanize a sweet little bird like Piney is very difficult, but it is illegal to keep unreleasable native birds.

One of the most disturbing trends throughout the world is the change in faces of little children. There are now much higher rates of cleft palate, underdeveloped skull and upper facial bones, underbite, overbite, crooked teeth, small eyes, facial tumors, and other changes to the facial features of newborn babies. Visible changes in bone structure have increased significantly in prevalence, as have many other health problems in children, including alarming increases in the following:

autism; childhood cancers; premature and/or dysmature births (failure to reach normal weight by full term); respiratory problems after birth; obesity; diabetes; autoimmune disorders; and most commonly now, heart malformations or other heart problems. In 2015, heart defects were reported to be the number one birth defect in children in the United States.

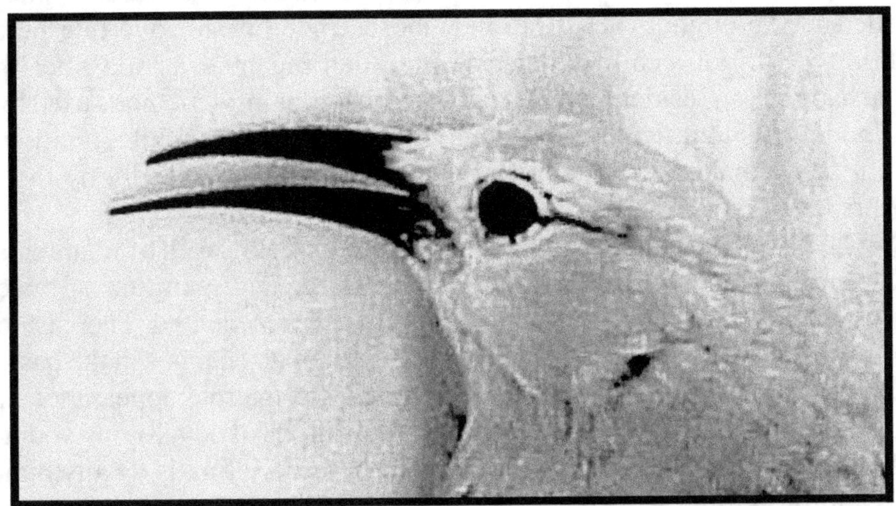

This shows the underbite and overgrown bills on Piney, the Clark's Nutcracker, three weeks after exposure to something in the rain caused neurological damage. Photo by Wayne Tree.

Not surprisingly, there is a close correlation between the increase in many of those health problems in children and increased prevalence of underbite and heart defects in white-tailed deer. Even more interesting, our 2015 study showed the correlation between the increase in birth defects and serious health issues in newborn children and the upsurge of Roundup® use was from 85% to 98.5% for the children's health issues we addressed. A very close correlation of 98.5% between the extreme increase in Roundup® use and the dramatic increase in autism was also found, although autism was not an issue included in our study. Another study by different researchers showed that autism is at least partly caused by a lack of calcium going to affected portions of the brain during development in the womb.

Between 2000 and 2015, while giving talks with the unreleasable birds I use for environmental education, I saw far more children with underbite than while teaching in elementary schools in Malta and

Missoula, Montana, between 1966 and 1976. In 2001, I read a scientific report regarding the sudden mysterious epidemic of underbite in young children all over the world, confirming my observations.

More recently, a dentist who specializes in children's dentistry told me overbite is now the most common facial malformation he is seeing in his practice. Interestingly, since 2007, this birth defect is also being observed more often in grazing animals, especially mule deer, white-tailed deer, pronghorn antelope, and moose. Underbite and overbite have serious effects on a child, being extremely detrimental to a child's health and happiness. Besides having to undergo often-painful methods used by orthodontists to attempt to mitigate the underbite or overbite, children with facial malformations are frequently teased unmercifully by their peers.

The pervasive changes in facial structure on both sexes of mammals and birds are unparalleled. Rapid change in the configuration of male genitalia in multiple mammal species is also unprecedented. There is no previous historical record of such rapid, widespread changes in the basic anatomy of developing young. The external and internal appearance of animals is now being devastatingly altered. Billions of developing young have died and billions more will likely die before we finally do anything to stop the killing and maiming of newborns, even those of our own species.

**Colorful rainbows
and unsightly birth defects,
caused by toxic rain.**

CHAPTER 6
THE CHANGING FACE OF EARTH

In addition to changes in animals, plants too have been subtly but acutely damaged. Extinction of plant and animal species is reportedly happening at a faster rate than at any time since the mass extinction that ended the reign of dinosaurs. What should be of concern is that many tiny organisms actually flourish in high ultraviolet radiation and chemically contaminated environments. Some species of fungi, algae, and one-celled organisms such as bacteria and oomycetes are especially well adapted to high radiation. They were evolving and populating Earth many millions of years ago, when high ultraviolet radiation was the norm.

In the early 1990s, exposure to much higher than normal ultraviolet radiation resulted in faster reproduction and consequent rapid mutation of several fungus species and of an oomycete (single-celled organism closely related to our cells) called potato blight by potato farmers. The mutated organisms had become less susceptible to chemicals commonly used on fields of grain, potatoes, and other crops to kill fungi and blight, resulting in a major increase in the use of fungicides. One was Vinclozolin®, a fungicide known to cause ectopic testes (not descended into the scrotum) in exposed newborn rats. Another was a nitrile fungicide called chlorothalonil composed of two cyanide molecules attached to a hexachlorobenzene ring. Cyanide is a deadly poison and hexachlorobenzene is an older type of fungicide banned by the EPA because it is a proven human carcinogen.

Both nitriles and cyanide cause serious disruption of thyroid hormones. Cyanide also damages the liver, making it less able to detoxify other ingested or inhaled chemicals. Thus, all those to which an animal is exposed are able do far more cellular damage than when the animal's liver is functioning properly. When they made chlorothalonil, scientists combined deadly cyanide molecules with molecules of a fungicide known to cause cancer. Is it any wonder that cancer is now epidemic?

In addition, there was an enormous increase in use of Roundup® (glyphosate) when corn and soy genetically modified to be resistant to the herbicide were planted nationwide in 1996. Another herbicide shown to be detrimental to normal fetal development, glufosinate ammonium (called glufosinate), was registered for use in 1993. Since the 1990s, use of both glyphosate and glufosinate has greatly increased in many countries worldwide.

Besides killing weeds, glyphosate kills and damages native plants and vital soil microorganisms. Glyphosate and its primary metabolite AMPA are now found in the majority of samples tested of air, water, snow, rain, mother's milk, urine, and processed foods. As a patented antibiotic, glyphosate in air, water, and food is likely contributing to the alarming increase in antibiotic resistant bacteria. Seed corn, sweet corn, soybeans, alfalfa, wheat, sugar beets, rice, rape, and other crops have been genetically modified to be resistant to glyphosate (Roundup Ready®), so it does not kill them when higher quantities and/or concentrations are sprayed on them. Unfortunately, many weeds have developed resistance to glyphosate. Consequently, large corporations are producing new genetically modified seeds to be resistant to other herbicides, such as 2,4-D.

The herbicide 2,4-D was mixed half and half with 2,4,5-T to make Agent Orange, infamous for its serious, long-term, detrimental effects on humans and land exposed to it during the Vietnam conflict. Besides being a known endocrine disruptor, 2,4-D causes serious chromosomal damage and has been linked to several serious illnesses, including breast cancer, non-Hodgkin's lymphoma, and neurological diseases like ALS. A 1990 study showed an astounding 50% increase in non-Hodgkin's lymphoma in Nebraska farmers exposed to 2,4-D. To make Agent White (at least as deadly as Agent Orange and also used in Vietnam), 2,4-D was mixed half and half with another herbicide, picloram. Agent Orange received all the attention when adverse effects of herbicide exposure to people in Vietnam became well publicized; Agent White was seldom mentioned.

Genetically modified crops have also been developed to be resistant to glufosinate. From 1994 to present, increasing amounts of glufosinate have been applied to Liberty Link® soy, corn, and cotton, the most common glufosinate ammonium-resistant crops. Exposure to glufosinate results in reduced glutamine and increased ammonia levels. It is similar to glutamic acid, a natural amino acid that can stimulate the cells of the central nervous system. Glufosinate has been shown to cause serious brain damage in study animals, likely because an excess of glutamic acid can cause death of nerve cells in the brain.

Between the summer of 1994 and 2001, millions of pounds of chlorothalonil and other fungicides, in addition to increased use of glyphosate, glufosinate, and multiple organochlorine herbicides, were applied to crops in North America, often sprayed into the air from planes or helicopters. Somewhat less fungicide use has occurred since 2002, but chlorothalonil remains the most used fungicide in the U.S. The use of several other thyroid hormone disrupting compounds has increased substantially since 2006, including that of Roundup® on new Roundup Ready® crops. Roundup® applications on wheat, corn, soy, and potatoes increased in the U.S. from 10 million pounds in 1995 to an almost inconceivable 180 million pounds by 2010. The use of insecticides made of thyroid hormone disrupting, brain damaging, synthetic nicotine, called neonicotinoids (neonics), also increased extensively in 2006, with drastic consequences to invertebrates, especially bees and native insect pollinators, as well as vertebrates.

Now that many genetically modified plants have been introduced into the environment, it has been discovered that the process of genetically modifying a plant's cells causes unexpected changes to the plant. Even though many plants have been genetically modified to be resistant to glyphosate, long-term effects from eating genetically modified crops were not adequately tested. Even short-term studies on rodents, cattle, and hogs showed they were extremely detrimental to the digestive system and other organs.

A study found eating genetically modified corn caused underdeveloped young, reduction in fertility, reduced litter sizes, impaired immune responses, and other serious health problems in rats and mice. Both genetically modified corn and glyphosate are in many breakfast cereals. If the detrimental health effects on children from eating breakfast cereals are at all similar to the effects found in rats and mice, this is likely a serious issue with regard to children's health. Also, scientists predict the catastrophic effects of genetically modified plants on biodiversity and the environment in general will be "longer lasting than nuclear waste." They are referring to many of the plants we depend on for food!

Another concerning impact of exposure to glyphosate is its effects on human sperm. It likely also damages the sperm of other exposed vertebrate species, especially that of other mammals. With regard to effects on females, Roundup's® main ingredient, glyphosate, even at very low exposures, disrupts the levels of an enzyme, aromatase, which is instrumental in the biosynthesis of estrogens. Disruption of aromatase can cause severe enlargement of breasts on women or udders on ruminants. When they suddenly become overlarge, women may need to undergo breast reduction surgery; the excess weight can actually damage a woman's spine. Always before, I had only heard of women who had surgery to enhance their breasts. It seems women must now heed the warning, "Be careful what you wish for."

With increased use of glyphosate on alfalfa in Ravalli County, I saw very obvious mammotrophic effects on four female mixed-breed milk goats I kept as pets for 12 years. The set of triplets were never pregnant so their udders and teats never had any reason to develop to the extent they did. The oldest, Blackie, had only one kid in 2004 when she was three years old, the only time she was bred. Her mammary development was normal at that time for a reproductive female. In summer 2011, the left side of Blackie's udder suddenly grew so large it became chafed from rubbing on the inside of her leg. By summer 2012, the back of her udder had developed large chemical blisters, and by that fall, the chemical blisters had become tumors. Because of her tumors, Blackie had to be euthanized. Two of my triplet does, two years younger than Blackie, also had unnatural udder enlargement but only one was as severe as Blackie's.

The use of neonicotinoids has steadily increased worldwide since their introduction in 1994. I doubt it is just coincidence that bats, bees, and other pollinators have experienced significant die-offs after neonics, especially Clothianidin®, began being used. Studies have recently shown that dust from fields where it had been applied killed all of the bees exposed to it. In another study, bees were simultaneously exposed to Clothianidin® and to the fungicide chlorothalonil. This combination was found to be a thousand times deadlier to bees than the neonicotinoid alone. Bees and other pollinators are now exposed to multiple environmental chemicals found in the pollen of plants on which they feed. The decline in bees and other pollinators leaves less of them each year to pollinate flowering plants, many of which provide food for millions of people. Visible effects on Earth's plant life from insufficient pollinators are somewhat subtle now, but will eventually be evident, changing the face of forests and grasslands everywhere.

Because they are made of nicotine-like compounds, neonicotinoids are extremely thyroid hormone disrupting, especially to developing fetuses. Bees are also becoming addicted to pollen containing the neonicotinoids, which then kills them. This is comparable to what cigarette smoking does to humans, except bees die much more quickly.

The combination of cyanide and nicotine in cigarette smoke often causes human newborns to be born with Fetal Tobacco Syndrome. This produces the same symptoms, including skull and facial malformations, as newborns with Congenital Fetal Hypothyroidism. Is it fair that every mother of all vertebrate and invertebrate species on Earth is forced to breathe and eat the very same chemicals doctors tell pregnant human mothers not to use? It is not likely a coincidence that with significant increases in use of neonicotinoids in summer 2006, as well as new increased use of glyphosate on Roundup Ready® alfalfa, the prevalence of underbite and other craniofacial malformations on examined white-tailed deer fawns was 70% in spring 2007, more than double the 33% prevalence in 2006.

Landowners and pesticide applicators use many different kinds of herbicides, insecticides, and fungicides, often combining them. Exposure to combinations of toxins have long been shown to be far more damaging to non-target plants, beneficial insects, and developing vertebrate young than exposure to just one. Pesticide combinations can damage plants and animals far from where they are applied. When toxins carried in snow and rain land directly on exposed skin of a sensitive animal or onto leaves and flowers of sensitive plants, they often cause extensive damage.

Honey, one of my favorite Nubian milk goats, born in spring 2000, was extremely sensitive to toxins in rain and snow. The long ears on this breed hang down so rain or melted snow drips off the bottom edge. Often toxic water collecting on Honey's ear tips damaged the skin, causing small pieces of her ear to disintegrate. Eventually, the tips of her ears were completely eaten away by the toxins, making them appear to have been bitten off. These poisons have to be very damaging to literally *eat* a live animal's ears, like something in a horror movie. I watched it happen, but was unable to do anything about it. The astronomical use of herbicides, fungicides, and insecticides beginning in the early 1990s, has continued to increase for over 20 years. This has been a very bad period for animals and animal biodiversity, resulting in the extinction of many species.

Between 1995 and 2012, pine beetles have killed large numbers of pine trees in many forests in the United States and Canada. The prolonged drought is blamed, but it is likely a combination of lack of moisture and immune system damage from herbicides continuously landing on and coating the trees' needles. Dehydrated trees with their immune systems damaged by continuous exposure to herbicides can no longer effectively ward off beetle attacks. Millions of dead trees found throughout forests are changing our forested lands from green to reddish brown or gray. Forests may eventually recover, but it will likely require many years and far less exposure to toxic chemicals.

Billions of pounds of dust carrying a virtual chemical soup are picked up from yards and fields and carried on weather fronts, to come down in rain and snow on all the oceans of the world. Runoff from fields carry pesticides, fertilizers, and other pollutants into streams and rivers, which flow into the oceans. Studies done only 20 years after organochlorine pesticides began being used in 1945 showed serious damage to life in the oceans. Again, we have failed to face up to the harmful changes we are causing, in this case to the face of the planet itself.

Regarding our ability to affect the looks of our planet and our oceans, massive areas of floating plastics and other garbage in the Pacific Ocean can now be seen from space. When dumped into the oceans, our garbage does not go away. It remains for decades or even centuries, much of it floating on the surface. Things like plastic eventually break down into toxic chemicals, adding to the chemical soup the oceans' water has become. Meanwhile, pieces of plastic kill millions of ocean animals including fish, sea birds like Albatross, and rare sea turtles. Dumping plastic into the ocean is completely unnecessary. The ocean is not a universal garbage dump, even though it has been used that way for years. It would be in mankind's best interest to begin an immense effort to rid the ocean of plastic and recycle the debris into bio-fuel, using bacteria to digest the waste.

New volcanic eruptions, wild fires, deliberately set fires, and the tremendous increase in human populations, with corresponding human carbon-dioxide-emitting activities, have combined to greatly increase atmospheric carbon dioxide. The greenhouse effect, as a result of more atmospheric carbon dioxide, methane, and other greenhouse gases, natural and man-made, has caused a far greater acceleration of polar ice and glacial melting than was predicted by researchers. Less and less ice

This shows Honey's left ear where toxins in rain caused skin on the tip to disintegrate. Her right ear had similar damage.

at both poles each year is changing the appearance of Earth as seen from space.

And just like many people, Earth is becoming broader in the middle. Melting polar ice releases fresh water, which flows to the equator. The loss of Greenland ice is believed to contribute significantly to rising sea levels in the Northern Hemisphere, changing the shape of many lands, with some areas disappearing completely underwater. The paradox is that melting ice has already revealed new landmasses. As large portions of Earth's surface are changed, millions of people will have to move to more habitable areas, in addition to the millions displaced by wars now and in the future. It is clear the consequences of a warming climate will reconfigure the shape of continents and islands. Fortunately, many people are now facing up to the fact that human activities are instigating irreversible, catastrophic changes to our one and only planet, but changes in our behavior to date are far too slow.

Burgeoning human populations are also causing unprecedented variations in enormous areas of both land and ocean. Billions of lights now shine from ever-larger regions of Earth's landmasses, completely altering the appearance of Earth at night. Massive amounts of temperate and rain forest have been removed, greatly changing the face of the land and resulting in mass extinctions of plant and animal life. Warmer temperatures, less rainfall, and removal of protective vegetation by human activities have caused existing deserts to become larger and new deserts to form, resulting in giant dust storms carrying pollutants around the world in fast moving weather fronts. All these factors are continuously and significantly changing the face of our planet, unfortunately seldom for the better.

It is crucial for all of us to work together to find ways to mitigate and reverse the damage we are causing to Planet Earth and to the plants and animals who share it. We must immediately find which endocrine disrupting toxins are the culprits in triggering changes in the faces of birds, mammals, and other animals. When young animals die of starvation or cannot stand, walk, or fly, or they die because their intestines fall through the hole that doesn't close where their umbilical cord was, they experience sad, horrible, painful deaths. This unjustifiable abuse of newborn animals is being completely ignored.

It is absolutely essential that we recognize and admit to the detrimental changes in the faces and bodies of children. What hormone disrupting toxins are doing to children could easily be classified as extreme child abuse. There was an amazing list to illustrate the decline in childhood health in an article I read in 2017 titled, "Our Nation's Sick Children: Do not Let Kids Become Statistics" by Kay Jennings. The article stated, "According to David Brownstein, the medical director of the Center for Holistic Medicine in Bloomfield, Michigan, children in the United States are getting sicker." He provided the following data; 1 in 3 children is overweight, 1 in 5 is obese, 1 in 6 has learning disabilities, 1 in 11 has asthma, 1 in 68 has autism, 1 in 10 has ADHD,

1 in 20 has food allergies, 1 in 2 has a chronic illness, and childhood diabetes is increasing so fast that 1 in 3 will have diabetes by 2020. All of these adverse health issues have been shown by hundreds of studies to be caused by exposure to various herbicides, insecticides, and fungicides. Most concerning, all have been shown in multiple studies to be caused by glyphosate alone at levels far lower than what is found in the processed foods many parents buy and feed to their children.

Adults must all plead guilty to allowing the atrocious deaths and horrendous suffering in the young to continue unabated. We must insist in the strongest terms that products that are the most disrupting to normal development be banned immediately. Safe substitutes are available. We must mitigate the almost unbelievably damaging changes we are causing to ourselves and other animals or we, as a species, will face serious consequences.

The astronomical use of hormone disrupting, cell damaging herbicides, fungicides, and insecticides beginning in the early 1990s, has continued to increase for over 20 years. This has been a very bad period for animals and animal biodiversity, resulting in the extinction of many species. Issues concerning adverse changes to Earth's surface and species' extinction are mostly well publicized. Even the overgrowth of bills on birds in Alaska is fairly well known. However, the high prevalence of multiple developmental malformations in wild and domestic mammals throughout the United States and all over the world has received almost no notice at all by the news media, and consequently very little by the general public.

It is extremely important for everyone concerned about future generations to be informed about the disastrous epigenetic changes in animal young and to recognize harmful changes in plants that we and other animals require for food. Many people also depend upon domestic animals for food. Most have domestic animals as pets. Cancer, which used to be almost unheard of in dogs, cats, and domestic livestock, now kills millions, usually at great cost to their owners. Obvious unhealthy changes in so many individual domestic animals should be of concern to everyone, especially those who raise them, those who love them, and those who eat them. Hopefully, if we pay attention to what animals and plants are showing us, we can immediately begin to mitigate the damage, especially to our children, and ensure future generations of humans continue to enjoy a life similar to what we have been privileged to experience.

**From a tiny bird's
bill to the whole Earth's surface,
faces are changing.**

Alan Nelson took this photo of an adult Rufous Hummingbird with malformed and slightly crossed bills in 2008. The Rufous Hummingbird population has been reported to be declining by two to three percent per year for several decades because of loss of habitats, drier weather where it nests and other threats along its 4000 mile migration route. They nest in northwestern United States, Alaska and Canada and winter in Mexico.

CORPORATION ALMIGHTY

Claimed by Corporation Almighty,
Their genetically modified seeds
Would help the farmers feed the world,
Filling everybody's needs.

Spread altered genes around the world.
Force them into every nation.
If they resist, we make it hurt,
Said the war administration.

To Corporation Almighty
Even heads of nations bend,
So tainted pollen from GMO
Plants are now on every wind.

Their scientists failed to mention
The severe collateral damage
And all the hidden side effects,
Impossible to manage.

And similar to eating fruit
From the fabled forbidden tree,
Causing deadly adverse changes
Not imagined there would be.

Genetically modified pollens spread,
Contaminating other plants.
Their catastrophic changes
Harming even tiny ants.

With modified alfalfa, rice,
Potatoes, soybeans, corn, and wheat,
There is little "normal" food
Left for anyone to eat.

The damage done to planet Earth
Scientists say is not a plus,
Lasting longer than nuclear waste
Or warming caused by us.

Unusual developmental defects were observed on several owls brought for rehab after 1997. The defects included short upper bill, crossed bills as shown on the Saw-whet Owl (top photo) and malformed eyes as shown on the fledgling Great Horned Owl (bottom photo). The young Great Horned Owl also had a narrow skull and disrupted feather development.

CHAPTER 7
FRIED LIKE A WEENIE IN A MICROWAVE

The high ultraviolet radiation caused by damage to the ozone layer as a result of Mt. Pinatubo's eruption resulted in a number of extraordinary environmental events. I kept a record of unusual phenomena that appeared to be directly connected to much higher than normal ultraviolet radiation, some of which were reported to me and others I personally observed. Since moving to Montana in 1963, this would be the third time I observed bizarre environmental phenomena involving large numbers of animals.

The first was the loss of a great many domestic calves soon after I moved to the Bitterroot Valley in 1969. A cluster of symptoms called Weak Calf Syndrome (WCS) caused high mortality at that time. In my 23 years on my father's ranch and his 50 years of working on his own and other ranches in South Dakota, we had never seen any symptoms in calves resembling those of WCS.

The second phenomenon was when airborne chemicals sprayed throughout western United States adversely affected large numbers of wild birds. Beginning in 1981 and lasting through spring of 1985, I received several birds of a variety of species who had hatched with extreme limb or facial malformations. These were consistent with severe fetal hypothyroidism during development in the egg. A toxic exposure to the female bird may have contaminated the contents of fertilized eggs prior to being laid. Another possibility is that thyroid hormone disrupting chemicals passed through the shell, exposing the embryo after the egg was laid. Most likely, it was both.

The serious effects caused game bird, waterfowl, and other bird populations to crash. Also, hunters were told they should bake their waterfowl or game birds in the oven, catch the fat drippings, and dispose of them like toxic waste. Supposedly, it was then safe to eat the meat.

After an insecticide, endrin, and an herbicide, 2,4,5-T, were banned from use by the Environmental Protection Agency (EPA) in 1985, more waterfowl and game bird young survived and there were no further malformations in hatchlings I received for care until 1996. Interestingly, during the 10 years between 1985 and 1995, there were also far fewer cases of Weak Calf Syndrome in other states and almost none in our area. This was likely not a coincidence. Throughout the United States, there had been a huge increase in endrin and 2,4,5-T use in 1969, continuing until the two chemicals were banned in 1985. Here in Montana, there was a major escalation in use of several types of pesticides on forests and fields in the 1960s, including those two plus DDT and 2,4-D.

Jack Ward, a Ravalli County veterinarian, had diagnosed and named the first case of WCS in 1964 and recorded an epidemic of WCS in RC calves beginning in spring 1969. It caused the deaths of hundreds of thousands of calves each spring from 1969 through 1985 in ranching areas throughout the United States. The use of DDT was banned in the U.S. in 1972, but that did not appear to decrease the number of cases of WCS. The areas where the most devastating outbreaks occurred were either downwind of or directly in areas where endrin was extensively sprayed in addition to 2,4,5-T and 2,4-D.

If young wild mammals were being affected, I did not see them, nor were any reported to me. Between 1969 and 1985, I lived in Malta, Montana, and then Missoula, Montana, where I taught elementary school classes. Consequently, I did not have newborns of either wild or domestic mammals available to examine. If mammals were as severely affected as wild birds I received to rehabilitate, the malformations would have caused death prior to or immediately after they were born, making it unlikely anyone would have seen them.

In 1996, two years after the period of much higher than normal ultraviolet radiation, I again began seeing malformations in hatchling birds. However, these were somewhat different and not as severe as those in the early 1980s. For some reason, I did not begin observing underdeveloped upper bills on birds until a year after we had seen large numbers of young mammals of multiple species with underbite, crooked legs, reproductive malformations, and other birth defects.

The huge increase in fungicide use, especially chlorothalonil, and the dramatic increase in use of Roundup® and other herbicides from 1994 through 1996, corresponds well with the sudden appearance of malformations in all vertebrate species observed. Hatchling birds appeared to be somewhat more resistant to those environmental toxins during the first two or three years in comparison to the effects on grazing animal newborns. This may have been because ruminants eat a great deal of foliage, so were more quickly exposed to damaging levels of the chemicals than birds who eat insects and seeds. For whatever reason, there was not a significant prevalence of short upper bills on hatchlings and fledglings brought for rehabilitation until spring 1999.

By then, I had a strong suspicion the many unusual malformations in newborn vertebrates that began in spring 1995 were likely connected in some way to the bizarre events I had observed in 1993 and 1994. That was especially true of the two most common abnormalities in mammal young. Specific malformations of male reproductive organs and epigenetic changes resulting in underdevelopment of upper facial bones were extremely high in prevalence. It was also true of the two most common malformations in fledgling birds, underdevelopment of upper facial bones and disrupted feather growth. Many of the malformations observed had not previously been reported in scientific literature, making it difficult to determine exactly what might be causing disrupted growth during pre- and post-natal development.

One of the first unusual phenomena I began seeing in February 1993, when ultraviolet radiation was abnormally high, was that developing pollen cones on our ponderosa pines were different. They had always been slightly curved outward from their point of attachment in a rosette-like pattern and were never branched. In 1993, those on our trees were twisted into bizarre shapes with enlarged, bulbous ends, like thick, fuzzy worms with fat heads. Sometimes they branched into double ends, looking like two-point deer antlers in velvet. I soon discovered pollen cones were similarly misshapen on all species of pine trees throughout western Montana.

After finding information reported by scientists who studied effects from the Mt. Pinatubo eruption, I concluded that the strange-looking pollen cones must have been caused by the high ultraviolet radiation present at that time. Cones of multiple pine species were being similarly affected over a very wide area.

A Canadian site on the Internet gave readings of ozone and ultraviolet radiation levels directly over each measuring station in Canada. (Scientists there have been measuring ozone levels since 1957.) The closest station to western Montana is in Edmonton, Alberta, 500 miles straight north of the Bitterroot Valley. An unusual weather pattern compounded the problem of thinning ozone in late March 1993, when the station in Edmonton recorded a springtime ozone value of 22% below normal for over two weeks. This low value equated to a historically unprecedented increase in ultraviolet radiation of 44% higher than normal over Canada and northern United States. Canadian scientists warned their citizens that just a few minutes exposure to such high ultraviolet radiation levels severely weakens the immune system as well as causing acute sunburn on exposed skin. As one Canadian scientist put it, "We were being fried like weenies in a microwave oven."

All through 1993 and until June 1994, we continued to monitor readings from the Canada measuring stations. For over a year, ozone values remained lower than normal, resulting in fairly consistent 15% higher-than-normal ultraviolet radiation levels, occasionally going up to 20%. Fortunately for all plants and animals, it did not exceed 40% again.

In spring 1994, pollen cones were once more misshapen. I collected those of various species from several areas, including near Yellowstone National Park where we vacation each spring. I sent the labeled cones to a scientist who was studying effects of radiation on pollen cones. He confirmed deformities on those from Montana and Wyoming were consistent with radiation damage. At his request, park rangers and others sent pollen cones to him from all over northwestern United States. All those he received showed similar effects of exposure to high ultraviolet radiation. At that time, the scientist was also studying radiation levels near nuclear power plants. He sent me a sample of similarly-shaped pollen cones from downwind of a nuclear plant located near where he lived in eastern United States. The mystery of the malformed pollen cones was solved.

Another phenomenon I began seeing in early spring 1993 concerned blue-green algae growing in the black rubber pans I used for watering animals. In less than a day it grew enough to thickly cover the sides and bottom of the pans. This unusual growth continued through 1994 and into 1995. I would scrape algae out of the pans in the morning. By afternoon the sides and bottom would again be covered with a thick growth. I consulted my sister, Pam, a marine biologist who knows the natural history of coral, algae, foramina, and other water organisms. She confirmed that blue-green algae grow and reproduce much faster when exposed to high ultraviolet radiation.

Vertebrates do not do as well, as evidenced by another disturbing occurrence. In April 1993, the top of the muzzle on my black Alpine milk goat, Jewel, became so sunburned that her skin was extensively covered with blisters. Even though I put salve on the blisters every day, it took nearly three weeks for them to heal. A week after her nose blistered, Jewel became quite ill and consequently lost the twins she was carrying. She eventually recovered, raising healthy twins the next year.

On June 11, 1993, a three-week-old female baby skunk named Rosie was brought to me with dog bite injuries on her back. Fortunately for the little skunk, a woman who was taking a morning walk found her lying on her side in a pasture, unconscious and hypothermic. It was mid-morning when Rosie was found, so she had been lying in direct sunlight for over four hours.

Rosie had warmed a bit while riding in the woman's car with the heater on, so was beginning to wake up by the time she and her rescuer arrived. The woman had wrapped her in an old sweater tucked into a small cardboard box. I placed the box on a heating pad to continue warming her. When I examined Rosie for injuries, I discovered her hind legs were partially paralyzed by the dog bite. I gave her warm milk mixed with strained chicken baby food. Rosie hungrily lapped it up, licking the bowl clean. A large cardboard box with a warm blanket for a bed and a shelter made of the sweater for her to crawl under made a safe and comfortable nursery. A heating pad on low remained under one end of the cardboard box to keep her warm while she slept.

Rosie was very gentle and trusting, not once threatening to spray or bite when I handled her. After several days of physical therapy for her partly paralyzed hind legs, she was again able to walk normally. She remained gentle and liked to sleep on my lap when I took a break to watch my favorite TV show. When she outgrew her cardboard box, I put her in a special pen for small mammals. It has a wire bottom, so animals like skunks cannot dig out. A wooden sleeping box containing her blanket was in the roofed area at the back of the pen.

On June 29, a young skunk slightly older than Rosie was found in a root cellar near Missoula. The little female had been trapped for at least three days before being rescued. She was thirsty and hungry but uninjured. I named her Petunia and put her in the pen with Rosie. Both seemed happy to have a friend. They would spend hours playing together until they tired and slept lying close together. Rosie remained gentle and came to me when I called her name. Petunia was much wilder as a result of being older when brought for rehab. Also, since Petunia was not injured, there had been no reason to handle her, so she did not become tame like Rosie.

The two little skunks looked like twins. The left ear had been sunburned on both, causing raised blisters on the top edge of the ear.

Presumably, in Rosie's case, it was the ear exposed to the sun while she was lying unconscious in the field. I did not know how Petunia's left ear became so badly sunburned, since it couldn't have happened while she was trapped in a dark cellar. The blistered ears healed, but on both skunks the skin was permanently thickened. Neither skunk's ear grew hair in the area scarred by the severe sunburn.

After they were old enough, I released the skunks in our yard under a brush pile. I put a pan of cat food and one of water nearby each day while they learned to catch insects, worms, and mice, the main items in a skunk's summer diet. Petunia left our busy yard for a new territory, where she made her home under a brush pile at the east end of our land. I put food there for as long as she stayed.

Rosie remained gentle and tame. She stayed in our yard, following me around when I did outdoor chores, coming to be fed and petted when I called her. She was so tame that for her safety, I put hay bales in our large deer pen so she could dig a den in the soil under them; it was warm in winter and cool in summer. She liked the deer fawns who lived in the pen each spring. When school children came to see the animals, Rosie would appear to be petted when I called her. She seemed to enjoy being the center of attention. Almost always, someone would ask if her scent glands had been removed. It got their immediate attention when I said no. Everyone assumes if a skunk can spray, it will. Rosie never had a reason to spray and to my knowledge never did. The edge of her sun-damaged ear remained thickened and hairless. She lived for eight years.

The two skunks and my goat were not the only animals who had blistering from sunburn in spring 1993. Two recovering Great Horned Owls being cared for by another wildlife rehabilitator were placed outside in a sunning box for approximately an hour and a half. Captive birds need periods of sun on their feathers to enable them to properly utilize the calcium in their diet. The owls were usually kept in a flight room with barred windows where they were not exposed to direct sunlight. The rehabber did not know the ultraviolet radiation was dangerously high. When she took the owls out of the sunning box to put them back into the flight room, she discovered their eyelids had become red and blistered. The rehabber immediately put salve on the injuries, but it took over a week for them to completely heal.

A few days later, I received a Great Horned Owl who had been found in an open field, sitting on the ground with a broken wing. Being exposed to the sun for an unknown time period caused it to have red, blistered eyelids exactly like the other owls. I called all the wildlife rehabilitators I knew in western Montana, warning them to watch for blisters on eyelids, ears, or faces of animals and birds brought to them. One stated quite emphatically that birds, especially owls, could not possibly get sunburned eyelids. Unfortunately, he was wrong.

Other eye problems in young animals during spring and summer 1993 were blindness and cataracts. I had not seen either in my previous 25 years of rehabbing animals. A male white-tailed deer fawn was brought to me on June 6, because he was found wandering around in circles in someone's yard. He was blind and starving, his eyes showing white lenses. A veterinarian's diagnosis was that the deer had a bacterial infection, which should heal in 10 days or less with the eye ointment he prescribed. The fawn's eyes were no better after 14 days of using the ointment, so I discontinued its use. Besides not helping the fawn's eyes, it caused them to itch. I kept him inside, away from any sunlight for about five weeks, and slowly the white lenses cleared so he could see again.

I was surprised and extremely pleased when the fawn's sight returned. I gave him several tests to make certain he could see well enough to survive in the wild, then put him in the deer pen with other fawns we were raising that year. He was released with them when all were old enough. I called him Mushroom, because I had to keep him in low light for so long. Mushroom lived quite a long life for a male white-tailed deer. We saw him for the last time in October 1998 when he was five years old. He had grown an impressive set of antlers. Bucks with large antlers seldom survive hunting season. We never saw him again after fall 1998 so assumed he was killed by one of the neighbors who hunt deer.

I could easily distinguish Mushroom year around from all other male deer. He had cut an identifying notch in his left ear going through a barbed wire fence soon after he was released as a fawn. Mushroom's eyes apparently functioned normally, as he managed to avoid vehicles, fences, wild predators, and neighborhood dogs. I have always wondered how many newborn animals died of starvation in spring 1993 because their eyes were damaged by the extremely high ultraviolet radiation.

Another example of an animal found starving because of an eye problem was a six-month-old mountain lion cub brought to me in summer 1993. He had a cataract on the lens of his left eye. A game warden eventually took him to the Montana Department of Fish, Wildlife and Parks wildlife rehabilitation center in Helena. Because of the cataract, they couldn't find a zoo that would take him, so the decision was made to euthanize him. Although it was a sad end to the little cat's short life, it was likely for the best. Most mountain lions are not happy living in a cage.

In 1994, Oregon rehabilitation facilities reported receiving 10 young-of-the-year birds with malformations, including missing eyes, crossed bills, and other bone abnormalities. That was one year before we began seeing similar birth defects in animals here in western Montana. Washington State University received what they described as "a rash of blind owls" in 1993 and 1994, but they had no funding available for studies to determine the cause. Interestingly, studies had already shown that exposure to very high ultraviolet radiation causes blindness. It was one of the primary warnings from the Canadian scientists.

In 1994, 1995, and 1996, when I went out to look at plants or on botany trips with other amateur botanists, we saw an unusually high number of white flowers on wildflower species that were commonly purple, pink, or red in color. There were white flowers on Blue-eyed Mary, Elephant Head, Spotted Knapweed, Oxytropis, Delphinium, Phacelia, and others, in quantities ranging from a few to a fairly large number. Leucistic flowers (lacking their normal color) were scattered throughout the population of normal-colored flowers. After 1997, almost all those we saw were normal in color, with only an occasional white flower, the usual prevalence.

Another observation of interesting effects on plants was the much faster growth of crust lichen on rocks on our land. The lichen colonies, which had grown almost imperceptibly for years, suddenly grew visibly much larger. Rocks with small round colonies in 1993, were nearly covered with them by 1997. Several, which I measured at monthly intervals, grew from one to three inches larger in diameter in just one summer.

In 1995, wildlife watchers began reporting many white or white-spotted (leucistic) birds and animals. A pure white red squirrel was seen regularly in a yard in Hamilton, Montana, and several other white squirrels and white chipmunks were reported in Montana. Several white bison calves were born since 1995 in different areas of the United States, causing great excitement in Native American communities. They consider a white bison to be sacred. However, none of the calves remained white as they grew to adulthood. Their hair turned reddish cream at six months and changed to the usual dark brown as an adult, thus the abnormal hair color was caused by leucism, not albinism. Albinos remain white their entire life.

In June 1995, a female white-tailed deer fawn was found starving near Victor, Montana, a small town not far from where we live. The fawn was mostly white with a more normal-colored head and neck, though her face and muzzle had more white hair than most. Her white body was dappled with small red spots making her color a light roan so I named her Roanie. Her shape was unusually wide and short for a deer, making her look much like a tiny roan calf. Her incisors and bite were normal. Both front and back legs were short, malformed, and crooked, so they had to be splinted to straighten them. The back legs required supports for nearly a month before her bones were straight and strong enough for her to walk normally. When Roanie was ready to be weaned, she was taken to a zoo in Red Lodge, Montana, where she lived for almost a year. She died suddenly of heart failure because of an enlarged heart, as found in a necropsy by the zoo's veterinarian.

Since 1995, I have necropsied many normal-colored white-tailed deer fawns, elk calves, beef calves, newborn domestic goats, and birds that had an enlarged right heart ventricle. For some reason, hearts of necropsied animals have had another unusual symptom since summer of 2006. Many, especially those of newborns, exhibited dilated lymphatic vessels on the heart surface, often in addition to an enlarged right ventricle. An enlarged heart is considered by medical professionals to be a dangerous health problem. State wildlife biologists showed no concern about heart defects we reported on newborn wildlife. At present, the most prevalent birth defects on children are reported to be congenital heart malformations.

In spring 2001, our second roan fawn, Allie, was born in Pattee Canyon, near Missoula, Montana. Allie also had crooked leg bones, similar to Roanie's. In addition, her lower incisors were round with a point on the top instead of being wide and thin like normal lower incisors in deer, other ruminants, and humans. Thirty million years ago, it was normal for some deer species to have round, pointed incisors, exactly like Allie's.

A third oddly-colored female deer, born in 1998, was often seen in the foothills of the Bitterroot Mountains west of Victor. That one was mostly cream-colored and appeared to have normal skeletal structure. She was born in the wild, surviving until the winter she was three years old, when she was killed and eaten by a mountain lion. All three were white-tailed deer. We haven't heard of leucistic deer in our area since 2001, but a fairly large number have been observed in eastern United States.

Beginning in 1994 and continuing to the present, bird watchers have observed and photographed many birds with white feathers where dark ones would normally be. Leucism produces birds who are as attractive as they are unusual in appearance. Feeder watchers throughout western Montana have reported white or partly white House Finches and House Sparrows at their feeders. I was told of American Robins in our county with white spots on their brown feathers in 2001, 2002, 2003, 2009, and 2010, and there are multiple photos of leucistic American Robins on the Internet. A Red-winged Blackbird, with cream-colored feathers where black feathers should have been, came to our bird feeder during winter 1995-1996. It had a black bill, black legs, and dark eyes, with red and yellow chevrons on the wings, indicating that only feathers that were normally black in color had disrupted melanin. Birders photographed several nearly-white Red-tailed Hawks in Montana between 2007 and 2013. The "Ghost Birds," being beautiful and unusual, are quite exciting to see and photograph, often attracting general public attention as well as that of birders. In recent years a large number of leucistic bird photos have been posted on the Internet.

Elevated radiation levels from man-made sources have been shown to cause a high prevalence of similar white feathers on normally dark swallow species. After the Chernobyl disaster in Russia, researchers found a significant prevalence of leucism in Barn Swallows nesting in the contaminated area. Many of them had white spots scattered over their dark body, similar to the white or white-spotted bird species being observed and photographed here in North America. It should be concerning that something is affecting young birds here during feather development similarly to those living in a nuclear disaster zone where they are exposed to very high radiation. Several other factors besides radiation have been shown to cause unusual feather color. These include unbalanced diet, old age, injury, disease, or a shock of some kind to the bird's system, including exposure to toxins.

There is a significant difference between leucism and albinism. Albinism is caused by changes in a gene which interferes with the production of a precursor to the pigment melanin, causing disruption of melanin production in all feathers and skin. In birds with albinism, the irises appear red because blood vessels are visible without melanin

Allie, the roan white-tailed deer fawn from near Missoula, Montana.

coloring to hide them, and legs and bills are pink because, without melanin, normal coloration is absent. If melanin disruption happens in specific feathers or in only some areas of skin, the condition is called leucism. In these birds, the color of the iris is always normal and legs and bill usually are. This condition occurs because some environmental factor disrupts the production of normal levels of melanin, but the bird's genes are not affected.

If a hatchling American Robin is exposed to toxins, the toxins themselves could interfere with melanin production. Also, effects of being poisoned could result in inability to digest food, lethargy, failure to food beg, or diarrhea, causing interference with proper development of the hatchling, including normal development of feathers and bones. If those symptoms last too long, the hatchling will die. If it recovers, the time period it was unable to digest food is considered a period of starvation or unbalanced diet. Thus, both poisoning and malnutrition can result in a bird producing feathers without normal melanin coloration. American Robins, House Finches, and House Sparrows are birds often reported with leucism. Those species nest where considerable amounts of unnatural chemical toxins (including lawn spray, insecticides, fungicides, car exhaust, and others) are present during the nesting season. Such exposures could easily contribute to or cause leucism and other developmental problems in sensitive hatchlings.

A consideration not often mentioned is that both toxins and radiation cause deleterious effects on the immune system, often resulting in autoimmune diseases and susceptibility to viruses and bacteria. Consequently, a bird's own immune system may attack cells that produce the precursor to melanin, or the immune system may somehow interfere with melanin going into developing feathers. Either could cause white or lighter-than-normal feathers.

Many studies of amphibians have shown for years that their populations are seriously affected by exposure to environmental toxins and high ultraviolet radiation. Prior to 1994, there were Western Toads in large numbers throughout Ravalli County. By the end of July 1994, many people in the county had noticed an almost complete absence of them in their yards. This was to me one of the most disturbing observations of the disruption of plant and animal life during the high ultraviolet radiation event here in western Montana. Western Toad populations have not recovered and remain much lower than before 1994. Researchers debated whether the sudden decline was due to high UVB radiation or if there was a combination of factors.

In other areas of North America, ozone depletion and water pollution by pesticides, PCB, and heavy metals have, alone or in combination, been shown to cause deformities and population declines in frogs, salamanders, and other amphibians. In studies of four species of frog exposed to lower levels of chlorothalonil than are now found in the environment, young of all four species were killed. As I previously said, a test of water from melted snow that fell in our yard on March 19, 1999, had 0.43 ppb of chlorothalonil and similar chemicals in it. That is over four times what it took to kill frog embryos and damage adult frogs in the studies. Therefore, chlorothalonil in rain falling onto amphibians' skin would likely have an extremely detrimental effect. Also, very few young toads who hatch from eggs laid in contaminated small ponds left from snow melt and spring rains are able to survive the exposure to chlorothalonil, significantly contributing to the sudden severe decline in toad population in our area.

Ravalli County's leopard frogs disappeared long before 1993, soon after the herbicide xylene, deadly to amphibians, was poured into irrigation ditches to kill weeds. No leopard frogs have been found in Ravalli County for many years, joining a growing list of animal species that have been completely extirpated here. Others are Columbia Sharp-tailed Grouse, fresh water mussels, and white-tailed jackrabbit. The grouse were over-hunted, as were white-tailed jackrabbit. Jackrabbit young did not survive to restock the populations because their sagebrush bunch grass habitat was sprayed with 2,4-D and picloram. Mussels died because streams and rivers were contaminated with multiple pesticides, to which mussels are very sensitive.

The porcupine population in our area is now declining so fast it may soon be on that list of extirpated animals. In summer 2015, a fellow rehabber received a three-month-old porcupine for care because he had neurological damage, causing him to tip over when he walked. Eventually, he was unable to move either hind leg. The little porcupine couldn't get to his food and water or remain upright to eat. Every couple hours he was placed in an upright position and food and water were held for him, hoping he would recover use of his legs. Unfortunately, he continued to deteriorate and the decision was made to euthanize him. Testing showed he had been exposed to Rotenone®, used to kill small rodents.

In October 1997, I spotted a young toad trying with little success to hop through thick grass near our house. He was a juvenile male who had hatched in a nearby pond, growing from a tadpole to a small toad during the summer. No foot had formed on his right hind leg during development, just one toe-like appendage where the foot should have been. This caused the little toad to have great difficulty hopping, especially in areas with thick grass.

I named him Lefty and put him in an aquarium with a shallow pan of water to sit in. It was a fairly cool day in October when I found the little toad. In a few more days, it was below zero outside, so I kept him in our house through the winter. He ate mealworms, crickets, and flies, growing quite rapidly on the abundance of food. The next spring, I showed him to Bryce Maxell, a biologist who studies amphibians. He confirmed that Lefty's right hind foot was malformed, not bitten off or injured.

Lefty accompanied me to many talks I gave during the winter with unreleasable birds I use for educational programs. He was a big hit with school children as well as adults. By spring, he was full-grown and could hop well enough to be released. At the time, we had a swampy area along Willoughby Creek, where toads congregated to mate and lay eggs.

Lefty, a Western Toad had an unformed right hind foot.

The males would sing to attract females, who deposited their eggs in the shallow pond there. When it was warm enough outside and before breeding season, I released Lefty in the pond. Since his leg deformity was not genetic, I hoped he would be able to attract a mate and help his species survive.

In fall 1998, I found another juvenile toad with underdeveloped toes on its right foot. An adult toad with an underdeveloped right eye lived in the flowerbed beside our house for three years, 2013, 2014, and 2015. The toad appeared able to successfully find and catch insects with only one functioning eye. We still see a few Western Toads in our yard each year and some young ones are surviving. It would be very sad to have the pretty and ecologically important Western Toad join our county's list of extirpated animals.

All the major factors (radiation, nitriles, nicotine, cyanide, multiple organochlorine herbicides, and glyphosate) to which animals have been exposed from 1994 to the present have been shown by multiple studies to cause serious disruption of thyroid hormones. For developing young, it takes only minuscule amounts of such chemicals to have a serious life-long effect. Even more harmful to the population as a whole, undesirable epigenetic changes with which they are born or hatched are passed on to several future generations.

Whether the decline in amphibian populations and the sudden appearance of the high prevalence of developmental defects in toads and frogs were caused by too much ultraviolet radiation, exposure to increasing levels of toxic chemicals, or a synergistic combination of those conditions has been extensively debated. However, more recent studies indicate the millions of pounds of pesticides used throughout the United States were, and still are, the prime factor responsible for both malformations and population declines in affected vertebrate species.

Glyphosate alone has been shown to cause multiple malformations, neurological damage, cancer, serious damage to digestive and immune systems, as well as other adverse health symptoms in amphibians, birds, and mammals. Reptiles in our area appear to be in decline, but I could find no studies showing the effects of glyphosate, chlorothalonil, other pesticides or high UVB radiation on snakes, turtles, lizards, or other reptiles.

In 2003, I was told of another alarming result of high levels of ultraviolet radiation in 1993 and 1994. When Bob and I were checked for skin cancer, the doctor mentioned that he had just lost a patient, a woman only 24 years old, to the deadliest form of skin cancer. He said there was an epidemic of this disease in young people between 16 and 25. When I asked if he knew why, he said exposure to too much sun during a person's lifetime is the usual cause, but he had no idea why so many people under 25 were dying from a cancer that used to be uncommon in young people. He had lived in this area for only two years so I told him what had happened in 1993 and 1994. The Ravalli Republic, a newspaper in Hamilton, Montana, had printed an article about the harmful effects of high levels of ultraviolet radiation, warning everyone to cover all exposed skin and wear broad-brimmed hats when going outside. Unfortunately, very few heeded the warning. Many people, especially children and teenagers, were and still are exposed to the sun for long periods when they go to riverbanks in the summer, often staying for hours to play in the sand, sun bathe, or swim.

I explained to the dermatologist that in summer 1994, because of the extremely high ultraviolet radiation, I asked at several area drugstores if they were selling more sun screen than usual. The answer was no. However, they said they could not keep up with the demand for sunburn lotion. Many people even complained of becoming sunburned through their shirts. Sadly, some who were severely sunburned in the summers of 1993 and 1994 have already died of skin cancer.

Plants and animals did their best to warn us of the deadly effects of high ultraviolet radiation. If a large volcanic eruption again disrupts the ozone layer, it will likely result in similar wide-spread high levels of ultraviolet radiation. Hopefully, the next time this happens, more people will pay attention to what animals and plants have shown us. Parents should at least try to keep their children out of the sun during such events. Young people should not have to die from unknowingly being "fried like a weenie in a microwave."

**With plants modified
genetically, consumer
pays with deadly change.**

CHAPTER 8
DYING TO WARN US

Ravalli County, Montana, used to be one of the most beautiful places in the United States. That was before unregulated, rampant development and multiple large subdivisions covered the fields, pasturelands, and forested lower slopes of the mountains on both sides of the Bitterroot Valley with over-sized houses. The irony is that realtors and developers attract people to come here by claiming we have clean air and water. They are apparently willing to let children and other young animals die to keep that false image alive.

Many kinds of wildlife live on our land, including Yellow-bellied Marmots. Over 100 were born in spring 1994, about the same number as each year for the previous several years. When more were born than could thrive on our land, we would live-trap 20 or 30 and take them to friends who wanted marmots released on their land. Since 1994, we haven't had to find new homes for any, and now only between 20 and 30 live here.

That year no young marmots survived to adulthood. Since then only a few have lived to come out of hibernation when they were a year old. In 1997, over 150 of the chubby little fur balls were born. When they were old enough to leave their nursery dens, we saw them running around in our pastures, playing and busily learning what foliage was good to eat. Beginning on July 6, an unusually long weather front came through, bringing cloudy skies with a drizzling rain that lasted for 10 days. By July 16, nearly every young marmot had died. Only six bedraggled, very ill youngsters remained. I managed to catch one of them with a net and found blood dripping slowly from its nostrils; it could barely breathe. I euthanized it and took it to my veterinarian to be sent to the Montana State Agriculture Laboratory's veterinarian for necropsy and testing. I wanted to know what kind of horrible disease had infected the marmots and appeared to kill only young ones. Within two days, the remaining five youngsters were gone, too. Every one of over 150 young marmots who had appeared completely healthy just two weeks before had mysteriously died.

Veterinarians at the lab reported they could find no bacterial infection or evidence of a virus in the young marmot I sent for testing. The digestive system was no longer functional, it had severe liver damage, and the lungs were hemorrhaging; the poor little guy was drowning in his own blood. The lab report said they did not know what killed the marmot, though the letter I sent with it stated very plainly I had euthanized it and what drug I used. More oddly, even after I had told them over 150 young marmots born that spring had died of whatever had killed it, they said maybe it was hit by a car. A car did not hit that marmot or any of the others who died in that two-week period. I paid $50 for the lab fee and postage and all I received was "maybe it was hit by a car!"

Most disturbingly, they also noted on the bottom of the lab report that there was no evidence of pesticide poisoning. I had said nothing about pesticides or pesticide poisoning to the veterinarian who sent the marmot to the lab. In my letter to lab personnel describing the symptoms of all the young marmots, I never mentioned pesticides or any other toxin. Unintentionally, the lab report indicated they suspected some kind of poisoning had occurred. A damaged liver, damaged digestive system, and bleeding lungs are all classic symptoms of exposure to a severe toxin. The only poisons marmots could have been exposed to on our land were whatever was in the rain, on foliage they ate, and the moist air they breathed during the extended rainy period. We do not use pesticides. Also, as only young marmots had died, whatever caused their deaths was far more toxic to recently weaned youngsters than to adults.

Just as alarming, two years before the deaths of the young marmots, I had seen several with bizarre limb malformations. Three had a completely unformed right front leg, so there was no leg at all on the right shoulder. One such affected animal might have been a fluke, but three with the same birth defect was a strong indication of disruption of fetal development throughout our marmot colony.

Both front legs were malformed on another little marmot, with no bones between the shoulder and front feet, which were attached directly to the shoulder. When it was old enough to go out of its den to eat plants, it had to push itself along with its hind legs while sliding on its chin. I caught and euthanized it, but did not bother to spend $50 to send it to the state lab. The lab personnel would likely have said the marmot had a normal variation or that birth defects are normal occurrences. That is what the State Agricultural Lab and the MDFWP Wildlife Lab have consistently said concerning malformations on hundreds of wild and domestic animals my colleagues and I have brought to their attention since spring 1995. The question is how can a veterinarian or a wildlife biologist truthfully consider a serious birth defect to be a normal variation, especially when it causes mortality?

After observing young marmots with severely malformed limbs, I began paying closer attention to all the other newborn animals I saw in spring 1995. Marmot youngsters are born quite early in warm, sheltered underground nursery dens dug by their mothers. Consequently, they come out to explore and play around the den entrances before most other wild mammals are born. Soon after young marmots began leaving their dens, my milk goats produced their babies. One female was born with crooked front legs and a severe underbite. Not long after the goats were born, I saw two unrelated white-tailed deer fawns with extremely crooked hind legs, which appeared to be attached to the hip at an odd angle.

Besides the birth defects I saw, bizarre examples in a number of domestic animals were reported to me. A local rancher had two mule foals, both female, born with severe underbite and other facial malformations. They were so badly deformed they were euthanized soon after birth. A friend had a lamb born with extremely malformed upper and lower jaws. With special feeding and care, it lived to be six months old. Dozens of calves and other domestic newborns died or were put down because of malformed legs, contracted tendons, misshapen heads, and other abnormalities. Many sheep, goats, foals, and calves were born with an underbite, like my baby goat.

Thus began the planet-wide virtual melt-down of normal fetal development in vertebrate species, including human newborns. The damage has been devastating and long lasting. After 20 years, it has become obvious the malformations are far more prevalent, severe, and widespread than damage caused to newborns by the high radiation released in nuclear power plant disasters. Unfortunately, nothing has been done to mitigate the sadistic, almost incomprehensible damage to young of many species and likely to many future generations.

A major obstacle to finding what is going wrong with the development of young animals is that the Montana Department of Fish, Wildlife and Parks has consistently denied there are developmental malformations in wildlife, especially wild grazing animals. Respected scientists we consulted between 1996 and 1999 gave multiple written statements saying animals we provided for their examination had one or more birth defects. The MDFWP biologists at the laboratory said what looked like a malformation to "untrained personnel" was an artifact of being dead. Then, completely contradicting themselves, the statement they sent to our Ravalli County Board of Health was that the accident-killed deer we sent to be examined had normal variations. MDFWP biologists have since repeatedly claimed obvious developmental malformations on wildlife are normal variations, even after we published three peer-reviewed studies. Our first two studies addressed the high prevalence of the most common birth defects and the third study, published in 2015, addressed health issues and birth defects in wildlife, domestic animals, and human newborns. It is clear that reviewers of the studies considered the issues we addressed to be real or the studies would not have been published.

On April 11, 1996, I was cutting up a dead male white-tailed deer to feed the unreleasable Bald Eagle, Golden Eagle, and Turkey Vulture I had at that time for educational programs. Bob had picked up the yearling buck beside a local highway where it died after being hit by a vehicle.

The birds were not particular about how their meat was cut up, as long as I didn't get it dirty. I cut off the legs and stripped out the back-strap for the eagles. The heart, liver, tongue, and testes were favored by the Turkey Vulture. After butchering hundreds of deer and elk for meat eaters in my care, it was a completely routine procedure. But that time it was anything but routine. When I lifted the left hind leg of the buck to cut it away from the body, what I saw was surprising and alarming. The deer had no scrotal sac at all. Except for four small teats, normal in both genders, the skin was completely smooth where the scrotum should have been. In 25 years of butchering deer, I had never before seen a male deer with no scrotum.

After recovering from my surprise at the young buck's condition, I went directly into my normal insatiable curiosity mode. I carefully dissected the groin area to find the testes. Both had descended through the inguinal canal during fetal development, but had stopped in a horizontal position between the outer skin and the body wall rather than forming the scrotum, which holds testes away from the warmth of the body.

Being born with no scrotum can occasionally happen to a male animal, so at the time I didn't realize it had wide-spread implications. Then just two weeks later, Bob came home with three male white-tailed deer, which were all killed in the same place by the same truck. Remembering the previous buck, which had no scrotum, I immediately checked the genitalia. The oldest, a three-year-old, looked completely normal and exactly as male deer had always looked, with testes held well away from the body wall by a normal-sized, bilateral scrotum. When I examined the two yearling bucks, I got a sick feeling in the pit of my stomach. One had no scrotum at all, just like the yearling I had examined on April 11. On the other, only the left half of the scrotum had formed. In medical terms, each half is called a hemiscrotum. The right side had not formed during fetal development on that buck, so the right testis was horizontal under the skin, as were both testes on the buck with no scrotum. All three males I examined in the month of April 1996, all born in 1995, had a serious birth defect of their genitalia. Although I thought three bucks with reproductive malformations was alarming, it turned out to be the tip of a gigantic iceberg and the beginning of a long campaign to get proper testing done to find the cause.

Six of the next seven yearling male white-tailed deer Bob picked up on roadsides in northern Ravalli County also had malformed scrota (plural of scrotum), including none, only one hemiscrotum formed, both hemiscrota as very short bumps, and one male with misaligned hemiscrota, with the left formed directly forward of the right. The latter condition was even more disturbing than short, half, or no scrotum because that specific birth defect had not been reported in the scientific literature. Apparently, it was something that had not previously happened in male mammals.

Several of the buck deer also had a very short penis sheath, like the ninth vehicle-killed yearling buck with malformed genitalia, which I labeled Buck # 9. Incredibly, of the 10 examined yearling male deer born in 1995 only one, Buck #10, had normal reproductive organs.

We had reported our observations of reproductive malformations in the first eight deer to the biologist at the Missoula Office of Fish, Wildlife and Parks. He told Bob to call him when another fresh carcass with malformed genitalia was found. Consequently, Bob immediately called him to report Buck #9 and said we had a second fresh carcass of a male yearling with normal genitalia for comparison. The biologist agreed that Buck #9's genitalia was malformed and Buck #10 was normal. He took both carcasses to the MDFWP diagnostic laboratory in Bozeman, Montana, to be examined.

Buck #9 had a tipped-back, misaligned scrotum with the right hemiscrota almost not formed, causing the right testis to be partly horizontal under the skin. All of his genitalia were far forward on the belly, almost to the umbilicus (the navel on a human). The penis sheath was only a half-inch long. Normally on a fully-grown white-tailed buck it is at least four times that long.

The lab report, not surprisingly, said buck #10 was normal. To my extreme consternation, the report on buck #9 stated, "The scrotum was rotated 90 degrees, but this appeared to be a postmortem change." That was contrary to what several independent veterinarians and biologists who specialize in wild ruminants had stated to us. They had confirmed our diagnosis that the condition was a birth defect. The head of the lab and the co-author of the MDFWP Laboratory report on deer furnished to them by Bob Hoy later told me in person that "impact trauma" from being struck by the vehicle caused the genitalia to just appear to be malformed to an "inexperienced observer." Interestingly, a postmortem change is not the same as change caused by impact, so the same official gave two completely different and false explanations for the obvious reproductive malformations with which Buck #9 had been born.

In spring 1998, the same biologist examined two live white-tailed deer fawns with misaligned hemiscrota I was rehabilitating. He stated to Bob and me that both male fawns had a congenital reproductive malformation. Inexplicably, from that day until his retirement, he would never address with me our observations of many other live males with misaligned hemiscrota of at least a dozen different species of mammal. I furnished him with multiple photos of many animals, including several of live male white-tailed deer with obviously misaligned hemiscrota. None of the deer or other animals in the photos had been hit by a vehicle and of course none had postmortem changes, as all were alive when photographed.

Something serious is happening to disrupt development of genitalia on so many male mammals. Because our observations were ignored by wildlife biologists and health officials, the prevalence of misaligned scrotum on white-tailed deer fawns born in recent years is near 70%, making this condition now the norm. A bilateral scrotal configuration, which used to be the norm in deer I examined at 100% prevalence, is now present on only 30% of male fawns born each year. According to biology books, a birth defect prevalence of over 5% is supposed to raise a red flag for wildlife managers. Over 70% should set off health alarms everywhere, but has received almost no attention. Misaligned hemiscrota have been observed, photographed, and reported on all other wild grazing animals, rodent species, and other mammals in Montana, and on wild ruminants in other states. Evolution was long thought to happen slowly. **This change in mammal genitalia may prove to be one of the fastest and most bizarre evolutionary changes ever observed.**

During winter 1996, Bob provided six carcasses of seven- to eight-month-old male white-tailed deer to the wildlife lab to be examined. None of those deer had any sign of a scrotum present on the external skin. External reproductive organs consisted only of the four teats and a short penis sheath. Officials at the lab said in their report that the deer had no visible scrotum because they were immature. That seemed odd, because all male deer fetuses I had removed from accident-killed pregnant does prior to 1995, had a large, completely visible scrotum, as well as quite a long penis sheath. One of the authors of the lab report later told me in a phone conversation that those six deer would have grown a scrotum when they were old enough. I should have asked him on what planet he took his biology classes!

All the biology books I checked and many wildlife biologists I contacted, including knowledgeable experts on white-tailed deer, said the scrotum is formed early in development on a fetus's malleable skin by the testes when they descend. Very small male fetuses I had removed from accident-killed does in the month of February in years prior to 1995 always had a fully formed scrotum containing the testes. If the scrotum is not formed on a male fetus at the normal time early in development, deer and most other mammals, including human fetuses, will never have a scrotum. They do not magically grow after a male mammal is born. I thought that was common knowledge. It seems inconceivable that the top biologists at a state wildlife laboratory would not know such basic biological facts. Maybe they failed Biology 101. However, something much more devious seemed to be behind their inane statements. It appeared they were likely cooperating in an intentional, wide-spread cover-up of wildlife birth defects.

Early in spring 1997, I removed 11 fetuses from accident-killed female white-tailed deer and sent them to the MDFWP lab to be examined. Some were normal and others had obvious malformations. Both the MDFWP Laboratory biologists and the state veterinarian at the

Montana Department of Agriculture Laboratory examined the fetuses. Two of the four females had underbite. One female and one male had hyper-extended front legs, meaning the legs are bent the wrong way at the joint in the middle of the leg, making it difficult for a newborn to stand up. One male had no scrotum even though he was long past the age it should have formed; another male had a short, misaligned scrotum. One female fetus had severely underdeveloped facial bones, missing facial muscles, and a crooked lower jaw. Her male twin showed completely normal development.

The lab report said they could find no malformations on any of the fetuses and the State Veterinarian stated emphatically in his report, "It would be helpful for the person collecting the samples to appreciate normal versus abnormal external characteristics." The State Veterinarian was admonishing me, as I was the person responsible for collecting the fetuses. His comments completely disregarded a letter from a local veterinarian that I sent to the lab with the fetuses. It stated the two female fetuses had underdeveloped upper facial bones, one of those fetuses had a crooked lower jaw, and the other had hyper-extended front legs.

Also prior to giving the fetuses to MDFWP personnel, I showed seven of the 11 to wildlife biologist Dr. Bart O'Gara (unfortunately now deceased). They were frozen when I showed them to him, but the malformations were evident. Dr. O'Gara gave me a letter beginning, "To Whom It May Concern" and went on to say, "One female fetus appeared to have retarded development of its ears and facial musculature; two fetuses appeared to have lower jaws slightly longer than upper jaws, the opposite of the normal condition – this probably resulted from shortening of the nasal bones and face; and one female fetus had front legs that were extended ahead at a strange angle -- being frozen it was impossible to determine the cause of the problem, but the legs resembled those of calves from domestic and bison cows that were poisoned by eating lupine."

Dr. O'Gara was absolutely correct about the cause of the underbite on the two fetuses resulting from shortening of the nasal bones and face, which includes the premaxillary bones; and interestingly, lupine poisoning causes thyroid hormone disruption. Dr. O'Gara also stated in the letter, "The above abnormalities were more than I ordinarily have seen per 100-200 fetuses, except in one very inbred pronghorn population. During the winter of 1962-63, I handled most of the fetuses from more than 4,800 elk shot in Yellowstone National Park. During

A live adult male white-tailed deer photographed by Eugene Beckes at the National Bison Range, has the left hemiscrota formed directly forward of the right and both are tipped backward. This is definitive proof that this condition occurs during fetal development, is that way for the life of the animal, and is obviously not "a postmortem change."

graduate school and 25 years in the U. S. Fish and Wildlife Service, I collected and studied thousands more from numerous big game species. Thus, I am not inexperienced concerning the appearance of normal and abnormal fetuses. I also collected and inspected 38 embryos and fetuses from white-tailed does on the Metcalf National Wildlife Refuge between 14 September 1990 and 7 January 1992. None were abnormal, but two (fetuses) in very old does collected in March and May were dead."

Dr. O'Gara's letter not only proves the fetuses we sent to the state laboratories had a high rate of developmental malformations, it gives strong evidence that such birth defects were not occurring on white-tailed deer in Ravalli County immediately prior to 1995. It also provides indisputable proof that personnel of the Agricultural Laboratory and the MDFWP Wildlife Laboratory falsely reported there were no malformations on any of the 11 fetuses we provided for them to examine.

With his extensive experience studying wild and domestic grazing animals, in no imaginable stretch of terms should Dr. Bart O'Gara have been called inexperienced. However, because I sent his letter to the State MDFWP Laboratory, he was subsequently included in the group of people deceivingly and insultingly referred to as "inexperienced observers" in the laboratory's report on Ravalli County white-tailed deer. That report, including reports from the Agricultural Lab (all stating that no birth defects were found on any of the 28 examined white-tailed deer carcasses provided to the lab by Bob Hoy or on any of the 11 fetuses) was released to the Montana governor, all appropriate state agencies, the media, local health departments, and other concerned citizens. Consequently, nothing was done to find the cause of the birth defects.

In June 1997, we received Skippy, an orphaned male fawn with crooked front legs and an underbite. He also had only half a scrotum. The left testis was in the left hemiscrotum, but the right one was ectopic. I had not yet learned how to stimulate underdeveloped bones to grow to normal by giving homeopathic cell salts, which was unfortunate for poor little Skippy. Even though he received the same goat milk formula as Firefly, his underdeveloped bones did not grow to normal size. The only difference was Firefly's formula had calc. phos. dissolved in it and Skippy's didn't. He had to live with an underbite and crooked front legs for the rest of his life, which as it turned out, was not long. He was killed by a neighbor during the 1999 hunting season when he was two years old.

Bucky, another deer we raised in 1997, was a male fawn who had a normal length bilateral scrotum. He had been hit by a vehicle, which broke his front leg. I applied a splint and his leg healed in a little over a week. The two fawns became good friends, remaining together until they were nearly two years old. At a year and a half old, Bucky's antlers had three points on each side, with somewhat unusual double brow tines on both. It may be of interest to trophy hunters that Skippy, at a year and a

The female fetus at the top with underdeveloped facial bones and muscles and a crooked lower jaw was sent to the MDFWP Wildlife Laboratory with its normal male twin shown at the bottom. The lab biologist stated that impact trauma (there was none to the face and head) caused the female fetus to look malformed to inexperienced observers.

half old, had pencil-thin single spikes, with the left being malformed and even smaller than the tiny right one. Over the years, I have observed many male white-tailed deer born with misaligned scrota who also grew undersized antlers, with the left usually much smaller than the right. Even when they live to be four or five years old many have small, uneven antlers. It strongly appears that when the right testis is ectopic or nearly so, it often adversely affects normal growth of the left antler.

Facial and genital malformations were two of several signs that developing young were suddenly experiencing disrupted organ growth. It is important to emphasize that very few of either of those types of birth defects had been reported in wild grazing animals prior to 1995. Except for one published case report on a white-tailed deer fawn in eastern United States, I could find nothing in the literature that even mentioned underdevelopment of the premaxillary bones in a grazing animal. It does seem odd that one fawn with an underdeveloped upper face warranted a case study, but the same malformation in the many fawns, young goats, foals, calves, sheep, birds, and other animals that we reported to local veterinarians, biologists, scientists at universities in Montana and other states, government officials, public health personnel, and others have been completely ignored. Those same entities have continued to ignore the increasing prevalence of multiple birth defects in deer and other animals, including humans, even after our four peer-reviewed studies were published.

I have suggested to people working for state agencies in Montana and other states that there is a gigantic cover-up of birth defects in game animals who are supposed to be protected and managed by state agencies throughout the United States and by provinces in Canada. The always angry answer is that there is no cover-up, with one exception. In fall 2013, after 17 years of reporting the increasing numbers of birth defects in game animals to state officials, I called a high-ranking official in the Montana Department of Fish, Wildlife and Parks, told him about the newest birth defects we had documented in big game animals and other wildlife, and asked if they wanted a written report with photos. He replied emphatically, **"Judy, the Montana Department of Fish, Wildlife and Parks will never admit there are birth defects on the game animals! It would interfere with selling hunting licenses."** Most people would agree that refusing to admit a proven high prevalence of multiple, easily-observed birth defects in wild game animals is, by definition, a deliberate cover-up.

It was several years after we began seeing underbite in multiple species of newborns before I found a veterinarian who was familiar with that specific abnormality in grazing animals. She worked with horses born with underbite in Colorado and knew that thyroid hormone disruption during development of an embryo or fetus can and usually does cause underdevelopment of facial bones, limb bones, the thymus and other organs, and sometimes the entire fetus. Fetal hypothyroidism is known to cause a whole range of epigenetic changes. Once I knew what to look for, I found a large number of studies on this problem and its effects on various vertebrate species. As I found and read the studies, it became clear that it was at least one very likely cause of the variety of symptoms we had been observing.

Many of the studies I read about thyroid hormone disruption were done on developing amphibians. It was found that deformities in amphibian species were directly connected to chemical exposure, especially to various pesticides. One-third of the 42 species of amphibians in the U.S. are in decline. A very important study published in 2010 by Alejandra Paganelli and colleagues, found that frog embryos exposed to the herbicide glyphosate, the main ingredient in Roundup®, were "highly abnormal." Glyphosate impaired retinoic acid signaling in cells of frog embryos. Retinoic acid is commonly known as Vitamin A. By itself, glyphosate increased retinoic acid activity enough that it resulted in deformities in cartilage of the head when embryos became tadpoles. Similar effects were found when chicken embryos were exposed to glyphosate. Interestingly, in three counties in Washington, a much higher prevalence than normal of anencephaly (failure of the brain and skull to develop) occurred in human newborns between 2010 and 2013. Drinking water there was contaminated by Roundup® run-off from areas sprayed near streams.

The definitive malformations are so prevalent and so severe on human fetuses whose parents live near fields heavily sprayed with glyphosate-based herbicides that there have been demands for a world-wide ban on products containing it. Disruption of retinoic acid, thyroid hormones, and other enzyme and hormone systems during development have all been shown to cause the type of craniofacial malformations now found in epidemic numbers in children and wild and domestic animals.

Monsanto, one company that produces glyphosate-based herbicides, has also produced many genetically altered food-crop seeds, including corn, soybeans, sugar beets, potatoes, alfalfa, wheat, and cotton. These modified seeds are being planted in countries throughout the world, including India and Africa. They produce crops resistant to glyphosate so Roundup® and other glyphosate-based herbicides can be applied directly to them to kill weeds without killing crops. Consequently, glyphosate-based chemicals are now the most used herbicides in the world, exposing all life on Earth to biologically significant levels many times each growing season. Expanded use of glyphosate is likely responsible, or at least partly responsible, for the alarming increase in prevalence of underdeveloped facial bones, heart defects, and reproductive malformations in mammals, and to the decline of amphibian populations all over the world. Many have completely gone extinct, so will no longer be able to do their part in maintaining balance in ecosystems where they once lived.

Biologists say amphibians are canaries in the coal mine for environmental changes, but frogs and toads are not the only animals dying to warn us. Many individuals of all families of vertebrates are being epigenetically changed during development. And many invertebrate species, including honeybees and other pollinators, are rapidly declining. Finding and proving the cause or causes of the developmental malformations and declining populations will be difficult. Multiple chemicals can disrupt normal functioning in the following: thyroid hormones, genes, Vitamin D3, Vitamin A, minerals, and important enzymes. Roundup® causes all of those issues by itself, resulting in a slow decline in health and eventual death. Some pesticides cause neurological damage, usually resulting in immediate death.

Developing young are now exposed to thousands of man-made toxins, in addition to higher radiation levels and natural toxins to which they have always been exposed, making it even more difficult to pinpoint the foremost cause or causes of developmental malformations. The epidemic of abnormalities of the head, face, limbs, heart, thymus, and other organs is likely a result of exposure to multiple toxins with multiple effects, but exposure to ultra low levels of glyphosate alone could cause most of the observed birth defects, based on what happens to study animals.

Several years ago, I sent photographs of developmental malformations in birds from our area to a scientist who tracks radiation-caused defects in birds and insects living in the contaminated zone at Chernobyl, Russia. Regarding the photos of birds with malformations from western Montana, he said, "We have seen a few strange lips on birds but nothing as extreme as the strange bills you are finding!" I also sent him our two studies of malformations in grazing animals. He then said, "You appear to have a very unusual situation happening. I would be very concerned given the extraordinarily high frequencies of abnormalities! Is anyone looking at the human epi data? Clearly you have identified a very nasty situation that appears to have been generally ignored as well. If you raise your voice, you are labeled an activist and lose all credibility."

It appears the malformations here in North America are much more severe than in the radiation zone within sight of Chernobyl. That is highly disturbing. Also quite troubling is his statement, "If you raise your voice, you are labeled an activist and lose all credibility." It is my opinion that everyone should be an activist for protecting and promoting the normal development of life. To have future generations, we must protect newborn children and all other newborns from the disrupted development that has been occurring.

The malformations I and other rehabbers have documented in animals from our area of Montana includes no eyes, small eyes, blindness, small skull, cleft palate, underdeveloped facial bones (especially the upper or lower jaw bone), malformed teeth, no limbs, short limbs, malformed limbs, contracted tendons, weak joints, heart malformations, immature stem cell development, herniated umbilicus, partially or completely underdeveloped thymus, partially or completely underdeveloped left thyroid lobe, hair loss, and many types of cancer. In addition to many of those symptoms, birds have malformed rhamphotheca (the covering of the bills), crooked sternums, disrupted feather development, malformed feathers, and disruption of melanin in growing feathers resulting in white feathers where dark ones should be. Also, many individuals of multiple mammal species have the malformed, underdeveloped external male genitalia already discussed. Nearly all listed symptoms we have observed are consistent with malformations on newborn animals in studies where thyroid hormones and mineral uptake have been deliberately disrupted. Mineral deficiencies alone have been shown by studies to cause severe fetal hypothyroidism even without exposure to multiple thyroid hormone disrupting toxins.

Wild young with the more severe symptoms of fetal hypothyroidism usually die before or soon after birth or hatching and are seldom seen. Consequently, prevalence in birds is extremely difficult to determine. Examination and proper testing by medical professionals have not been conducted on young of wildlife or domestic animals from our area. That needs to be done to determine whether internal changes during development that cause health problems like diabetes, high cholesterol, brain damage, or internal reproductive malformations are present at birth. Unfortunately, prevalence of such developmental changes in vertebrates, especially human newborns, increased significantly in 2007 and after. Rates of autism, diabetes, obesity, high cholesterol, asthma, heart defects, and many kinds of cancer in young children appear to still be rising.

Also, in the time period between 2007 and present, I have observed several female white-tailed deer with serious symptoms of thyroid hormone disruption, which is most commonly caused in ruminants by multiple mineral deficiencies. I could easily distinguish them from other female white-tailed deer living on our land by their rough hair. Over a two- to three-year period, each of them would become more and more emaciated until she looked like a walking skeleton. None of them had fawns after they began looking unhealthy. The last time I saw each of those does, she was extremely thin with rough hair, and walked as if arthritic. When the doe failed to return, I assumed she died from the effects of mitochondrial disruption and metabolic acidosis that thyroid hormone disruption causes. If young breeding-age female deer were dying in this manner throughout their range, thousands may have died. If the fawns they failed to produce while they were slowly dying are factored in, the numbers of deer lost are significant. The symptoms of severe mineral deficiencies that began occurring in wildlife in 1994 had the highest prevalence from 2006 to 2013. However, I saw two such does in our yard in summer 2017, so they are still dying to warn us.

Wild pollinators, including bees, butterflies, other insects, and many invertebrates besides insects are disappearing. Pine trees, fish, and birds are dying in massive numbers. The pine trees have been dying for several years, killed by bark beetles, likely in part due to their weakened immune response as a result of wind-drift herbicide exposure. In addition, there have been massive numbers of unexplained bird, fish, and marine mammal deaths in North and South America, Europe, and other areas of the world in recent years.

In a fish die-off in January 2011, hundreds of thousands of menhaden, croaker, and spot fish died in Chesapeake Bay in Maryland. During the same month, far away in Paranaque, Brazil, what was estimated at a hundred tons of dead fish, mostly sardines, washed up onto the beaches. One hundred tons of a small fish is a number of individuals that is very

This female white-tailed deer illustrates the serious effects that mitochondria disruption, metabolic acidosis and mineral deficiencies cause in a grazing animal. The photo was taken in late summer, when she should have been in prime condition.

hard to imagine. Other areas of South America also had dead fish washing up on the coasts. Inability to get enough oxygen to keep cells alive is a reported cause of massive die-offs of both fish and birds. Low oxygen levels in the ocean is becoming more of a problem, and it is due to several factors, including ocean warming, introduction of agricultural nitrogen fertilizers into estuaries, and natural cycles in ocean water. Toxic algae blooms also cause death of marine life, as does the massive amount of plastic we have dumped into our oceans.

So many dead fish and birds made people everywhere wonder for a short time what is happening in the natural world. Their concern comes none too soon and unfortunately did not last long. Meanwhile, studies suggest more than 5,000 people a day (over one million per year) die from exposure to chemicals in the United States alone and, according to the World Health Organization, 19,000 a day worldwide (12.6 million per year) die from pollution of all kinds. If their bodies were piled on a beach like the dead fish or fell dead in yards like the birds, maybe someone would actually take notice!

We are in a race to determine which toxins are responsible for the birth defects, oxygen depletion, and increasing mortality, and end their use before all vertebrate life is irretrievably damaged. Alarmingly, there seems to be a concerted effort to keep the dire seriousness of this catastrophe from the general public. I have been given a number of reasons for why this is done, but none are worth dying for. Meanwhile, each day millions of individuals, wild, domestic, and human, are dying, which should show us the complete insanity of spreading enormous amounts of multiple deadly toxins into the air, water, and food we and most other organisms need to survive.

Miners used to take a canary in a cage down into the mine to warn them when toxic gases were released into the air. If the canary began gasping for breath or fell over dead, miners knew they needed to get out in a hurry. For many years, "canaries" have been dying by the billions to warn us we are poisoning the environment of the entire planet. This is adversely affecting much of life on Earth, most severely during stages of development in the egg or womb. Unfortunately, unlike the miners, we can't leave the mine to find safety. We have only one planet, so there is no uncontaminated place to which we can escape. Our only alternative is to stop polluting and start house cleaning!

**Animals in vast
numbers die to warn people
about pesticides.**

CHAPTER 9
ELKIE'S AMAZING ANTLERS

In spring 1999, a man who found a newborn male elk calf lying beside a road, alone and starving, brought it to us for care. The road ran along the edge of Painted Rocks Reservoir south of Hamilton, Montana, in the Bitterroot National Forest. I named the adorable, gangly calf Elkie, which it turned out must be a universally common name for a young male elk.

Elkie had severe underbite, with premaxillary bones so much shorter than his normal-length lower jaw that he couldn't close his mouth over protruding lower incisors. The malformation may have kept him from suckling his mother's small teats, as he was a very hungry youngster when he arrived. In addition to underbite, his right front leg was bowed inward and both hind legs had weak pasterns so he had difficulty walking and could not run at all. The leg abnormalities likely made it impossible for him to keep up with his mother in the rough mountain terrain where he was born. She either abandoned him or they had somehow become separated and were unable to reconnect. However it came about, the little elk was an orphan about three days old when the man brought him to us.

I gave Elkie a big bottle of goat milk with a bit of whipping cream and the two homeopathic cell salt tablets, calc. phos. and bioplasma. As required for our rehabilitation permits, Bob reported to the local game warden by phone that we had received an elk calf. At that time, the Montana Department of Fish, Wildlife and Parks took them to their rehabilitation center in Helena, Montana, where they were raised and released when they were old enough. Elk calves become quite tame so have to be taken to a remote area where there are few or no people. In 2004, their policy changed and any elk calf or deer fawn who cannot be returned to its mother is supposed to be killed.

Unfortunately for Elkie, the warden said he would come get him the next morning. That did not give me the necessary two weeks for homeopathic cell salts to stimulate growth of his facial bones to normal length. It takes less time for legs to straighten and tendons in the joints to strengthen, after which the young animal can walk and run normally, but he wouldn't have time for that, either.

Elkie enthusiastically drank a big bottle of formula containing the two cell salts every three hours the rest of that day and during the night. He had apparently missed several meals since his birth. I went out early the next morning to feed him and take photos to document his strange-looking toothy mouth and crooked legs. When the warden came to transport Elkie, I gave him a sack of the cell salts (with a letter containing instructions on how often to give them) for Steve McMorran, who was in charge of the MDFWP wildlife rehab center. The warden assured me he would pass them on, but he apparently forgot. I called Steve a week later to see if there was any change in Elkie's face and legs. He had not received the letter or tablets and Elkie still had an underbite. Steve said his wife often used homeopathic remedies and could get some calc. phos. 6X when she went shopping that afternoon. He assured me he would give them to Elkie and let me know whether there was any improvement.

I also asked Steve about Janey, a newborn female elk calf we had gotten the day after Elkie was taken to Helena. A game warden took her there four days after Elkie. We never knew where Janey came from because she was dropped off at a realtor's office on Highway 93, the main highway through the Bitterroot Valley. The realtor's secretary called Bob, asking him to come get her. She was healthy and well fed, apparently kidnapped from her mother rather than orphaned.

We didn't know where Janey's mother was, as the person who left her at the realtor's office did not say where they found her. Consequently, we couldn't take her back, which would have been much better for Janey and her grieving mother.

Bob had immediately contacted the game warden to let him know we had another elk calf. The only thing I could find wrong with Janey was the location of her four teats. They were visibly quite far forward of the normal groin area. This was a common birth defect on ruminants, wild and domestic, between 1995 and 2001. It does not affect their survival like an underbite often does.

I called Steve a week or so after my first call to ask about Elkie and Janey. Steve told me both were doing well and that he had gotten another female calf. I thought that was fortunate for Elkie, because when they were released together in the fall, he would have two cows in his ready-made harem. When they were a little over a month old, I again called

Steve to check on the elk calves, especially Elkie. He said Elkie's mouth was normal and all four legs were straight. Steve had known homeopathic remedies can work, but was extremely impressed that one homeopathic cell salt would stimulate crooked legs to become straight. He was even more surprised that underdeveloped facial bones could grow to create a normal bite, especially with an underbite as severe as Elkie's had been. He had never before heard of that happening.

I didn't hear any more about the three elk calves until the next year. On September 26, 2000, a biologist who worked in the Helena office called to ask if I knew where the male elk calf we sent to the wildlife facility in spring 1999 was originally found. From what the biologist told me (and what was in various regional newspapers every day for the next two weeks) I was able to piece together the adventures and misadventures that had befallen Elkie, Janey, and the other calf following their release the previous fall.

After they were weaned, Steve had taken the three elk in a horse trailer to the Dearborn area north of Helena, where they were released on a ranch. He had picked an area of light hunting pressure since they were habituated to humans. Unfortunately, the three youngsters soon found their way to the Bowman's Corner area along Highway 200. People driving the highway would stop, call Elkie to their vehicle, and offer grain or feed pellets they carried just for him. Over the winter, the three elk had become a major attraction for many people in the area. However, that spring Elkie apparently became quite a nuisance to local homeowners. He began going into their yards where he would knock over lawn sprinklers, chew on garden hoses, and nibble on flowers. His antics began to irritate people, but everyone insisted they did not want anything to happen to the young troublemaker. From stories told to newspaper reporters, Elkie was a regular Dennis the Menace of elk calves. The two females were less bold and kept their distance from people, not approaching cars and remaining well away from homes.

With much good will from local ranchers and homeowners, all three calves had survived the 1999 hunting season. Dearborn area residents reportedly had many playful encounters with Elkie and his two-cow harem. They remained in good condition due to people providing grain and other treats all winter and throughout the next spring and summer. Interestingly, everyone who fed, photographed, or came in contact with the three elk, called the young bull Elkie, the name I had given him.

In spring, with plenty of extra food, lots of minerals in the soil where he was released, and likely inherited genes for large antlers, Elkie's first antlers began growing – and kept on growing! The sustained rapid growth was nothing short of astounding. Elkie's body had grown a good deal too, but looked small compared to his overly large antlers, especially when they were in velvet. By late summer, he had an amazing rack for a smallish one-year-old bull. Male elk of that age usually have just one main tine, essentially one point, called a spike, on each side. On some youngsters, the spike forks, making two points on each antler. Yearlings almost never have a large number of tines, but Elkie did. After shedding the velvet and polishing his antlers, Elkie's awesome rack was revealed. Each one had five large tines with many small short ones forking off, giving each antler 11 points for a total of 22, unprecedented and possibly a world record for a yearling elk.

Members of the deer family, including elk, moose, and caribou in the United States and cervid (deer) species in other countries, are unique among mammals in being able to regrow a body part. Antler bone is one of the fastest growing living tissues known. How they grow so fast, essentially replacing an entire body part in a relatively short time, has long intrigued scientists. Researchers hope studying their growth will someday make it possible for doctors to stimulate limbs or other injured tissues to regrow in humans. Recent research suggests that stem cells, with the ability to develop into many specialized cell types, are fundamental to the process. Estrogen, testosterone, and other hormones are thought to trigger growth of the stem cells. Researchers are attempting to better understand the chemical signaling pathway behind the process of antler regeneration, hoping it may someday be used to develop new treatments for human diseases.

In most species of the deer family, males shed and regrow new antlers each year. Female elk, moose, white-tailed deer, and mule deer do not normally grow antlers at all, although there are exceptions in which hormone dysfunction occasionally causes a female to grow antlers. Caribou and reindeer are the exception, with females having permanent antlers. When antlers first grow, they are essentially a bone covered with skin laced with blood vessels. These carry nutrients to the tips and sides of the growing antler to build more bone, enabling it to grow quite rapidly. The skin, called velvet, covering the antler during growth has a coat of thick, soft, fur-like hair to provide insulation and protection for the sensitive, growing tissue.

After antlers have reached full growth, the bone hardens and the velvet dies and is rubbed off on small bushes and trees. Rubbing on trees and bushes colors the white bone with sap, often polishing the antler with a variety of shiny, attractive browns, depending on the types of trees and bushes used for rubbing by the individual. Once the velvet is gone and the antler is highly polished and colored, they are beautiful and formidable weapons for fighting during mating season. The clash of antlers in fights between bull elk can be heard for miles. The victor wins the right to mate with many females, thus passing on his superior genes. In late winter, after breeding season is over, the bone between the pedicles and the antler base disintegrates and the antlers drop off. Pedicles are raised areas of bone located on the skull above the eyes. In spring, new antlers begin to grow from them, becoming full-grown in three or four months.

By August, Elkie began herding the two young cows like adult bull elk herd those in their harem. A rancher reported seeing him mating with Janey. The other young cow disappeared the last week of September. No one knew, or would admit to knowing, what happened to her. She was with Elkie and Janey when they were photographed near Highway 200 just outside of Augusta, Montana, on Saturday, September 23, 2000. Elkie walked up to the truck belonging to the photographer, but when the two young cows approached, he herded them away. Sometime before the photographer took photos of the three elk, someone had spray- painted both of Elkie's large antlers with fluorescent orange paint. A concerned rancher trying to ruin them as a trophy may have done the painting, likely hoping to prevent Elkie from being killed during the hunting season that was soon to begin.

Unfortunately, what it did was bring him to the attention of MDFWP officials who worked in the Helena office. Apparently without asking Steve at the Rehabilitation Facility whether he knew anything about the elk, they sent a warden out to bait Elkie and Janey into a horse trailer on Monday, September 25. They were kept in a pen at the facility until Wednesday, when both were killed and their bodies sent to the MDFWP Laboratory in Bozeman. Meanwhile, on Tuesday, MDFWP officials issued a big press release to the Helena Independent Newspaper about their capture, with all kinds of speculation as to where the elk had come from and why they were so tame.

Apparently, Steve McMorran told them on Monday, right after the elk were captured and two days before they were killed, that he had

Elkie at one and a half years old had large antlers and a normal bite in this photo taken and sent to me by a MDFWP biologist. Elkie's baby picture showing his severe underbite is on the cover of this book.

released them the previous fall, after raising them at the MDFWP Helena Rehab Facility. The Helena biologist called me on Tuesday morning, asking where the two elk calves from Ravalli County had originally been found.

I told her Elkie came from Painted Rocks Reservoir, but that I didn't know exactly where in Ravalli County Janey had been found. During the ensuing conversation, I learned the teats on the young cow who was captured with Elkie were forward of normal, so I knew it was Janey. The biologist said MDFWP department heads in Helena had decided Elkie didn't look right and needed to be tested to see if he was a hybrid. They also wanted to test both elk for Chronic Wasting Disease, even though they had no symptoms of any kind. There was no reason to kill the elk to do either test. Officials knew exactly where they originated and the biologist stated the elk looked healthy and in excellent shape.

Somehow people in the Dearborn area where Elkie and Janey had lived for a year learned they had been recaptured and euthanized. Many angry people called to find out why Elkie was killed. The MDFWP personnel gave them the made-up story about the possibility of a male hybrid elk escaping from a game farm, breeding with a female elk, and thus polluting the native Rocky Mountain Elk gene pool. The same bogus story they released on Tuesday ran in a Helena newspaper, The Independent Record, on Wednesday, September 27, 2000, saying they had to kill Elkie because he might be a hybrid European Red Deer, and he might have Chronic Wasting Disease.

According to the newspaper article, a spokesman for MDFWP said officials had no idea where the elk came from or why they were so tame, again proposing they had escaped from a game farm. They also admitted there was a rumor the elk may have been released from the Helena Rehab Facility, but they did not know if this was true. All of this was totally fabricated, since they knew full well the elk had been raised by their own employee, Steve McMorran, at the MDFWP Wildlife Rehab Facility. He told them on Monday that he had released those two elk and one other female the fall before.

Elkie and Janey may not have survived another hunting season, but they would have made two families a freezer full of meat. After carcasses are taken to Bozeman for testing, they are destroyed. Several months later, the MDFWP released a report saying both elk were negative for Chronic Wasting Disease and of course negative for Red Deer genes, definitely no surprise to those of us who knew the truth.

A statement in the first Independent Record story about the elk being captured gave a good clue as to why MDFWP officials were willing to sacrifice them for no apparent reason. That story ran on Tuesday, the day before Elkie and Janey were killed. Until a friend sent me the article from the Helena paper, I couldn't figure out what purpose there could be for the weird story about Elkie. What I had not known was that in an upcoming election, voters would be given the opportunity to decide whether or not to ban new game farm licensing and end the shooting of captive game farm animals. The foremost argument being made by opponents to game farming was that farm-raised animals could and do escape and breed with native species. The premise was that escaped elk could pollute the native gene pool with non-native genes. They were also concerned that game farm animals would spread diseases, including Chronic Wasting Disease. Thus, if Elkie was even suspected of being a game farm escapee, it would be free publicity for voting in favor of the bill. The MDFWP was not a fan of game farms, but they could not actively campaign for passage of the ban. However, they could and did use Elkie and Janey as a scare tactic.

On Thursday, September 28, the Helena Independent Record reported that the elk were killed on Wednesday, repeating the bogus nonsense. On the same day that exact story by the same reporter, Eve Byron, was on the front page of the Missoulian, to which we subscribe. Until I read the story in the Missoulian, I did not know they had actually killed the elk on Wednesday. I had stupidly thought that, when they learned the truth, they would simply take them out to a remote area and release them. A great deal of effort and money had been spent to raise the elk, so it did not seem reasonable to kill them just because Elkie had unusually large antlers. In fact, big, beautiful antlers would seem to be an excellent reason not to kill him and to preserve his genes.

The Montana Wildlife Federation is a nonprofit group that supported the ban on game farming. Their spokesman was quoted in the article as saying that the MDFWP was not ready to tie Elkie to their cause because he might be a natural hybrid, whatever that could be. I do not think there is such a thing as a natural hybrid, with only one species of native elk in Montana. Some quotes in the story were so preposterous and humorous they would have made me laugh out loud if I had not been so devastated over the completely unnecessary deaths of Elkie and Janey. I was extremely angry about the lies told about them. Most of all it was heartbreaking that they had killed Janey for no reason at all. She was neither a nuisance nor a danger to humans, which unfortunately could not be said about Elkie, with his huge antlers and his propensity for causing trouble.

After his antlers grew so large, it was hard for Elkie to poke his head in the windows of vehicles without causing damage. That was, of course, the fault of people who had encouraged that behavior in the first place.

This bad habit could have been used as a somewhat legitimate precautionary reason for killing Elkie, but it was never mentioned in the media. In a new story on Friday, titled "Guilt by Association: FWP Kills Elkie's Pal," the Independent Record ran a story about Janey being shot and killed by "officials with the state Department of Fish, Wildlife and Parks." Their reason for killing Janey was "because Elkie had been intimate with her." I suspect a lot of ranchers considered that statement quite amusing.

If that was not ridiculous enough, the article went on to say, "It will take about a month for the tests to be completed. In the meantime, Korn's [an MDFWP official] office is chasing down rumors, including one circulating that asserts it was FWP that released the animals to the Dearborn area in the first place about a year ago, after they spent time in the state's animal shelter." The article also said, "We're looking at the paperwork to see if, in fact, it [Elkie] came from the shelter," Korn said. "If we get confirmation they [all three elk] came from the shelter, then we need to look to see if they were at a game farm prior to that." That statement was completely absurd, meant to deliberately confuse the public. The state's animal shelter only rehabilitates wild animals, not animals from game farms. Besides, shelter personnel, especially Steve, would have known if any of the elk came from a game farm. Elkie and Janey certainly didn't. There seemed no end to the absurd explanations for why the elk were so callously killed.

What did the article mean by the reference to "chasing down rumors?" I had talked directly to the biologist in charge on Tuesday, and told her Elkie and Janey were newborns when they came to me. Regarding confirmation as to whether the elk had been at the shelter, the biologist had also talked to Steve McMorran, the manager of the state's wildlife shelter, on Monday, the day the captured elk were brought to the facility. But the statements became even more bizarre as they went on to say, "The death of Elkie has angered hundreds of people, including many Dearborn area residents. They believe the state should have postponed killing the animals until it found out their breeding and where they came from." The important point is the MDFWP officials knew Elkie's and Janey's breeding and exactly where they came from and they knew it on Monday. They reconfirmed the elks' entire history on Tuesday, but still the MDFWP Laboratory biologist killed both elk on Wednesday.

A quote from one of the ranchers, Harold Adams, who had fed Elkie and his two-cow harem, was heart-rending. "The biggest thing I see this animal did wrong was befriend humans, then we put it to death. This is so frustrating. And what are they going to do now? Quarantine the entire area? This is almost like they're playing God. It breaks my heart.... Now, when I go out there, the only thing I can think of is this animal was put to death because it came up to me." To put Mr. Adams' mind at ease, the young elk was not killed because he walked up to him. Elkie was killed for a far more sinister reason: political manipulation of the public.

On Election Day, the ban on game farm expansion and pen hunting was passed on its merits, in spite of the fact that many western Montana newspapers, except the one in Helena, printed the whole truth about the Elkie and Janey tragedy. The Independent Reporter never did print the truth concerning the history of the elk. It opened my eyes to the fact that if state officials would not tell the truth about just two lives, I am not likely to ever get them to tell the truth about the birth defects affecting millions of lives, including those of children. This entire unfortunate fiasco made me ashamed to belong to the human species.

On Friday September 29, the Missoulian reporter, Daryl Gadbow, printed the whole true story about Elkie and Janey. He was angry that the article from Helena reporter Eve Byron, which had been printed in the Missoulian, was so completely false. Daryl's story was on the front page, along with the toothy baby picture I had sent to him when Elkie was a calf. The article even reported how Steve had fixed Elkie's underbite and crooked legs with a supplement while Elkie was at the Helena Rehab Facility. On October 3, the Ravalli Republic ran an article by Buddy Smith titled, "Mysterious Elk Had Roots in Bitterroot." His article also told the whole truth. Strangely though, in that article, a MDFWP spokesman said that what concerned them about Elkie was his large antlers and that his rump patch was reddish, lacking the distinctly caramel-cream color of a Rocky Mountain Elk. In spite of his large antlers, Elkie was only one and a half years old. Wildlife agency personnel should have known yearling Rocky Mountain Elk retain the reddish color until they mature. If Elkie had lived, his rump patch would have eventually turned the adult caramel-cream color.

If Elkie had kept growing large antlers with multiple points each year and if each year they were more massive, he would have been an astounding trophy by the time he was four or five years old. We can only imagine what valuable scientific information he carried in his genes to enable him to grow such an unprecedented amount of new bone so quickly. The greatest tragedy may turn out to be Elkie's irreplaceable genetic information, now lost forever for a perceived political gain. This again shows that extremely important information can be learned from our animal friends, if we just pay attention.

Many people loved Elkie for his mischievous but gentle disposition and were impressed by his huge antlers. He was killed because those amazing antlers made him a convenient and expendable political tool. Possibly the epigenetic changes in his genes that resulted in him being born with developmental malformations also resulted in his antlers growing so unusually large at a young age. Another possibility is that the cell salt electrolytes helped trigger the unusual antler growth. Large antlers may be beneficial to male elk during breeding season, but Elkie's resulted in a premature death, so weren't at all beneficial to his survival.

Sadly, Janey was killed for no reason other than, apparently, MDFWP officials considered "being intimate" a capital offense. If she and Elkie had produced a male calf, it would have carried his genes and possibly also grown large antlers at a young age. What really seemed unfair was that the disgruntled public cared only about Elkie being killed. Hardly any complaints were made about the MDFWP biologist euthanizing a healthy female elk without grounds that were justifiable or even rational. I guess sexism even exists for elk.

**Truthiness is that
facts are less important than
what people believe.**

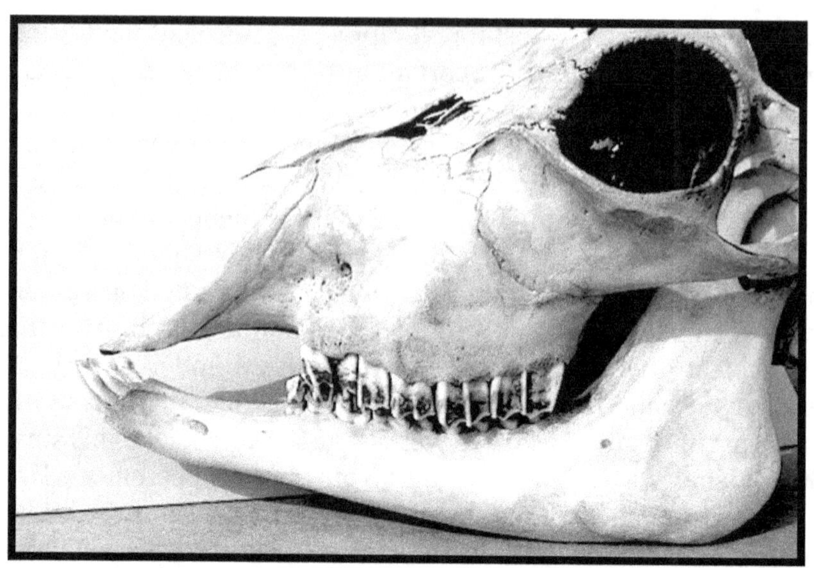

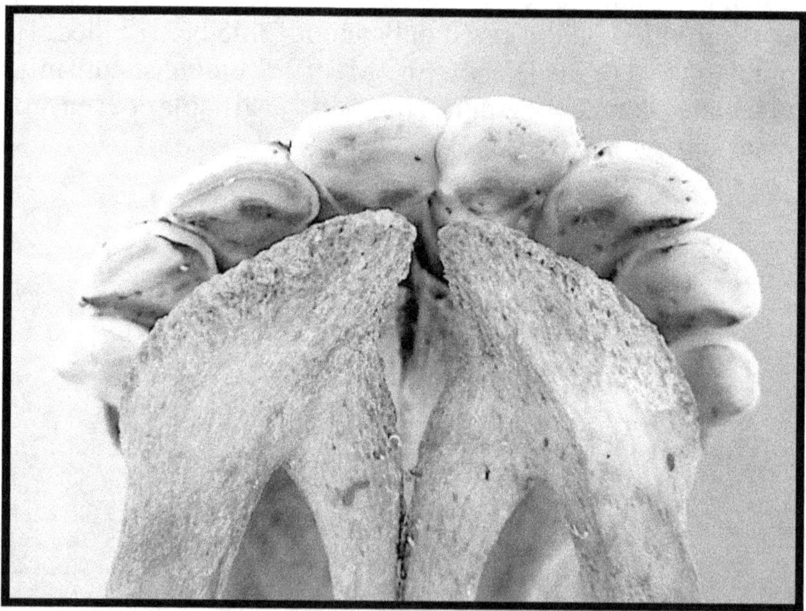

When a domestic goat has an underbite (top photo), the birth defect is said to be caused by "bad genes." This is not true! The premaxillary bone being too short and narrow is actually caused by disruption of necessary calcium to the fetal facial bone cells during development in the womb. The lower photo shows the same birth defect from a top view on a male bighorn sheep. With multiple birds and mammals being born with this defect, it can't be genetic!

CHAPTER 10
ALMOST ROADKILL

One morning, the first week of June 2000, I received a phone call from a Montana Department of Fish, Wildlife and Parks Game Warden named Terry, who lived and worked in Philipsburg, Montana. Terry had rescued a two- or three-day-old mule deer fawn who had been hit by a car. The two bones in his right hind leg between knee and ankle (tibia and fibula) had been broken and somewhat shattered. Terry explained on the phone that a veterinarian in Philipsburg had examined the fawn and told him the leg could not be put in a cast, so the fawn would have to be euthanized.

Fortunately for the fawn, Terry decided to check with me. I told him I had successfully immobilized the leg with the same bones broken in a friend's sheep; it had healed just fine. We decided we should give the fawn a chance, so Terry drove 150 miles to bring him to me. On the way, he named the fawn Willy.

After two tries I finally succeeded in completely immobilizing Willy's leg with splints and a whole lot of vet wrap. When I was done, his entire hind leg was held firmly in place and could not be moved. Willy could still walk, mostly using his three good legs. He kept his balance by touching the toes of his broken leg to the floor. Even with his leg immobilized, Willy could lie down to sleep or get up to suckle and hobble around.

I put him in our six-foot by six-foot intensive care kennel with deep straw on which to sleep. It is in a room in the basement of our house, where I could watch him closely and he would be warm. Every three hours day and night, he drank eight to 12 ounces of goat milk with two tablespoons of whipping cream added. At each feeding, I put a tablet each of calc. phos. 6X and bioplasma in the milk after warming it.

Willy was quiet and cooperative, ate well, and grew so fast that I had to loosen the vet wrap around his body every three days. When I did that on the twelfth day, I checked the area of the break to see if it was healing. Amazingly, both bones were straight and solid, with strong calcification where they had been injured. Veterinarians say it usually takes six weeks for a bone to heal. Willy had two broken bones in his leg and one was actually shattered.

I carefully removed the vet wrap and splint. The leg was somewhat stiff, so Willy still just barely touched the tips of his toes to the floor on his first day of freedom. In two days, he was using his leg normally except for a slight limp. By the 16th day after being injured, Willy seemed fine so I put him outside in our large deer pen. He proved his leg was well by doing his unique four-footed mule deer bounce, called stotting, up and down the full length of the 120-foot deer pen three times without stopping. He bounced around trunks of young cottonwood trees growing in the pen, like a quarter horse in a pole-bending race. He was obviously thrilled to be able to run again. And likely, after two weeks in our basement, he was happy to be out in the beautiful spring sunshine.

Early each morning in July, after they finished their bottles, we let Willy and the white-tailed deer fawns we were raising out of the deer pen to learn what plants to eat and how to survive in the wild. All the fawns came running when we called them for their bottle of milk at noon. At their evening feeding time, we put them back into the pen to keep them safe. By August, they were old enough to be out full time. They always came back for their milk, morning, noon, and evening. Willy was never late for any feeding. He was usually standing in our front yard waiting for us to come out with his bottle. By September, he was larger than his older, white-tailed deer companions and was ready to be weaned.

Terry had said when he brought Willy to us that he wanted to return him to the area where he was born. I called to let him know Willy was ready to go back home to the forest near Philipsburg. We were hoping he would find a small herd of mule deer to join, or possibly even reconnect with his mother. We have only white-tailed deer living on our land. Occasionally, a small herd of mule deer will pass through, but we had no permanent resident herd for Willy to join. It was much better for him to be released where he was born.

On the morning Terry came, Bob and I lured Willy into the deer pen with grain and closed the gate. Terry arrived around 9:00 a.m. with a large plastic pet kennel for transporting him. Willy was very cooperative, coming immediately when I called him. All we had to do was guide him as he walked into the kennel. It took all three of us to carry it to Terry's truck and lift it up into the bed. Willy had grown to be quite a husky deer. I thanked Terry for giving him a chance at life and Terry thanked me for fixing his leg and rehabilitating him. Although I would miss Willy, I was thrilled to have him on his way home to a normal life in the wild.

Willy found and joined a small group of mule deer with two adult females and two fawns. I was pleased that he had other fawns for companions. Young deer are extremely social and have great fun playing together. Terry occasionally saw Willy during the winter. Then, as most yearling males do, he left the females to join a group of bucks for the summer and Terry lost track of him.

Willy joined the many animals, including people, who owe their fast recovery from injury, illness, or chemical poisoning to the cell-stimulating effects of homeopathic cell salts. I wish the veterinarian who pronounced the death sentence on Willy could have seen him stotting up and down the mountainsides after he returned home. I think it is important that veterinarians and doctors understand how homeopathic cell salts can and do help patients recover much faster. That they stimulate the cells of the animal's body to work at optimum levels was clearly demonstrated by Willy's fast and complete recovery from almost being road-kill.

**Deer prancing on moon-
lit snow are unaware the
snow contains toxins.**

LISTEN TO THE WILDLIFE

Where are the newborn elk calves?
Biologists wanted to know.
They looked under grass and bushes.
And they looked under melting snow.

They searched the land by walking.
They searched the land by air.
But hardly any elk calves
Could they find anywhere.

They put the blame on cougars,
Wolf, coyotes, and the bear.
They put the blame on causes,
That were not even there.

"Do not blame us," said mother wolf,
To the wildlife management crew.
"The calves are sick or dying,
And our pups are dying too."

"It's the same for us," said antelope,
Bighorn sheep, and all the rest.
"Our young ones can no longer pass
The survival of the fittest test."

"We birds no longer look like us,"
Sadly chirped the chickadees.
"Our bills are crossed and our
Feet and legs have deformities.

"Biologists, start looking up,
Something bad is in the air.
Our babies aren't surviving
And it really isn't fair.

"Our eyes are always burning
And breathing causes pain.
Many of us go to sleep
And do not wake up again.

"We have tried to warn you,"
Shyly said the white-tailed deer.
"How will people stay alive
If we're no longer here?"

CHAPTER 11
CHANGING THE FACES OF FOALS

When I was young, school children sang a song about all the pretty little horses. Since 1995, many newborn foals are no longer pretty. In fact, some are born quite homely because of underdeveloped skull and facial bones or crooked legs. I have been told about high numbers of horse, mule, and donkey foals born with underbite in the same areas of Montana where many other grazing animals have that birth defect. Judging by photos posted on the Internet, this is happening nationwide.

According to horse ranchers, in 2001 a large number of foals were born in Ravalli County with underbite; some had crooked leg bones, with approximately 50 foals reportedly shot by their owners because of birth defects. That same spring, there was a very high rate of underbite in fawns of our study animal, white-tailed deer, live and accident-killed, and on other mammals and birds who were brought for rehabilitation.

Often foals born with debilitating malformations are put down, but not all with underbite are euthanized. A friend who works with horses checked the mouths of those on a ranch in Ravalli County in 2008 and found that eight of the 19 she examined had underbite. At another ranch, six of 10 horses she examined did, too, for a total of 56% with underbite on 25 horses. The animals were of different ages and a variety of breeds, removing the excuse of abnormal parental genes, considered a reason by many ranchers for birth defects in their foals.

In 1995, a horse breeder and his wife moved to a ranch near Corvallis, Montana, nine miles south of where we live. On the land neighboring their main pasture was a large mint field. Farmers who grew mint in Ravalli County used special chemicals on the plants during the growing season, including: Terbacil®, Bentazon®, and Atrazine®, all herbicides; Acephate®, an insecticide; and Omite®, an acaricide to kill mites. The horse rancher had 12 paint mares, two stallions, and some younger stock. In spring 1996, they lost all but one of the 12 foals born to their mares. Eleven died or had to be euthanized because of birth defects.

The owners bought a ranch in Oklahoma as soon as they could find one and moved their horses there immediately. All their mares were again bred to their stallions and every foal born the next spring was completely normal. They had never had a malformed foal prior to moving to Corvallis, where pregnant mares were pastured next to the heavily-sprayed mint field. Having their mares exposed to pesticides cost the horse owners between $50,000 and $100,000 in just one year in feed, lost revenue, and having to relocate. In spring 2001, most of the mint fields in Ravalli County were cleared and other crops planted due to a severe drop in mint prices. In the states west of us, many potato fields that were normally sprayed with chlorothalonil were also cleared and planted with other crops that did not require so many pesticides, especially fungicides. Most foals born in Ravalli County between 2002 and 2006 were normal, with only a mild underbite on those who had any birth defect at all. Many are still being born with underbite, but since 2013, there have been no reports of foals with severe facial malformations.

A foal born at a new neighbor's place in spring 2001 was the last example of a foal with an extremely malformed face that I saw. The neighbor's daughter called early one morning to ask if I would come and look at her newborn filly, who had been born with no eyes and a malformed mouth. Unfortunately, if the "make an eye" gene(s) is not turned on at the correct time during development, eyes will not be formed in a developing fetus and nothing can be done for the animal after it is born.

I rushed to see the foal. She was standing beside her mother and from the rear looked like a pretty bay filly. But when she turned around, I could see her face was shockingly ugly. Her muzzle and the front of both upper and lower jawbones were extremely malformed. No eyes looked out from the small eye sockets. A veterinarian had been called to euthanize the foal, because she could not suckle and, of course, she was blind. The neighbor let me have the body so I could photograph the malformations and do a necropsy. Her internal organs appeared normal, including heart, lungs, and thymus, those most often adversely affected or malformed in many newborns. Local horse ranchers had previously reported several severely malformed foals to me, but, unfortunately, I did not have the opportunity to examine them.

Between spring of 2000 and 2003, Kezia Coon, the daughter of another neighbor who lived a mile west of us, had four mares who produced four filly foals, all born with an underbite. None of the mares had an underbite. Two of the mares, both pregnant, were given to Kezia by owners who no longer wanted them. She had purchased the fourth mare, a purebred Morgan, to pull her buggy. She bred the Morgan to a purebred Morgan stallion.

The first mare to foal had belonged to Kezia for 16 years. She had received the half Arabian and half Quarter-horse cross, a yearling, as a gift on her eighth birthday. With a bit of advice from me, Kezia trained the bay filly when she was three years old, riding her in area horse shows for several years. Until Kezia was old enough to get a job and buy the Morgan mare, she was her only horse.

In 1999, Kezia bred her then 15-year-old Arabian-Quarter Horse mare to an American Warmblood stallion. This breed is a combination of Thoroughbred, Percheron, and Hanovarian. A filly with a fairly severe underbite was born on August 21, 2000. The lower teeth protruded in front of the upper ones exactly one-half inch. Other than the underbite, the foal was beautiful. Kezia asked several of her mother's rancher friends if they knew why a foal would have an underbite and if anything could be done for it. They all told her inbreeding causes that particular birth defect and it is not good to keep a foal with it. A horse with a bad underbite can't graze very well, so requires special feed all of its life. In addition, the foal would be unsalable when it grew up. They said it should be euthanized.

When the foal was 10 days old, Kezia's mother Diane remembered something I had told her in 1998 about Firefly. I had explained that giving the fawn calc. phos. 6X several times daily had been responsible for causing her facial bones to grow to normal size and configuration. Because Diane's Angora goat herd produced over 100 kids each year, I had given her a bottle of the calc. phos. 6X in case any baby goats were born with an underbite. She had either used it all or misplaced it, so she told Kezia to call me. As soon as I hung up the phone, I put my bottles of calc. phos. 6X, and bioplasma in a sack, grabbed my metric ruler and camera, and rushed over to measure and photograph the foal's mouth.

I had Kezia hold the filly while I gave her one tablet each of calc. phos. 6X and bioplasma. Then I measured the underbite and took photos with my 35 mm camera. I asked Kezia if it had changed noticeably in the 10 days since the filly was born. She said it had measured a half-inch at that time. I found there had been no change. I suggested she give the foal one tablet of each cell salt at least three times every day, also asking her to report any improvement so I could photograph the stages of progress.

Twenty-three days later, Kezia called to tell me her filly no longer had underbite. I immediately went over and took photos of her mouth, which was normal with the top edge of the bottom middle incisors fitting directly against the back of the upper incisors. Her upper facial bones had grown to perfectly match her lower jaw.

I sent my film to be developed, excited to have before and after photos of the complete mitigation of a fairly severe underbite in a foal to show my veterinarian. When they came back, there weren't any developed photos. The film had stuck, not advancing in the camera; all photos I had taken on that roll were ruined. I was disappointed, but there was nothing I could do. I still had Firefly's before and after photos and also several of goat kids born with underbite. Their facial and premaxillary bones had grown to normal size after receiving homeopathic cell salt tablets, producing a normal bite. When I told Kezia about the camera malfunction, she too was disappointed. I asked her to call me immediately if any more of her mares had foals with an underbite.

I had to wait until April 25, 2002 for the next foal, another filly, to be born. The mother was a Mustang, registered as an American Indian Horse born in the Prior Mountains of Montana. She had been caught as a yearling in a BLM (Bureau of Land Management) roundup. The people who adopted her gave her to Kezia because they were moving to a place where they would be unable to keep her. They knew Kezia would take good care of the young horse. She knew nothing about the sire, except the foal was conceived south of Hamilton, Montana, where the mare was pastured after being adopted from the BLM Adopt-A-Mustang program. Three weeks before the foal was born, the owners moved her to a different pasture, two miles north of Corvallis, Montana. Kezia brought the mare to her place a few days before the foal's birth so she could monitor her and check the foal for underbite immediately after it was born. I made certain she had plenty of cell salt tablets to give the foal.

Kezia watched the birth on a beautiful, sunny spring afternoon. As soon as the mother had licked the foal clean, she checked its mouth. Finding the little mustang filly had an even worse underbite than the previous foal, she put the two cell salt tablets on the baby's tongue. She also measured the deformity and called to tell me the underbite was 9/16 inch. Unfortunately, Bob and I were just leaving on an overnight camping trip. I told Kezia I would come to take photos as soon as we returned in two days.

At that time, Kezia was working during the day, so could give the new foal the cell salts only twice daily, morning and evening. Almost exactly 48 hours after the filly was born, I went to measure the underbite and take photos. Her upper facial bones had grown an amazing amount in that short time. The underbite measured just slightly over 4/16 inch from the top edge of the lower incisors to the top of the upper incisors, less than half what it had been when Kezia measured it at birth. In 11 more days, at 13 days old, the filly's bite was completely normal. Kezia called to let me know I could take after photos. The little filly was adorable, with a beautiful face and head and a perfect bite. She was a soft dun color with zebra-like stripes on her slim legs and the black stripe down the middle of her back that defines most of the Prior Mountain wild mustangs. She grew up to be one of Kezia's favorite horses.

We are concerned about wild mustangs who live in the Prior Mountains. Are they also having foals with underbite and other symptoms consistent with mineral deficiencies and fetal hypothyroidism? Has anyone ever checked the captured mustangs for underbite or crooked legs? These birth defects would have serious consequences for wild horses. A foal with underbite would not be able to bite off sufficient grass, so after it was weaned it would likely be undernourished, especially in winter. A foal born with crooked legs would not be able to run from predators or keep up with its mother and the rest of the herd, causing it to die soon after birth.

Kezia's third foal with an underbite was born to a black mixed-breed mare. She was given to Kezia late in fall 2002 and foaled during the night of December 16. The people who gave her the mare didn't tell Kezia she was pregnant. Because it was a large mare and quite fat, the pregnancy didn't show, not even immediately before the birth. The night she foaled the temperature dropped to around 20 degrees below zero, the coldest of any night that winter. The next morning, Kezia found the female foal dead and nearly frozen solid in a corner of the corral. The mare had not even had time to clean it before it froze. The foal had an underbite, the soft tissue of its muzzle and lips was malformed, and it appeared to be somewhat premature. She would have been an ugly mare, if she had lived. Even if cell salts stimulated her upper facial bones to grow to normal, the soft tissue around her mouth would still have been malformed and unsightly. This tissue was normal on the first two fillies, so when their upper jawbone grew to its proper length, they were beautiful.

Kezia bred her pretty, registered Morgan mare to a registered Morgan stallion. Both had champion bloodlines. The mare was fairly old, at 22

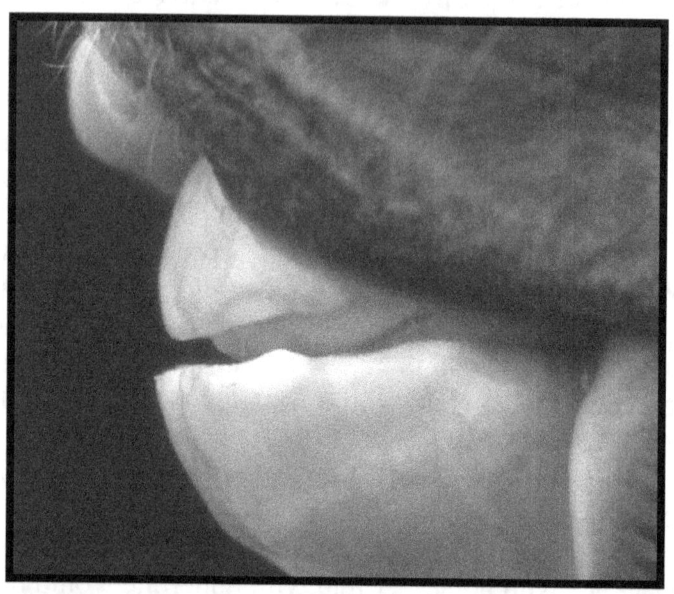

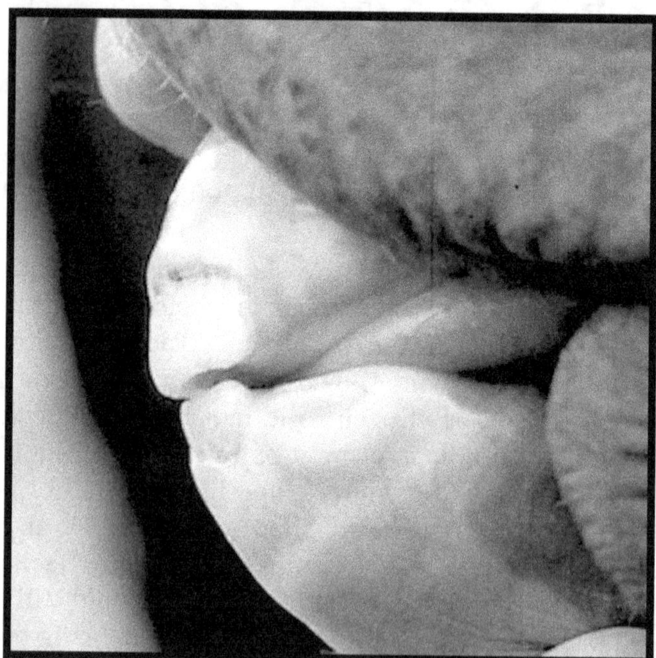

The underbite on this American Mustang filly was 9/16 inch at birth. It was slightly over 4/16 inch 48 hours after she was given cell salts beginning at birth, upper photo. She had a perfect bite at 13 days of age, lower photo.

years of age, when she had the fourth foal with underbite to be born in Kezia's small herd of four mares. She took very good care of her horses, fed them well, provided minerals, and kept their feet trimmed and shod. There was no apparent reason for the birth defects. We had proven the malformations had nothing to do with inbreeding by stimulating the upper jawbones of the live foals to grow to normal. At that time, I had not been able to find a veterinarian or anyone else who could propose a possible cause of underbite and disrupted development of the upper facial bones in so many animals and so many species. Thus, the reason for foals to have an underbite was still a mystery.

Eventually, I was told that a Canadian veterinarian was studying large numbers of foals being born with underbite and other birth defects in Saskatchewan. Dr. Andrew Allen had published several studies about foals with Congenital Fetal Hypothyroidism. When I called Dr. Allen, he said underbite, or brachygnathia superior, was a common and definitive symptom of Congenital Fetal Hypothyroidism, caused by the fetus being exposed during development to thyroid hormone disrupting environmental toxins ingested or inhaled by the mare. The thyroid disrupting toxins are carried in the bloodstream directly to the developing foal, replacing thyroid hormones in receptors of fetal cells. The toxins do not do the jobs of directing cellular growth that thyroid hormones do. Consequently, the fetus has disrupted development, with certain bones targeted. We still do not know for certain why specific facial and limb bones are most often affected. However, disruption of the Sonic Hedgehog genes by exposure to certain herbicides, especially glyphosate in Roundup®, is strongly suspected as the main cause.

Kezia's fourth foal, the twelfth born to her purebred Morgan mare, was a pretty, almost black filly born May 5, 2003. Her underbite measured only 3/16 inch, much less than the other three foals, and the soft tissue of her muzzle was normal. Kezia gave the two homeopathic cell salts to the foal each morning. On the seventh day after the filly was born, her bite was normal and her face perfect, just as we had come to expect. Kezia was very busy, as she had two or three jobs when the foal was born. She didn't call to tell me about the new filly until after her facial bones had grown to normal, but did measure the underbite immediately after the birth, when she gave the first dose of cell salts.

Cell salts seem to jumpstart cellular function in newborns, especially muscle, bone, and nerve cells, so they work at optimum levels. Newborns of all mammal species to which I have given them immediately after birth are able to stand, walk, and suckle much more quickly than young not given the cell salts. I found the time from birth to standing and suckling in newborn goats was 20 to 25 minutes without cell salts. Those given cell salts immediately after birth required only 10 to 15 minutes, a significant difference especially important in vulnerable wild young.

After Kezia successfully caused the underbite in her three live foals to grow to normal, I discussed the problem with local large animal veterinarian Dr. Jack Ward. He told me the underbite in foals he had treated right after birth lessened somewhat after injection of a large dose of Vitamin D3. However, he admitted that none of those foals grew to have a completely normal bite like the American Mustang filly, whose before and after photos I showed him. Since Vitamin D3 is technically a hormone, this is another indication underbite is caused by hormone disruption during fetal development. Thus, disruption of Vitamin D3 in the young animals appears to be another possible contributing factor for causing abnormal bone development.

I also searched old veterinary books, finding no mention of underbite in grazing animals. I could find nothing in the literature to indicate that underdeveloped skull and jawbones in horses, mules, deer, goats, or any other species have previously been caused to grow to normal by giving them a homeopathic pill. Surgery on the lower jaw to shorten it had always been required to correct the bite of a foal born with underbite, according to all veterinarians I consulted prior to discussing the problem with Dr. Allen. However, the underbite they described resulted from the animal being born with a longer than normal lower jaw, which is caused by a genetic defect in both parents. That birth defect can't be remedied with cell salts because it is impossible to cause a longer than normal jawbone to become shorter by giving the newborn a pill.

The effectiveness of cell salt treatment on all three foals was quite apparent, even when they were given only once daily. During the period from birth to 10 days of age on the first filly, when cell salts were not being given, the underbite did not measurably change. The facial bones only began to grow to normal size after calc. phos. 6X and bioplasma were administered twice a day. It then took the bones 23 days to grow to normal and the bite to be perfect, at which time the filly was 33 days old. The facial bones on the second filly, born with the worst underbite, took 13 days to grow to a perfect bite after both cell salt tablets were given twice daily starting immediately after she was born. The third filly, a purebred Morgan with only a slight underbite, was given the two cell salt tablets only once daily, with treatment beginning immediately after birth. Her facial bones required only seven days to grow to normal size.

An important aspect shown by this evidence is that beginning treatment with cell salts during the period of accelerated growth immediately after a young animal is born appears most efficient in promoting fast growth to a normal bite. However, beginning treatment when the foal was somewhat older, even though it took the bones slightly longer to grow to normal, was equally effective, since this also resulted in producing a completely normal bite. Being able to stimulate bones with disrupted growth to reach normal length proves the disruption of development to major bones is not the result of genetics. The DNA of the parents does not pass brachygnathia superior to the foal. Also, all the foals were different breeds, but still had the exact same malformation. This completely nullifies claims of local ranchers and some veterinarians that the underbite problem in newborn foals, or other animals such as deer and elk, is caused by inbreeding or because it happens in certain breeds or species.

In March 2012, a woman from Michigan called me to ask about using cell salts to help her newborn filly who had a very severe underbite. At birth, the foal could not close her mouth because her upper face was so short the lower lip could not fit over the lower incisors to contact the upper lip. I told the owner, who had found me through Internet research, about the cell salts and where to get them. She began giving calc. phos. 30X tablets to the foal, every day at first and then intermittently. She was unable for various reasons to continue giving them every day. After several months, the foal's upper face had almost grown to normal, with the lower incisors just slightly in front of the uppers. A photo showing how she looked at that time was attached to her thank you note, even though the foal's bite was still not quite normal. The last photo the woman sent was of the filly as a yearling. Her upper facial bones had grown so her incisors fit together in an almost perfect bite, allowing the filly to graze efficiently and live a normal, productive life.

Kezia and I are hopeful that by telling the story of how she helped her three newborn fillies grow to normal, more people will give homeopathic cell salts to all foals born with an underbite instead of killing them or letting them grow up with a debilitating defect. A tablet each of both homeopathic cell salts, calc. phos. 30X and bioplasma, can be given several times a day. At the very least, one tablet of calc. phos. 30X should be given at least once a day. I've found calc. phos. 30X works better at stimulating disrupted bone growth than calc. phos. 6X.

A mare has to carry a foal for 11 months. It is such a waste to "shoot, shovel, and shut up" when a foal is born with underbite. Also, euthanizing newborn foals and burying them without reporting them to health officials has not been helpful in promoting efforts to find the cause of the malformations. We need to quickly prove what is causing the birth defects and stop its use so newborn foals will again be pretty little horses.

**A hypothesis
is as good as the data
on which it is based.**

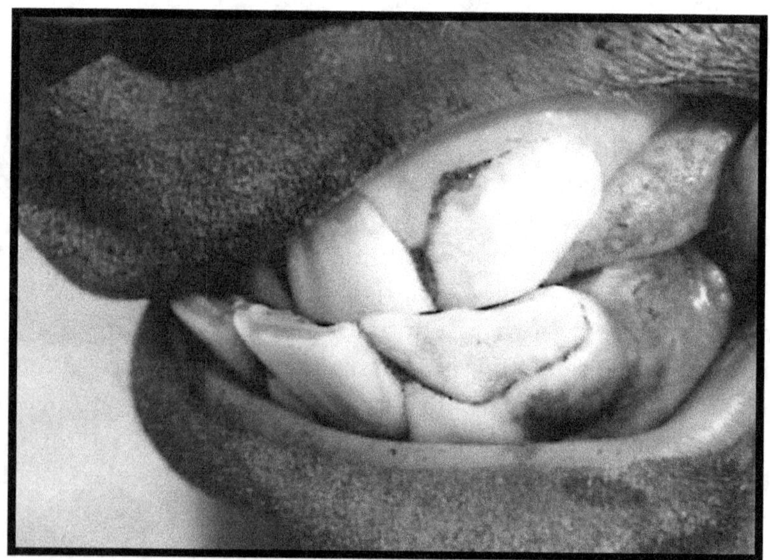

This shows the bite on a seven-month old female foal not given calc. phos. tablets. She had an underbite all of her life.

CHAPTER 12
MAKING FEATHERS GROW

A hatchling Cliff Swallow was the youngster who helped me learn to mitigate Avian Keratin Disorder, the name given by researchers to disruption of feather and bill development. Consequently, I and other rehabbers can usually make feathers that suddenly stop growing begin to grow again. Most grow to be normal in length on fledglings with that defect alone. On some individuals, a few of the feathers also develop in an upside-down position or at odd angles. Even when those feathers become the size they should be, they do not provide adequate lift or necessary function for maintaining normal flight.

The little swallow and its four siblings were brought to me as two-week-old hatchlings on August 2, 1998. At that time, their feathers were just beginning to emerge from the sheaths. A young girl, with the help of her mother, had rescued the babies from drowning in the Bitterroot River. A boy had thrown a rock at the nest, knocking it into the river. Fortunately, it flows quite slowly in late summer so the kind woman and her brave daughter were able to retrieve all the babies before they floated away. Even so, they had been completely soaked in cold water.

It appeared the hatchling swallows had survived a difficult three days. The nest where they lived was attached to a cement beam under the bridge on a main county road. Each day in summer, a number of people swim in the river near bridges. Almost every year, malicious, uncaring people, usually young males, knock down swallow nests so they can watch hatchlings drown. People do not understand we desperately need swallows, swifts, and other birds who eat billions of mosquitoes and other small insects. Mosquitoes carry deadly diseases that can be transferred to our livestock, pets, and us, as well as to wild animals. For example, in spring 2016, there was a worldwide health scare over the Zika virus, which, in addition to other dangerous viruses, is spread by mosquitoes. Birds help protect us from such diseases by greatly reducing populations of carrier insects. People who are caught killing swallows, swifts, or other migratory birds can be fined as much as $10,000 for each bird killed, but juvenile boys or older bird-killing vandals are seldom caught or punished. Unfortunately, swallow populations appear to be in serious decline, so every bird is precious.

All five swallows were quite lethargic and showing respiratory distress by the time their rescuers arrived at our house. The woman said she and her daughter had quickly taken them out of the water; she didn't think any of them had gone under the surface or inhaled water into its lungs. After hearing that, I asked whether the county weed control truck had sprayed near the bridge recently. I needed to know if the swallows' obvious respiratory problems were from inhaling water into their lungs or from exposure to herbicides. The woman said the county had sprayed both sides of the road two days earlier.

After thanking the mother and daughter for their good deed, I examined each of the swallows while making them comfortable in a nest of soft rags. A small aquarium placed on a heating pad became their temporary home. Because they might have been poisoned and were wet and cold, I gave each of them half a tablet of both calc. phos. 6X and bioplasma at their first feeding. I continued giving them cell salts every three hours until they fledged. Their food consisted of both baby bird food and mealworms, the usual diet I use for hatchling swallows. Whenever the babies food-begged to tell me they were hungry, I gave each a cropful of food and a few drops of water.

After a few days, all but one appeared to have completely recovered from the herbicide exposure and their fall into the river. Emerging feathers on their bodies and heads appeared fully grown after nine days. At that time, I put them in a flight box where they could practice flying and learn to land on branches. After a few days there, I transferred the five swallows to a flight room. That was when I discovered that the seven outside primary feathers on both wings remained quite short on one of the young birds.

Primary feathers are essential for flight, but these were less than a quarter inch long. They had apparently stopped growing several days earlier, although all of the other feathers were fully grown. Until I picked it up and spread its wings, the short feathers were not noticeable. The swallows always sat still with folded wings when I fed them in the flight box. Because the little swallow could not fly, I had to return it to the flight box in the bird room.

The young Cliff Swallow with short primary feathers was the first bird to have disrupted feather growth as a fledgling in my care. In previous years, beginning in 1996, I had received several birds with underdeveloped primary feathers, but all were post-fledglings or adults. They had only two or three primary feathers underdeveloped, not all of them. When I discovered this little swallow had such seriously underdeveloped feathers, even after receiving cell salts several times daily, I had no idea how to make them grow. Apparently, cell salts had not prevented disrupted feather growth, nor had they stimulated the feathers to grow to normal length.

Disruption of feather or bone and bill growth appears to be the result of exposure to herbicides sprayed near nests containing recently hatched birds. Since caring for the five Cliff Swallows, I have received many hatchlings with underdevelopment of facial bones or feathers. Every one I saw with those malformations had been exposed to a known application of an herbicide or combinations of herbicides, as the young swallows had been two days before they were knocked into the river. Combinations containing 2,4-D appear to cause the most disruption of normal growth in young birds and to mammals after they are born.

I have found several studies since receiving the Cliff Swallows that say hatchling birds exposed to organochlorine pesticides or other endocrine disrupting toxins were shown to have disrupted feather or bone growth. This is because the organochlorine herbicides, insecticides, fungicides, and other commonly used organochlorine chemicals disrupt normal functions of thyroid hormones, extremely important in directing growth of bones, organs, scales, feathers, or hair in developing vertebrates, including human newborns.

After considering the problem with the little swallow's feathers, I came up with the hypothesis that disrupted feather development may be initiated by the affected cells not receiving adequate minerals needed for normal growth. Hoping to help the little bird, I decided to give him a few drops of oral liquid electrolytes instead of water at each feeding, which was about every half hour. In past treatment of dehydrated or injured birds, my electrolyte combination always produced an observable beneficial effect on an animal's health, including its immune system.

After five days in the flight room, I released three of the four swallows who could fly. Their body, wing, and tail feathers were all fully-grown and they were healthy. The fourth youngster had fully developed feathers and could fly, but its severe respiratory problem remained. It could not maintain flight more than once or twice around the flight room, after which it began panting with its mouth open. Often it would have to flutter down to the floor to rest. I took it back to the flight box and put it with the fledgling with underdeveloped feathers, so they could keep each other company.

I gave both birds several drops of Pedialyte®, rather than water every half hour when I fed them. I also gave them a tablet each of bioplasma and calc. phos. 6X every two hours with their food. I hoped my electrolyte combination would at least boost the immune system of the swallow with breathing problems, thus helping heal its lungs.

Unfortunately, there was no improvement in the swallow's lungs, but after four days of giving Pedialyte® in addition to the cell salts, I was delighted to see the underdeveloped feathers on its sibling begin to grow again. In another four days, they were twice as long as when they had stopped growing. Three days after that, the feathers had grown to half their normal length, and six days later, the little swallow could fly. I put it back into the flight room to practice take offs and landings and build up its flight muscles. After two days there, the swallow's primary feathers were nearly fully-grown. Even though its tail feathers had been somewhat damaged while it was flightless, it was able to fly very well. It could take off, land, and travel many times around the flight-room. Three days later, the primary feathers were all normal in length so I took it out into our large field and released it.

It was late summer and large flocks of swallows were beginning to congregate in preparation for their migration south. I wanted the fledgling swallow to be able to join one of these flocks. Swallows catch flying insects. Newly released fledglings usually begin snapping them out of the air as soon as they have flown around with wild swallows for a few minutes, and are able observe them catching insects. When I released the swallow, he joined several who were flying back and forth over our field. With my binoculars, I could see large clouds of small, gnat-like insects in the air above the field. Swallows would circle through the insect swarms, snapping them up by the mouthfuls. Eventually all of them flew out of sight toward the river.

The swallow with damaged lungs did not recover and its breathing became more labored. A few days after its last sibling was released, it died. I could only hope the others fared better and would live through their two long migrations to return in spring and raise young of their own. After releasing young swallows, I watch them as long as they are visible through good binoculars. Once I lose sight of them, I never recognize them again.

What I learned from making the feathers grow on the little Cliff Swallow helped me save many birds in the years since, especially Red-tailed Hawks, Osprey, and American Kestrels. Fledglings of those three common raptors seem to be quite often affected by disrupted feather growth. With the same mixture of the two homeopathic tablets and liquid electrolytes, I have stimulated disrupted feathers to grow to normal length on several individuals of each of those species of raptor, as well as on songbirds of multiple species.

One of the most unusual cases of disrupted feather development I have seen came to me the year after the swallow's feathers grew to normal. I received two hatchling American Robins because the parents disappeared, leaving their babies to starve. One hatchling had no pinfeathers growing on its body and was somewhat lethargic. Its sibling had normal pinfeather growth and, although somewhat underweight, appeared healthy. As usual, the lawn near the nest had been sprayed with herbicides, this time, five days prior to my receiving the hatchlings. It is likely their parents died after walking in the toxin-covered grass while catching worms to feed themselves and their young ones, often the case when people bring me orphaned hatchlings.

I gave both robins cell salts and electrolytes every three hours. It took a week for pinfeathers to begin growing on the bare hatchling. Oddly, it took much longer for its head feathers to grow to normal size than for those on its body. When all of its feathers were fully grown, the young robin looked like an adult, with brown back and solid red breast. Its sibling looked like a normal robin fledgling with a speckled chest. They did not look at all like siblings when they were ready for release.

Another strange example of disrupted feather development was failure of feathers to grow on the body of a hatchling Brewer's Blackbird. Blackie's little body was almost completely featherless when I received him in summer 2010. His head and neck feathers were still in the pinfeather stage and appeared to be growing normally. Wing and tail feathers were in the circular keratin tubes, called sheaths, in which feathers grow. But the areas of his body where fairly well-developed pinfeathers should have been growing had only a few scattered sheaths that contained down feathers. His entire body was nearly bare. If he hadn't been found beside a walking trail in Missoula, he would have died of hypothermia during the night. Because he was out of the nest, his mother would not have been able to cover him to keep him warm.

As soon as Blackie arrived, I began giving him the combination of two homeopathic cell salt tablets dissolved in electrolytes several times a day. In about two weeks, what looked like a normal number of pinfeathers had grown in the feather tracts on his body. By that time his head and neck feathers were fully grown, as all the others should have been by four weeks of age. After another 10 days, his body feathers had grown enough so he could safely be placed in a flight room to practice flying. Oddly, his wing and tail feathers did not have disrupted growth. On most affected birds, those are the feathers most often impacted. Because Blackie's had normal growth, he could fly even though his body feathers were not fully out of the shafts. His fully developed wing and tail feathers, with short pinfeathers on his body made him an extremely odd-looking bird. By the second week in August, his body feathers were finally fully grown and, because he had been practicing in the flight room for two weeks, he could fly very well.

I put a fledgling Red-winged Blackbird who was recovering from a cat bite in the flight room with Blackie to keep him company. Both youngsters could fly but, being fledglings, needed to practice catching live insects. I released many various-sized grasshoppers in their room every morning, as well as providing a dish of mealworms. Young blackbirds eat a lot, so it is essential they become proficient at catching a large number of insects each day. Blackie loved catching grasshoppers and would go after them while I was still in the room. It was fascinating to watch him run after a hopper, catch it in his bill, crunch down on it to kill it, and then swallow it whole. Both young blackbirds could eat between 10 and 20 grasshoppers in just a few minutes. Catching 200 or more grasshoppers a day with a net was great exercise for me.

Release day was August 21, a beautiful summer morning when Blackie was eight weeks old. It had taken almost twice as long as normal for him to grow all of his feathers. When he finally did, he was a handsome little guy. I turned Blackie and Red, his Red-winged Blackbird friend, loose in our hay field where several Brewer's Blackbirds spent their days hunting insects. A small stream of irrigation water flowed nearby on the edge of the field and many grasshoppers and other insects lived in the field. The two youngsters remained with the Brewer's Blackbird family until they all joined a large mixed flock of migrating blackbirds a couple weeks later.

Several years later, in July 2017, a lady named Dani called me concerning problems she was having with four fledgling European

Starlings she had raised from small hatchlings. Someone had found the babies and taken them to her because she likes raising birds. She hadn't previously cared for starling hatchlings so she checked the Internet to learn what they can be fed. The formula was moistened dog food mixed with mashed boiled egg, human baby cereal, and a small amount of water. Her husband bought a bag of dog food for the young birds and put it in a container. He didn't keep the bag and, unfortunately, they didn't remember what brand it was. Many of the cheaper dog foods containing corn, wheat, and/or soy have been tested and found to contain biologically significant levels of glyphosate.

Even though I know what serious problems glyphosate exposure can cause in developing young, the effects of the dog food diet on all the hatchling starlings left me stunned. They were leucistic, with large areas of white feathers in their wings and white tail feathers with a darker band on the tip. Normal European Starlings are completely brownish-grey with a light patch on the throat. On two of the fledglings, the primary and secondary wing feathers had stopped growing when very short, with one wing affected on one of the birds and both on the other. Of course, neither of those birds could fly at all. On the other two, the mostly white primary and secondary feathers had grown to normal length. However, the flat vane on either side of the central shaft of each flight feather didn't have normal conformation so the feathers did not provide adequate lift when the birds flapped their wings. Neither of those birds could maintain flight for much more than 20 feet and could barely get three feet off the ground.

I offered to care for the four starlings while Dani and her family were on a camping trip, so had the opportunity to observe them for three weeks. I attempted to stimulate normal feather growth on the two with underdeveloped wing feathers, as I had on other birds. The underdeveloped feathers on the starling with both wings affected began growth on most of his primary and secondary feathers. Several grew to almost normal length, but were upside down, like some of the primary feathers on Piney, the Clark's Nutcracker, had initially been. The little male could then fly-hop up to perches more easily, but could not actually fly. The other starling's disrupted flight feathers on its right wing eventually grew to almost normal length so it could fly, but not well.

Those four starlings provide strong evidence of what biologically significant levels of glyphosate can do to hatchling birds continuously exposed for almost their entire post-hatching developmental period.

Blackie's body was quite bare on the day I received him for care.

Blackie's feathers were fully grown after he was given the electrolyte combination.

Unfortunately, as we do not know what brand of dog food was used, I can't look up tests for glyphosate and its main metabolite AMPA in the specific product used. Whatever the level was, it certainly had disastrous effects on the feather growth in all of the hatchlings, causing them to be unreleasable. The starlings remained in my care until Dani and her family returned from their camping trip, when I returned them to her. She kept the starlings for another month, feeding them mealworms, Purina Game Bird Startina®, and water with the electrolyte combination in it. She released them during the day in her yard. The birds would go back into their large cage to get food and water. Eventually they all were able to fly quite well and joined the other young starlings in the area.

Many people intentionally poison migrating blackbirds, starlings, and other birds because they eat grain or fruit. Those same birds also eat billions of grasshoppers and other crop-devouring insects. It is much cheaper environmentally to let birds eat insects rather than spraying large areas with deadly insecticides. Allowing them to have some of our crops during their migration is a justifiable reward for destroying so many crop-damaging insects. Without birds, insects would eat all the crops humans and their livestock need. In fact, if most insect eating birds go extinct, humans might only be able to raise enough food to survive for a short time. It is thought rapidly increasing insect numbers would eventually defoliate nearly all plants on earth, at least until insects and plants reach a balance. In the interim, most vertebrate species, including humans, would likely die of starvation, resulting in mass extinctions.

Unfortunately, similar to the insect eating birds, beneficial insects are also in severe decline. Insects provide many services worth billions to the economy, such as cleaning up dead animal and plant material and pollinating our crops and millions of other plants vital to the ecosystems in which they live. Where studies were done in Europe, insect populations declined by 80% in the last 40 years. I have also seen far fewer spiders on our land in recent years. Insecticide spraying to protect food crops causes death to beneficial insects or inability to reproduce and can cause nerve or brain damage to many developing invertebrate and vertebrate young. Crop damaging insects become resistant to insecticides fairly rapidly, resulting in use of much stronger toxins and more damage to beneficial invertebrates, as well as to vertebrates, including human newborns.

For example, a new study of seed eating birds using White-crowned Sparrows shows neonicotinoids and chlorpyrifos, both widely used insecticides, interfere with bird orientation and feeding. The researchers found that **"wild songbirds consuming the equivalent of just four imidacloprid-treated canola seeds or eight chlorpyrifos granules per day over 3 days could suffer impaired condition, migration delays and improper migratory direction, which could lead to increased risk of mortality or lost breeding opportunity."** Mortality and lost breeding opportunity would significantly contribute to declines in affected bird populations. Chloropyrifos was supposed to be banned by the Environmental Protection Agency because of the severe damage it does to the brains of children. Unfortunately, because of politics, that did not happen. The consequences of not protecting birds who reduce insect populations naturally are drastic effects on the biodiversity of the planet and possible extinction of mankind. Thanks to all the birds who eat insects, so far we are still here.

**Pesticides sprayed now
change future generations;
damage DNA.**

CHAPTER 13
A HAWK GETS HIS WINGS

In mid-July 2002, two fledged Red-tailed Hawks were found on the ground under a nest near Missoula, Montana. It was reported that one, a male, had been there for three weeks. The other, a female, had been flying around with their parents for the same amount of time, returning to the nest at night. The parents had continued feeding both youngsters.

When they first saw the male on the ground, concerned nearby homeowners reported to Montana Department of Fish, Wildlife and Parks that an injured hawk was under the nest tree. The department secretary told them it was just learning to fly and that its parents would take care of it. A week later, the people again called the FWP office to tell them he was still on the ground under the nest, with three other hawks flying around. Again, the secretary said the bird was probably fine. Three weeks after they left the nest, the people reported that both young hawks were on the ground and neither appeared able to fly. FWP finally called a Missoula small-bird rehabber, who picked up both fledgling hawks and brought them to me because I have facilities for large birds.

As soon as I received them, it was apparent why the young male had not been flying around with his family. Except for two feathers on his left wing, his primary and secondary wing feathers and all of his tail feathers had stopped growing when they were between one and two inches long. His was the worst case of disrupted feather development I had seen in a raptor up to that time. Others I had received with underdeveloped feathers had only the outer three to five primary feathers affected. Three years later, I received a female American Kestrel with almost as severely disrupted wing feather development.

In August 2017, an Osprey chick on a local nest, which had a web camera, died while being watched by several hundred people. I had observed the Osprey family on the website two days before the chick died, after a concerned woman reported to me that something was wrong with the dwarfish baby. Called Squirt by the nest watchers, he had malformed wings with no actual feather development on his wings or tail. His wings were still completely covered in down and no tail feathers were visible, while his normal sibling, a female judging by its size, was completely feathered and ready to fledge. Squirt now has the distinction of being the most severe case of disrupted feather development I have observed on a raptor. His failure to grow to normal body size may have been because he was not fed as much as his much larger sibling. It also may have been a result of his obvious thyroid hormone disruption, usually due to exposure to a toxin during development in the egg or immediately after hatching.

There are multiple methyl switches on the sides of DNA. These epigenetic "marks" on the genome tell genes when to activate and when to turn off. They also dictate the strength of gene expression. In developing animals such as baby birds, methyl switches triggered by special chemicals produced in their cells are supposed to turn specific genes on at the proper time to activate growth of various parts. For example, a switch on the DNA signals the start of a complex sequence of actions to produce eyes. When switches are given the proper chemical signals, they trigger various parts of a developing animal to be formed at the correct time, place, and size.

There are also certain switches that continue to work throughout the animal's life. For example, in birds, specific methyl switches turn on cells that make feathers grow to normal size. Feather growth switches also activate replacement of worn feathers at the proper time. Each year certain feathers in a bird's wing and tail are signaled to loosen and fall out, called molting. The switches then activate feather-growing cells to make replacement feathers. Raptors usually lose only one or two feathers at a time from their wings and tail, to avoid interfering with their ability to fly and hunt. They also molt many body feathers each year, taking several years for complete replacement.

Epigenetic switches controlling feather growth can be caused to malfunction by outside influences, such as environmental toxins, high radiation, or malnutrition. If one or more of these factors cause switches to turn off prematurely, feathers can cease growing. This phenomenon is one of the issues included in Avian Keratin Disorder, since feathers are made of keratin. On grazing animals, like cattle, horses, and deer, similar conditions are disrupted hoof development or failure of hair to grow normally. Their hooves and hair are made of keratin (as are fingernails, toenails, and hair on humans).

Somehow, the young female Red-tailed Hawk had shattered her right humerus, the bone between the shoulder and elbow. Upon closer examination, I found she also had a large, fast-growing tumor under the skin from her lower face down the side of her neck. It almost completely blocked her esophagus, making it nearly impossible for her to swallow food or water. The cancer likely had something to do with her bones being brittle, resulting in the wing being badly shattered. After a thorough examination, I sadly concluded it was in her best interest to euthanize her, rather than allowing her to suffer any longer. Her wing bone was shattered so she would not be able to fly again. With cancer of the throat, death was inevitable. What was most disturbing was that such a young hawk had cancer advanced enough to create such a large tumor.

After giving the young male my electrolyte combination, I offered him several mice to eat. I named him Arkie because he reminded me of an archaeopteryx. His parents had done a good job of feeding him. He was in good weight and, other than very short wing and tail feathers, appeared to be in good condition and healthy. Malnutrition was obviously not the reason for his disrupted feather development.

I fixed a large cardboard box with a thick branch through the sides for a perch and put him in our dark basement room with two other male fledgling Red-tailed Hawks who had been brought in the day before. They were also receiving treatment for Avian Keratin Disorder, but their disrupted feather development wasn't nearly as severe as Arkie's. The other two were found on the ground under their nests in two different areas of Ravalli County. On both birds, the four outside primary feathers were much shorter than normal, so they couldn't fly well enough to get off the ground. The rest of their feathers showed normal growth, including their tail feathers. I called them Sky and Willow.

After receiving Arkie, I had three large boxes sitting in a row, each with a fledged Red-tailed Hawk undergoing treatment for disrupted development of their feathers. I could not help but wonder what was affecting otherwise healthy young hawks so severely, and causing disrupted feather growth in so many during the same time period.

Four days after Arkie arrived, I received two Osprey fledglings with underdeveloped outer primaries on both wings. They came from different nests, both within 10 miles of our place. I was able to release them back to their parents with feathers fully grown in eight days. Getting five fledgling hawks with disrupted feather development made me wonder how many young ones had died that year. If they were not

Arkie first arrived for rehab, all his flight and tail feathers had stopped growing while still short except for two normal length flight feathers on his left wing.

found soon after their feathers stopped growing, they would remain on the ground until they starved or were killed by predators.

Because of what I had learned while stimulating the Cliff Swallow's primary feathers to grow, I was able to begin treatment on the five fledgling hawks as soon as I received them. Every three hours for three days and nights, I had to place a tube down the throat of each hawk and, with a syringe, squirt the electrolyte mixture into their crop. It was not an easy task. They did not particularly like to have their mouths forced open and a tube shoved down their throat. By the time their three days of treatment was over, I had several bite marks on my fingers and hands.

They also received all the mice they wanted to eat each day. After three days of intensive treatment, I put them in a flight room and continued giving them cell salts by putting tablets in their mice immediately before each feeding. In a week, the under-developed primary feathers on Sky and Willow had grown to normal length so I released them at their respective nest sites. That way, the parent birds,who had remained near the nest caring for their other young, could teach them to hunt.

Arkie's wing and tail feathers were fully grown three weeks after beginning his treatment for Avian Keratin Disorder.

Arkie's wing and tail feathers had grown to almost half their normal length after 10 days. Because they were so short, it took nearly three weeks for them to grow to full length so he looked like an ordinary juvenile Red-tailed Hawk. Arkie was then transferred to a rehabilitator who was also a falconer. He trained Arkie to hunt, and released him. It had taken much longer than usual but Arkie was able to live free and fly wherever he wanted. He had finally gotten his wings.

When they are hunting,
Red-tailed Hawks can face the wind,
hovering in place.

This shows the left wing of the female American Kestrel with disrupted growth of all the primary feathers, causing her to be unable to fly when she fledged from the nest.

CHAPTER 14
STRANGER THAN FICTION

Blondie the coyote, Kitcat the baby bobcat, and Firefly the white-tailed deer fawn showed me how to use homeopathic cell salts and electrolytes to bring about amazing recoveries not previously recorded in medical literature. I began describing to rehabbers and other people how my electrolyte combination helped animals recover from specific developmental defects and some other adverse health issues. Many successfully used it on animals in their care. Meanwhile, I continued to use the combination on birds and mammals I received, many with problems I had neither seen before nor found in my search through online and other published reports. Some of the developmental malformations we were finding in young animals were so unusual I had not ever seen them mentioned in science fiction, let alone scientific papers. In addition, many of the recoveries I observed, as well as some reported to me by other people, were quite stunning.

An example of another rehabber successfully mitigating a developmental defect was on a pre-fledgling Eastern Blue Jay hatched near Chicago, Illinois. A young woman who volunteered at a wildlife rehabilitation center in northern Illinois came to visit me in spring 2003, while she was in our area of Montana visiting friends. I shared with her how we give homeopathic cell salts in combination with common electrolytes to make underdeveloped facial bones, skulls, bills, and feathers grow to normal. She had not yet seen a malformation like those I described in young birds at the center where she volunteered.

The day after she arrived home in Chicago, she went to the rehabilitation center. Amazingly, just that morning, an orphaned fledgling Eastern Blue Jay with underdeveloped upper facial bones and short upper bill had arrived at the center. The woman immediately emailed me to get my recipe for the electrolyte combination. Two days later I received the following message: "Thanks for the information on the cell salts. The little Blue Jay's beak stopped its abnormal growth after we gave it the cell salts and electrolytes. Its beak is now normal. Thanks for the tip." I wasn't surprised. I had expected the young jay's upper face to grow to its genetically-programmed normal size. I and other rehabbers in western Montana had successfully helped many hatchling birds' faces return to normal growth, restoring upper bills to normal length, almost always in two days or less.

However, something quite astounding that actually was a surprise happened in spring 2003. I received a call for help from a rehabber east of Missoula. Carl Bock, who lives near Potomac, Montana, had rescued six newly-hatched Canada Geese who had somehow become separated from their parents. Four were normal, healthy hatchlings. The other two had a quarter inch oval hole in the upper bill between the nostrils. The holes were large enough so Carl could look down through them and see the goslings' little tongues.

After finding the parents at a nearby pond, Carl returned the four healthy youngsters to their care. The two goslings with holes in their bills were having trouble eating and drinking, so he did not want to release them, thinking they would likely die. After three days in his care, the malformed goslings had shown no improvement. They were still gasping and shaking their heads when they attempted to eat or drink. They also were extremely reluctant to go into the water or swim, not healthy behavior for a baby goose. One of the main defenses of young waterfowl is their ability to swim and dive to safety under water when attacked by predators.

The fourth morning after finding the two goslings, Carl called a mutual friend and master falconer, Jim Chaffin, to ask if he had any ideas on how to help them. Jim gave Carl my phone number, suggesting he call immediately. I had not previously seen or even heard of that type of birth defect in the bills of birds, let alone tried to remedy the malformation. Hoping the cell salt and electrolyte combination might help the goslings, I explained how to make the solution to put in their water. I also told him where to go in Missoula for bioplasma, instructing him to dissolve one tablet in the liquid electrolytes each time he replaced the goslings' water.

That afternoon, Carl drove to Missoula, found the store, and bought a bottle of bioplasma. Upon arriving home, he mixed salt, baking soda, and potassium chloride as I described, and put a good pinch along with a tablet of bioplasma into the goslings' water pan, stirring until all ingredients were dissolved.

I had asked him to take before photos and, if the malformations changed at all, to take after photos. I did not really expect any improvement in such a severe defect, but knew it wouldn't hurt the goslings to give them the electrolyte and cell salt combination. I even considered it remotely possible, with emphasis on remotely, that my electrolyte combination might stimulate the keratin of bills to grow and close the holes. The only way to find out was to give it to the goslings and observe what happened.

Because it was an hour's drive to town and back, Carl had gotten behind in his feeding schedule for the other animals he cared for at that time, including several wolves. He decided to wait until morning to take before photos, but did change the goslings' water before he went to bed, dissolving a pinch of dry electrolytes and a bioplasma tablet in the water for the second time.

The next morning, Carl readied his camera and picked up a gosling to photograph the hole in the bill. Where it had been, there was a lighter area on a smooth, solid bill, with no hole remaining. He picked up the other gosling and found the same thing, no hole in its bill. His amazement was evident in his voice when he called to report what had happened. I was extremely and pleasantly surprised. I certainly did not expect the comparatively large holes in the gosling's bills to grow completely closed in only eight hours after bioplasma and electrolytes were first given. The holes had not changed at all in the four days Carl had the goslings, so the rapid, overnight closure of the holes was even more surprising. Unfortunately, there were no photos of the goslings' bills, before or after. Carl was so amazed the holes had completely closed in one night, he forgot to take photos of the light spots where the holes had been.

After the holes in their bills grew closed, the two little goslings were able to eat and drink normally. When Carl put them in a large pan of deep water, they dove under the water like goslings are supposed to do, swimming around completely submerged, coming up with a splash. The next day, Carl took them to the pond where their parents and siblings were and released them. It was not far from where Carl lived, so he was able to watch the goose family until the goslings were full-grown and began to fly. The adults were good parents and all six babies successfully fledged.

In the years since Carl remedied his two gosling patients, several domestic goslings with that birth defect have had the hole in their bill grow to normal after being given the bioplasma and electrolyte combination. It is hard to believe a hole in a hatchling's bill can heal at all, let alone grow completely closed so quickly.

Another astounding recovery after administration of both cell salts, calc. phos. and bioplasma, happened in 2009. A white-tailed deer who lived on the property of my friend Gary had twin male fawns. One was born with contracted tendons on both front legs, so the fawn could not straighten them to walk normally. He could barely stand well enough to suckle and became exhausted when he had to walk more than a few feet.

The handicapped fawn's ability to walk appeared to deteriorate as the days passed. Because he could not travel well, the doe and both babies remained near Gary's home where the fawns were born. After three weeks had passed with no improvement, Gary and I concluded we definitely needed to do something for the malformed fawn. We did not want to catch or touch him, because doing so might make his mother abandon him or result in injuries. Gary had been giving the doe a cup of grain twice each day to help her get enough nutrition to feed the fawns and to keep her close so he could monitor the defective twin.

Because his family used cell salts, Gary had both calc. phos. 30X and bioplasma. After discussing the problem on the phone, we decided to try something I had not heard of before, which was to give the cell salt tablets to the doe in hopes the minerals would go into her milk and be ingested by the fawn when he suckled. We surmised this might enable the malformed fawn's cells to somehow cause the tendons to loosen. The fawn would then be able to straighten his front legs and walk normally. We also both thought that was expecting nothing short of a scientific miracle. As with the hatchling geese with holes in their upper bills, I was quite skeptical that our plan would actually work, but as with many scientific experiments, you do not know what will happen until you try.

Cell salts seem to work best on abnormalities when given immediately after the young one is born. Because this fawn was three weeks old, I was concerned we had missed our window of opportunity. An even bigger question was whether there even *was* a window of opportunity to make contracted tendons loosen so the youngster could walk normally.

After our phone conversation, Gary immediately began giving the mother three tablets each of calc. phos. 30X and bioplasma in her grain every morning and night. Luckily, the fawns were both with the doe the first morning, so Gary was able to take several photos of the abnormal one struggling to stand and walk beside his mother. He didn't see either

Gary Mazade took this photo of the white-tailed deer fawn with contracted tendons at three weeks of age, before cell salts were given to his mother.

fawn the rest of that day, but in late afternoon, the doe came to eat her grain containing the six tablets of cell salts. The next day she came both morning and afternoon, but again the fawns were not with her. The third day, the doe came to eat in the morning, also without her twins. Gary was beginning to be concerned that something had happened to them.

Late that afternoon Bob and I could hardly believe what Gary called to report. When the doe came for grain, both twins were following her. Totally astounding to me, Gary could not tell which one had been born with contracted tendons. Both fawns had straight legs; both could walk and run and leap over rocks and brush. Almost as surprising, it was only the third day of giving cell salts to the doe.

About a week after the handicapped fawn had recovered, we went to Gary's place to see them. Both fawns looked healthy and normal. I wanted to take some photos, but since they could run and were not accustomed to me, they wouldn't let me get close enough. I could easily tell them apart with my binoculars because of their individual spotting, which I had memorized from Gary's earlier photos. Several days after the fawn began walking normally, Gary was able to get a distant photo of the twins that clearly showed normal front legs on the recovered fawn. Everyone who knew about the fawn was surprised by his complete recovery and that it occurred so quickly, even suggesting it was stranger than fiction.

What was to some the most important, and possibly most remarkable, case of recovery from a serious birth defect, was in a little three-year old girl. On a bright sunny morning in spring 2002, a woman brought three hatchling Mountain Bluebirds for me to raise. They came from a nest box in the woman's yard. One of the parents had been found dead near the nest; the other had not come to feed the hatchlings for several hours and was eventually also found dead. All of the hatchlings had underdeveloped skull and upper bill, with the upper bill shorter than the normal lower bill. After I held up each hatchling to examine them, I told the woman all three little birds had underbite. I asked her who had sprayed herbicides near their nest box two days before. After looking at me a bit like I was from outer space, she said her neighbor had sprayed his lawn two days before and the nest box was on the fence dividing the two properties. She asked in a very concerned tone, "How did you know the lawn was sprayed?" I told her I had seen underbite on many hatchlings after they had been exposed to lawn spray. The bluebirds' underbite appeared to have been caused about two days before she brought them to me. She thought the spray might have killed the parent birds, to which I agreed. Toxins in lawn spray killing one or both parents is a common reason rehabbers receive hatchling songbirds for care, and most of those exposed to lawn or roadside herbicide applications have an obvious underbite within two days.

The woman asked if I could do anything about the underbite on the birds. I assured her that if they recovered from being poisoned by the herbicides, their faces and bills would be normal in about two days. Upon hearing that, the lady took out her pen and a tablet and asked how it was possible to make their faces grow to normal. After writing the information about calc. phos. 6X and where to buy it, she asked if it worked on young mammals. I told her it did, but a newborn mammal's facial bones usually take from two to three weeks to grow to normal, not two days like the bills on hatchling birds, because mammal young grow more slowly.

I answered all her questions concerning my use of cell salts on both birds and mammals while I made the young bluebirds comfortable in their box. Then she asked me to come to her car and look at her three-year-old daughter. I had thought she wanted to know how to make domestic animal babies grow to normal, not her own child. I didn't even know a little girl was in the car, since my focus had been on the bluebirds and answering the woman's questions.

When we arrived at the car, I immediately saw the little girl had an underdeveloped upper face and skull. It was approximately the correct size for a one-and-a-half-year-old child. Her lower jaw was normal size for age three, but much too large to match the underdeveloped upper face and jaw, resulting in a fairly severe underbite of about three sixteenths of an inch. I told the mother I didn't know whether the bones could be stimulated to grow to normal on a child who was three years old. I also assured her it wouldn't hurt to try the calc. phos. 6X, as visible effects on young mammals had been highly beneficial, including good digestion, thick shiny hair, and strong bones, teeth, and hooves.

After the woman and her daughter left, I took the hatchling bluebirds to our house and gave them food, liquid electrolytes, and cell salts, my usual remedy for exposure to herbicides. All three survived. In just two days, their faces and bills had grown to normal as I had predicted. All were released when they could fly and eat by themselves. I completely forgot about the woman and her daughter. Since I was at our barn when they came, I didn't write down her name and address as I usually do when people bring me birds.

One summer day in 2004, almost exactly two years after the woman brought the bluebird hatchlings, she arrived at the barn and handed me a box containing an injured adult American Robin. At first, I didn't remember her. As soon as I had finished examining the robin and returned it to its box, the woman said, "I want you to come to the car and look at my daughter." When she said that, I remembered who she was. I asked if she had tried the calc. phos. 6X. She smiled and said yes. I asked if there was any effect. With an even bigger smile, she said I should wait and see.

When I got to the car, I could hardly believe my eyes. The little girl, then five years old, was beautiful. Her upper face and skull had grown to match the rest of her face. She didn't look at all like the child I had seen in 2002. I asked her to smile and was thrilled to see she had a perfect bite. Also, as I predicted, her blond hair was thick and shiny. Because I was so surprised at the change in her appearance, I neglected to ask the mother how long the astounding transformation of the underdeveloped facial bones took. I could tell the mother was extremely pleased with what she had done. Having a normally developed face would completely change her daughter's life. I have always regretted not asking for before and after photos. It would have been nice to have photographic proof of the almost unbelievable change in the little girl's face as a result of being given calc. phos 6X tablets.

After over 10 years of first using calc. phos. 6X and then 30X to quickly stimulate underdeveloped bones grow to normal in faces of hatchling birds and newborn mammals, I received a hatchling House Sparrow in summer of 2011. It had been found on the ground near a house. After placing it in a box and looking for a nest in nearby trees, the people called me. I couldn't tell from their description what kind of bird it was. When they arrived, I told them it was a House Sparrow hatchling. They are cavity-nesting birds so it likely fell out of a nest in the eaves of their house directly above where it was found on the lawn, and not from a nest in a tree.

When I saw the little sparrow's underbite, I asked if herbicides had been applied to their lawn in the previous two days. They said it was done the morning before. I took the hatchling out of the box and showed them the short upper bill. After explaining what herbicides used on lawns often do to hatchling birds, I thanked them for bringing it to me. I told them I usually could get the face and bill to grow to normal and, when it was full grown and able to eat on its own, I would release it.

After giving the hatchling a crop full of baby bird food, water, and a tablet each of calc. phos. 30X and bioplasma, I tucked it into a cloth nest lined with toilet paper in a small box placed on a heating pad. Because it had been poisoned, which disrupts normal thyroid hormone function, it was not able to maintain heat and energy. In order for a hatchling exposed to toxins to be able to digest food properly, it has to be kept warm.

The little sparrow quickly recovered and, after two days of receiving the cell salts in its food, its bill was normal in size and length. Fortunately, I remembered to take a before-treatment photo right after I fed it the first time. About a week later, I finally remembered to take another photo showing its bill had grown to normal. By that time the little sparrow had pinfeathers on its head and body and its large dark eyes had opened. It had changed in just a few days from being quite homely to being extremely cute. When it was old enough to fly and could eat by itself, I released it in our yard. It had been practicing flying in the flight room with three House Finch fledglings I had received for care the day after the sparrow arrived. The finches were a few days older than the sparrow, but once they all fledged and began flying, they were close to the same size. I put them together so the sparrow would have company and because young birds learn from each other. Those raised in a group have better survival skills than a bird who is raised alone.

The astounding growth to normal of the little girl's upper facial bones, amazing closing of holes in the bills of hatchling geese, growth to normal of underdeveloped facial bones that Firefly and many other mammals and birds had at birth, rapid improvement of the fawn with contracted tendons, and many other remarkable recoveries I have witnessed really do seem almost stranger than fiction. This is evidenced by an absence of reports in scientific literature of similar recoveries from such malformations, and most importantly, by the complete disbelief of nearly all medical doctors and most veterinarians, when I tell them about homeopathic cell salts and how they stimulate cells to function properly, promoting normal growth in newborns with certain developmental malformations.

Chemicals to which young ones are exposed during development disrupt normal function of mitochondria in cells. In humans, this is called mitochondrial disease, and animals in which the mitochondria are adversely affected typically also have metabolic acidosis. Mitochondria are the power packs in animal cells. They make the heat and energy necessary to keep the animal alive, growing, and able to function in a normal manner. If insufficient energy is produced by mitochondria, it often causes mortality in the animal, especially if it is a newborn.

Toxins such as those in pesticides also directly cause metabolic acidosis by disrupting an animal's cellular communication. Metabolic acidosis means bodily fluids are less basic or, to put it another way, slightly more acidic than is favorable to good health. This condition severely affects the ability of cells to take up nutrients, vitamins, and especially minerals, which they require to function optimally and do all the things they do every nanosecond of the animal's life.

Developmental malformations such as those described in this book are often the result of nutritional deficiencies resulting from mitochondrial disease and metabolic acidosis. The type and severity of the defect and when it occurs are dependent on the timing of exposure to toxins, both to the parents (especially the mother) and to developing young. The seriousness of the defect and what genes, and thus what

This hatchling house sparrow has a dished area between the eyes and its upper bill is visibly shorter than the lower bill.

The hatchling sparrow a week later, after its skull and upper bill had grown to normal.

organs, are affected also depend upon the stage of growth the young one is in at the time of exposure.

Minerals have a positive charge. Cell salts, being an electrolyte, simply produce a negative charge inside the cells, stimulating them to uptake minerals and other positively charged nutrients. That enables cells to do whatever job in the body they are genetically programmed to do, when they are supposed to do it.

Recoveries like those I have described might seem to some people too good to be true. Some suggest that magic, religion, or something of that nature is involved. However, the effects cell salts have on living cells are easily explained by simple science, even though sometimes the results actually seem stranger than fiction.

**All life depends on
water from rain that may be
too toxic to drink.**

A RANCHER'S LAMENT

Those chemical reps claimed Tordon®
So safe you can drink the swill.
Then laughing, said "If you relieve
Yourself in creeks, the fish it will kill."

They said if I used Tordon®
It would rid my land of weeds,
And since it lasts for years and years
It will kill all sprouting seeds.

I sprayed it here, I sprayed it there.
Then to my consternation,
I started coughing all the time
And my eyes got granulation.

Everywhere I sprayed the stuff,
Carefully following the label,
Jackrabbits and small mammals died.
"Tordon® is safe" is just a fable.

Now the skies are empty.
No birds to sing at dawn.
No wild friends to brighten life,
All of them are gone.

The above effects of Tordon® were reported to me by my good friend Bill Ohrmann, who was a rancher near Drummond, Montana, and an amazing artist. I wrote the poem for him using what he wrote to me in a letter concerning what happened to him and to the wildlife on his land when he sprayed Tordon®, a combination of picloram and other herbicides, often 2,4-D.

Even a fox in
beige camouflage can't slip through
toxic grass unscathed.

CHAPTER 15
BALD EAGLE REUNION

Wildlife rehabbers often receive birds and mammals who have broken bones, usually as a result of being hit by vehicles. By spring 2005, I had begun using the stronger homeopathic cell salt, calc. phos. 30X. Some people insist it should not work as well because there is less calcium phosphate in it than in calc. phos. 6X. Actually, homeopathic substances are considered stronger when there is less of the original present, because the ingredients are diluted and shaken more times. If a bird or animal is given calc. phos. 30X and bioplasma three times a day, it takes approximately one half the time for a bone to heal as it does when they are not given the two cell salts. With calc. phos. 6X and bioplasma, healing time is two-thirds as long. A shorter healing time is important for rehabbers because the sooner splints can be removed from an injured bird or mammal, the better the prognosis for release.

In early spring 2005, I received a fox pup who was hit by a vehicle, breaking the bone between her shoulder and elbow. The man who brought the fox pup had thought taking her back to her parents' den was the correct thing to do, until he saw she was injured. It is always best to leave young mammals of all kinds with their mother or parents unless they are obviously hurt or starving.

Most birds have little to no sense of smell, so young ones like American Robins who have fallen out of an open nest in a tree, jumped out of the nest prematurely, or are blown out by strong winds can be placed back in the nest. If it has been destroyed, a makeshift nest made of a loose weave basket or a plastic container, such as a nest-sized margarine tub, can be substituted. The replacement nest must have a number of one-quarter to one-half inch holes poked or drilled in the bottom so rainwater can easily drain out. Dry hay can be used for nest material; green grass or anything that retains moisture should never be placed in a nest. With wire, the basket or margarine tub can be tied to a tree branch in a protected area, always with branches above it for shade and cover. It is important to watch from a distance after putting babies into the new nest to be sure their parents have found and are feeding them. When young birds are hungry, they food-call, making it easy for parents to find them in the new location. If adults do not return to feed them, it is time to call a wild bird rehabilitator.

Because mammals have an acute sense of smell, animals like fawns, small bunnies, foxes, and other mammals should be left alone and not touched unless they are injured or in danger. A fawn lying on a road where a car might hit it is an example. If a fawn or other young mammal has to be moved, gloves should be worn with clean newspaper or paper towel wrapped around the gloved hands while picking it up and moving it to a nearby spot that is safe. Only the paper-covered gloves, not skin or clothing, should touch the animal. Cuddling or petting transfers unnatural scents onto them, making them easier for predators to find. Newborn mammals are naturally scentless, which helps hide them from predators as long as they remain motionless. A fawn should be left within 100 feet or so of where it was originally found. That makes it possible for the mother to call to it and find it when she returns to feed her baby. Small bunnies old enough to hop around are usually just out exploring. They should be put under a nearby brush pile, woodpile, or other suitable place where they can hide or escape from predators. In the case of any young animal who is ill or hurt like the fox pup, the best thing to do is to immediately take it to a wildlife rehabilitator.

Upon her arrival, I gave the fox pup my electrolyte combination, which she quickly lapped up. When she was finished drinking, I splinted her leg, completely immobilizing it. I made a soft bed with a thick blanket in our large plastic dog carrier. She was so small and emaciated she needed extra heat to maintain her body temperature. I put a heating pad under a back corner of the carrier, giving her the option of a warm spot or cooler area. A bowl full of pinky mice (babies without hair, easier to digest than older mice) mixed with chicken baby food was at the front of the kennel beside a bowl of electrolytes, so she could eat and drink anytime. I put cell salts into liquid electrolytes four times a day, ensuring she would get the electrolyte combination whenever she drank. I also mixed the two cell salt tablets into her mouse pieces and puppy food whenever her food bowl needed refilling.

After two days of eating all she wanted several times a day, she had visibly grown. The afternoon of the second day, when the vet wrap around her fast-growing body was becoming too tight, I cut it. By putting pieces of tape across the gap, I was able to make the wrapping looser without removing it or allowing the leg to move. On the third evening,

I put longer strips of tape across the space in the vet wrap to make it less tight.

When I loosened the vet wrap on the morning of the fifth day, I felt the bone in the area of the fracture. To my astonishment, it had solid calcification at the break area. Calcification had even completely encased the small pieces of shattered bone. With the leg stable and with no movement in the break area, I was able to completely remove the vet wrap. The pup favored the leg the rest of that day, indicating it was still tender. By the next afternoon, she walked with no limp at all. The young fox was released when she was about half grown and old enough to find her own food. We have several brush piles in which released small mammals can hide. I continue to provide food until they have learned to find or catch food for themselves.

I thought healing a shattered bone in only five days might be some kind of record, but I do not know if the Guinness Book of Records has a category for that. It was clear that calc. phos. 30X helped to heal bones even faster than calc. phos. 6X, though I knew it would take more tests to be certain. After healing many bones since, I have definitely found that fractures heal in approximately half the time when calc. phos. 30X is given as opposed to when no cell salts are given. Three people have reported to me that, when taking calc. phos. 30X, their broken bones healed in three weeks. Their doctors confirmed it and were extremely surprised at the speed of healing, especially in older people. Three weeks is one half the time most doctors say it will take for a bone to heal in an adult human.

Soon after the little fox's leg had healed, I had a chance to test calc. phos. 30X on another broken bone. It was mid-morning when I received a call from a wildlife biologist in Polson, Montana. A high wind in that area the previous night had blown down a large Bald Eagle nest near Flathead Lake. One pre-fledgling baby had been killed by the fall. The other eaglet, a female, had two broken bones in her wing tip. The biologist asked if I would be willing to take the eaglet and try to heal the wing. I said I would be happy to fix her wing and that it would take about five days for the bones to heal. Wing tips are easy to splint and usually heal fairly fast, even without cell salts. Since I was going to give the eaglet calc. phos. 30X, I asked the biologist to plan on returning the youngster to her parents in six days. I hoped the eagle pair would remain near where the nest had been, so they could find her and resume feeding her. They could then also teach her the hunting and survival skills she would need after she fledged, which is something I can't do.

Polson is about a four-hour drive from our place, so the biologist transporting the eaglet did not arrive until early afternoon. The bird was healthy and had been well fed by her parents. I gave her the usual electrolyte and cell salt combination by tubing her. A syringe holding the fluids is attached to a tube and used to force fluids directly into the bird's crop.

After splinting the wingtip to immobilize the broken bones, I fed the eaglet eight large mice. Bald Eagles usually prefer fish, but I didn't have access to fresh fish for her. Fortunately, she liked mice just fine, judging by the nine to 12 large mice a day she ate. Four times each day, I gave her the electrolyte/cell salt combination. While her wing was healing, Flathead area biologists built a manmade nest consisting of a plywood platform with a circle of sticks and branches, with hay in the middle for bedding, in the same tree as the original nest had been.

In the five days her wing was splinted, the eaglet ate well and her wing and tail feathers finished their growth. The afternoon of the fifth day, I removed the splint and found both bones were completely healed and well calcified as I had predicted. My confidence in the cell salts' ability to stimulate bone growth was validated. I immediately emailed the Polson biologist that his eaglet was ready to go home. The next morning, his coworker came to get her and she was put in the replacement nest that afternoon. Fortunately, her parents had remained nearby. Soon after the eaglet called to them, her father brought a fish and her parents resumed caring for her as if she had never been gone. As I hoped, it was a successful reunion. It took several days of wing flapping for her to build up her flight muscles prior to fledging. A little over a week later, the fledgling was flying around the nest area with her parents. Over the winter, they would teach her all the eagle survival skills she needed to learn, such as fishing, hunting, and where to find food in different seasons. This is the type of successful rehabilitation we always hope for. Who doesn't like a happy ending?

**Regal Bald Eagles
were brought close to extinction
by weakened egg shells.**

CHAPTER 16
SAVING SHA'RE

Sha're was about a week old when she was brought to me in the second week of June 2003. She was the sixth fawn we received for care that year, the last year Montana Department of Fish, Wildlife and Parks allowed my husband and me to care for game animals at our rehabilitation center. They suddenly changed their policy in 2004 to one stating that all young game animals who cannot be placed back with their mothers were to be shot, instead of rehabilitated and released as before. Their reason was a belief that caring for deer fawns and elk calves could spread Chronic Wasting Disease. It seemed an odd policy since no newborn ungulates have ever been diagnosed in Montana with Chronic Wasting Disease.

There was no public outcry against this new policy. State law decrees that game animals belong to the people of the State of Montana. There is something seriously wrong with a society that hesitates to euthanize a vicious dog who has bitten a child or killed a person's pet or livestock, but does not protest the shooting of an innocent young fawn or elk calf that has lost its mother to an accident. Deer and elk are as intelligent and loving as domestic pets and more deserving of life than a vicious dog. Unfortunately, many of the policies established by people in positions of power are for convenience, not fairness.

In 35 years of raising young game animals, Sha're (pronounced Shah-*ray*) turned out to be one of the hardest to keep alive. She appeared to have a dysfunctional immune system, as do many wild and domestic animals born since spring 1995. Our friend Dan Severson, a pharmacist and rancher working with veterinarian Jack Ward, found that beef calves with what is called Weak Calf Syndrome had an underdeveloped thymus. I found in necropsies on accident-killed deer fawns, elk calves, and other mammals that many wild young are also born with an underdeveloped and/or damaged thymus. If this gland is compromised in any way, a newborn's immune system can't do its job of shielding it. Thus, if the young animal has contact with a diseased animal, inhales dust particles covered with bacteria, viruses, fungi, or environmental toxins, or is exposed to toxins through the mother's milk or in other food it eats, its damaged immune system is unable to protect it, resulting in illness and often death.

The thymus could be likened to a school for T-cells (cells processed by the thymus gland that actively participate in immune response). The thymus is responsible for educating naive T-cells, which travel in large numbers from bone marrow, where they are produced, to the thymus. If a newborn animal has no thymus or an underdeveloped or damaged thymus, it is as though the school has burned down. The naive T-cells are spread through the young animal's body by its circulating blood, often attacking its own cells while failing to protect it from toxins and disease organisms. When that happens, a young animal is said to have an immune dysfunction. Juvenile rheumatoid arthritis (JRA), lactose intolerance, and inflammatory bowel disease (IBD) are the most common types of immune dysfunctions I have observed and treated in young mammals.

In 2016, two of the five white-tailed deer fawns I necropsied had no left lobe of the thyroid gland, in addition to an underdeveloped thymus, underbite, and other developmental defects. The left thyroid lobe was smaller than the right in many necropsied deer, especially since 2007, but I hadn't seen an animal with one side completely unformed prior to the two fawns examined in 2016. Thyroid hormones dictate growth of brain cells, bones, muscles, thymus, reproductive organs, and all other organs in a young vertebrate animal during its development in the egg or womb. When thyroid glands, or the hormones they produce, are unable to function properly, an almost unbelievable range of adverse health effects and malformations can occur.

Bill Dorrety was a very knowledgeable laboratory technician at the veterinary diagnostic laboratory he owned for several years in Hamilton, Montana. He verified that the thymus glands I provided for him to examine from calves, deer, and other young animals were underdeveloped, had tissue damage, or both. Studies have reported that underdeveloped thymus in young mammals is connected to exposure to environmental toxins or to nutritional deficiencies. Both factors cause disruption of thyroid hormones during development and often the consequent disruption of thymus development.

Sha're was found near Pinesdale, Montana. Her mother may have left her to die because the baby was extremely ill. Inflammation of her intestine and bowel indicated she had been having an acute allergic reaction to her mother's milk. Because of severe diarrhea, she was quite dehydrated and, like Firefly, Sha're was starving. She also had an underdeveloped skull and upper jaw causing underbite, similar to Firefly though not as severe. Sha're could close her mouth over her lower teeth and her face looked fairly normal. But with the front of her lower lip parallel with the front of the upper lip, rather than tucked in behind the upper lip, it was easy to see she had an underbite.

Because her symptoms were strongly suggestive of autoimmune disorders, I suspected Sha're's thymus was not working properly. The only way I could determine whether live newborns in my care had an underdeveloped thymus was by observing their symptoms. Because homeopathic cell salts seem to help the immune system function in a more normal manner, I immediately placed a tablet each of calc. phos. 30X and bioplasma directly in Sha're's mouth. Then, every half hour for two hours, I had her suck a small quantity of liquid electrolytes from a bottle. When Sha're indicated she was ready for food by making hungry fawn calls, I let her have five ounces of goat milk with a tablespoon of whipping cream added. She eagerly drank it and wanted more. I did not want to overfeed her, so she had to wait three hours before getting more milk. In the middle of the three-hour period, I gave her more of the electrolyte combination, continuing this routine for several feedings. By the next afternoon, she was able to drink eight ounces of milk every three hours without any sign of distress or pain. She no longer had diarrhea and her stool was free of mucus and blood, indicating her digestive system was functioning normally. I continued to put the two cell salt tablets in her milk formula at each feeding to keep it that way.

At a local health food store, I bought thymus capsules to give her twice a day, hoping they would help her thymus function more normally. I slipped a thymus capsule into her mouth just before offering the nipple, so she swallowed it with her first swallow of milk. I also put half of a crushed selenium tablet in her milk twice each day. Selenium is a mineral necessary to both the thyroid gland and the immune system. As soon as I began giving these supplements along with the cell salts, Sha're improved even faster. She began gaining weight and had much more energy. Her face and skull began looking more normal, Also, like other newborn mammals treated for underbite at birth, Sha're's lower incisors were completely contacting the dental pad in less than two weeks.

For a while Sha're's health seemed fine. She ate well, ran, played, and acted like the other fawns. Strangely, on the morning of July 7, when I went out to feed the fawns, she was unable to stand or walk. Her legs were partially paralyzed, as if she had some kind of nerve damage that prevented her from controlling her leg muscles. I checked the inside of her eyelids and found Sha're's conjunctiva was showing a severe reaction, strongly indicating a toxin exposure. What she might have been exposed to that would cause paralysis was a mystery I have yet to solve.

After finding Sha're could not stand or walk and had likely been exposed to a nerve damaging toxin, I gave her a bottle of the cell salt and electrolyte combination. By nightfall, her stool was runny and contained blood, indicating her digestive system was again being seriously affected. I continued to give the liquid electrolyte combination between milk feedings until the diarrhea was gone, which took three days.

Fortunately, Sha're's legs began working by mid-morning of the next day; she was able to get up and walk, although still a bit wobbly. Whatever was in the air on July 7 had to be very toxic to cause such severe disruption of her muscles and nerves. According to toxicologists and other scientists I have consulted, paralysis and incoordination can be symptoms of exposure to commonly applied pesticide combinations or to certain insecticides. In her book *Silent Spring*, Rachel Carson described similar paralysis on test roosters exposed to a fungicide and herbicide combination. The toxins had to come from somewhere else, because we do not use any herbicides or other pesticides on our land.

After three or four days, Sha're appeared to have completely recovered. She was eating grain and learning to browse on the grass, weeds, and tree leaves in the deer pen. By the last week of July, she had put on weight and grown taller. She progressed so well I hoped to begin letting her out of the deer pen during the day. The other five fawns we raised that year had been going out every morning, beginning the second week of July. When the fawns were hungry, they came to get their milk and we always led them back into the deer pen at night. Because I needed to sleep, I fed them only once in the middle of the night. Night feedings are important for deer fawns. Mother deer usually feed their newborns at night, giving them a final meal just before daybreak, and then do not return until late afternoon or at dusk. This is basically opposite of the feeding schedule of a human raised fawn. It is also one reason fawns are thought to be abandoned, and so are sometimes kidnapped by well-meaning but uninformed people. When fawns are old enough to remain with their mother full time, they suckle when hungry.

On July 29, between 12:30 and 3:30 in the afternoon, I saw or was told of other paralyzed or severely uncoordinated animals: a young male squirrel I was raising; two newly fledged wild pigeons living in our barnyard; a friend's two roosters; and several other animals reported to me later. Sha're's legs also became paralyzed again. All of the affected animals experienced a sudden inability to control their limbs. The birds could not walk or fly. Sha're was unable to stand, even if I tried to hold her up. She could not make her legs work at all, similar to the July 7 incident but worse. The joints just above the hooves on her hind legs were swollen and felt hot. The inside of her eyelids was so red and swollen that the conjunctiva of the lower lid was protruding out from under the eyelid. Her usually bright brown "Bambi" eyes were dull. I moved her to our indoor intensive care kennel and gave her all the remedies for thyroid hormone disruption I had used when she was younger. In two days, she was able to stand and walk, but was still quite uncoordinated. Her soft reddish hair began falling out on both sides of her body and on her legs where the joints had been so swollen. This is what happens to people's hair when they get chemotherapy.

When Sha're had become paralyzed on July 29, other symptoms she exhibited were nearly identical to those listed for an immune system dysfunction in children called Juvenile Rheumatoid Arthritis (JRA). She had swollen joints for several days, but after a little over a week, the swelling went down. The hair on her sides and legs took about three weeks to grow back, but was whitish tan in color, making her look rather ghostly in bright moonlight.

Sha're did not get diarrhea on July 29, but she did have both blood and mucous in her stool, indicating her intestines were inflamed. After five days, when she was able to walk and the swelling in her legs went down, she was returned to the outdoor deer pen. However, it was quite clear I was going to have to postpone her release to the wild until I was sure she was not suddenly going to become paralyzed again and thus vulnerable to being killed by predators. As it turned out this was a good plan.

All through August, Sha're ate well, looking and acting like any other healthy fawn. She had regained the weight lost while paralyzed during the end of July. She was a sweetheart to care for, always coming when I called her and always happy to see me. By the end of August, we were no longer putting the five older fawns in the pen at night, but they still came for their bottle three times a day. Sha're was alone except for

Sunny, a large female domestic rabbit. Sunny lived in the deer pen, safe from foxes and coyotes. Sha're and Sunny had become good friends. They slept side by side or with Sha're's chin over Sunny's back and Sunny tucked tight against Sha're's chest. When Sunny hopped around eating grass, Sha're followed her. I recently read in an article that evolutionary biologists and anthropologists, especially those doing animal research, referred to animal friendship as the "F" word. This proves scientists at least have a sense of humor about things they do not want to admit. Until recently scientists didn't believe animals could actually have friends, especially from different species. Sha're and Sunny acted in every way like very good friends.

I checked on Sha're several times a day, and spent extra time with her when I fed her. It was clear she missed her fawn friends, even with Sunny to keep her company. On August 22, Sha're's legs again became partially paralyzed, though not nearly as severely as on July 7 and 29. Fortunately, I was still giving her thymus pills and cell salts, so the only symptom she had August 22 was walking with her front legs bent, as though the tendons in her joints had suddenly become contracted. She had trouble walking all that day, but by the next day, her legs were back to normal.

On the same afternoon (August 22), a friend's pet dove, ironically named Fawn because of her color, also became quite severely paralyzed. Fawn could not flap her wings, stand, or walk. Her owner called to ask if I would try to make her well. I said I would, adding Fawn to the other animals for which I was caring. She responded well to the electrolytes, cell salts, and MSM (methylsulfonylmethane, a natural sulfur) I tubed directly into her crop several times a day. I also had to feed her by tubing her, as she could not walk around or remain upright without being supported. Oddly she was able to fly before she could stand on her legs, but after about a week of intensive care, Fawn was completely well. When my friend came to take her home, I sent cell salts and electrolytes with her, with directions on how to use them. Fortunately, she never became paralyzed again. My friend sent me a Christmas card from Fawn each year for the rest of the little dove's life.

Several other animals, including dogs, horses, and calves were reported to have suffered sudden paralysis of the hind legs on August 22. I was not told whether those animals recovered. The two roosters I had treated after the July 29 episode became paralyzed again, this time much worse. My friend brought them back to me, but after many days of

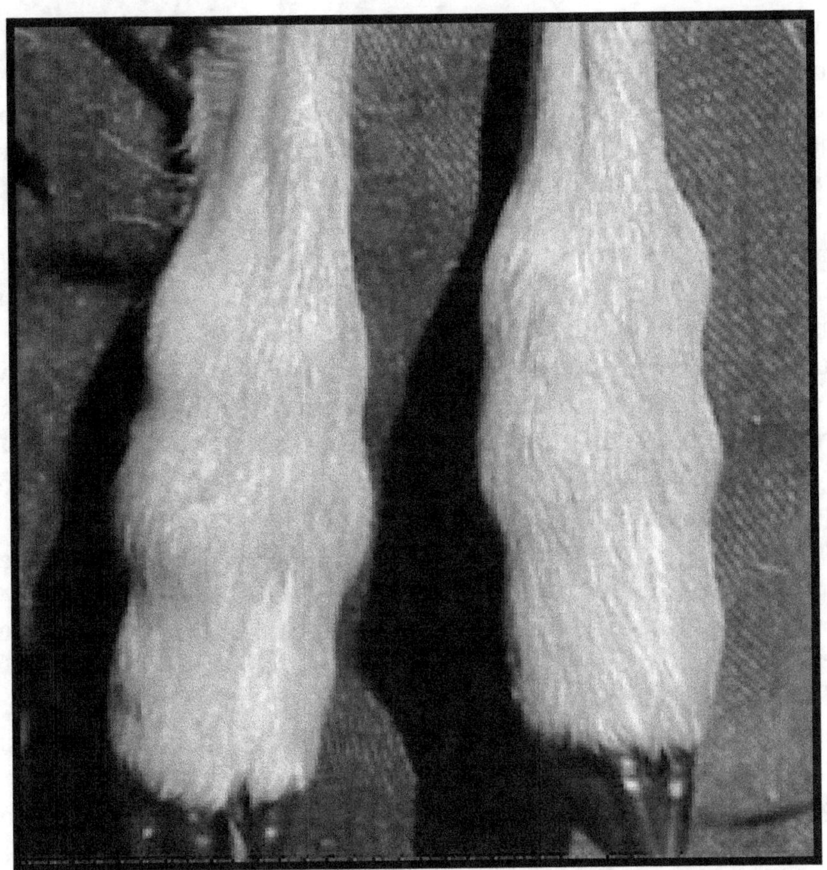

The swollen joints just above the hooves on Sha're's hind legs.

treatment, I was unable to make them well. The second bout of neurological damage to the roosters appeared much more severe than the first, as described by Rachel Carson in her book *Silent Spring*. The roosters had to be euthanized because they were unable to walk without falling.

We did not have a *Silent Spring* in 2003, but we certainly had a "paralyzing summer." Nurses reported to me that many people from Missoula and Ravalli Counties went to emergency rooms in Missoula and Hamilton on July 29 and August 22 with symptoms similar to those in wild and domestic animals, including some with partial paralysis. Most people had severe lower abdominal pain, as well as vomiting and diarrhea. Several doctors removed their patients' healthy appendix, thinking they had appendicitis. A few people reported to me that they had the same symptoms on those two days, but said they "toughed it out" at home without seeking medical attention. Neither doctors nor veterinarians had any explanation for the sudden bizarre symptoms.

I still do not know exactly what toxins made so many animals simultaneously exhibit such serious neurological effects. Whatever caused the symptoms must have been toxins carried on the wind, possibly from a state to the west of Montana. The area where symptoms occurred was so large the toxins could not have been from a single local event. I thought it was quite scary to have so many people and other animals affected at the same time, but officials, including those from county health departments, did not appear concerned. At least they were not concerned enough to ask the Environmental Protection Agency to do testing. If toxins are drifting with wind from other states, the EPA is the only one with jurisdiction to do anything about it. Local officials would have no control over what toxins are being applied in other states. Fortunately, we have not had another episode of neurological damage as severe as those that occurred in summer 2003. Because no testing was done, the cause of the paralysis and other symptoms was never determined.

Finally, on September 5, came the long-awaited day when Sha're could be released during the day with the other five fawns. Poor Sunny was very lonely without her, but Sha're liked being free to follow her fawn friends around our property. The male twins, Jack and Daniel, acted like big brothers, and Sha're never strayed far from them. Mac, the other male fawn, did not need another baby sister, since he already had two. The females, Sugar and Samantha, were both single fawns from different areas. Mac, Sugar, and Samantha were always together, so the six fawns acted like two sets of triplets.

The names of the fawns, except for Sugar, may sound familiar to some and, except for Sugar, all came from the Bitterroot Valley. I named Mac, the first to arrive, after MacGyver because I was a fan of the MacGyver television show. "How would MacGyver have done this?" is a question I frequently ask myself. Interestingly, a few people who have held a bird while I splinted a wing or leg have asked if I took lessons from MacGyver because of my unique methods.

One of the best MacGyverisms I have invented is using the hollow end of the shaft of a wing or tail feather to splint a bird's leg that is broken in the featherless, scaled area directly above the foot. I select a feather shaft slightly larger in diameter than the leg to be splinted. The shaft piece can easily be cut the right length with scissors. I cut the shaft in half, pad each piece, put a half on each side of the bird's broken leg and secure it with strapping tape. The feather piece must be larger in diameter than the leg to make room for the padding and not be too tight. Another long strip cut from the side of a feather shaft, a light stiff wire loop, stiff plastic strip, or stiff strip of Styrofoam cut from a Styrofoam tray should be taped on the outside of the leg, over the feather shaft splint, to keep the leg facing straight forward. The material used depends on the size and strength of the bird. It must be strong enough so the bird can't break it, but light enough so the bird can support itself and walk with the splinted leg. The outside support must go across the joint above the break and just past the foot. I splint the foot in a natural forward position and secure it so it can't twist sideways.

A feather shaft is extremely lightweight, but very strong. For small songbirds, wing feathers from a chicken, duck, hawk, or similar-sized bird are usually exactly the right size. Larger wing feathers from an eagle, hawk, turkey, or goose are just right to splint a shore bird, rail, magpie, jay, or other bird with a similar size leg.

For larger birds like crows, ravens, chickens, ducks, turkeys, geese, hawks, and owls, I use the plastic tubes that syringes come in to keep them sterile. I cut the correct sized tube in half or sometimes less than half, round the corners, pad each half, and tape the two pieces into position on each side of the break. As with the feather-shaft splints, a long strip of stiff but lightweight material must be taped on the outside of the leg across the joints to hold the leg straight. A feather shaft also works to splint a bird's wing tip. The halves of the shaft have to be trimmed to make a concave splint that, when padded, fits on each side of the broken wing tip bones. It seems quite appropriate that the best splinting material for certain broken bones on small birds is a larger bird's feather shaft. Even MacGyver would have to appreciate that.

In 2002, we had gotten a satellite dish to receive more television channels than our three local stations. One of the programs we could subsequently receive was Stargate SG1 on the SciFi Channel, starring none other than the star of MacGyver, Richard Dean Anderson. Stargate SG1 immediately became one of my favorite programs, prompting me to name the fawns we received in 2003 after characters on the show. Jack, the leader of the Stargate SG1 team, played by Anderson, and his team, consisting of Samantha, Daniel, and Teal'c, would travel to other planets through the Stargate. Daniel's wife, Sha're, lived on the first planet the team visited. The SG1 team often ended up saving all life on

Earth, and sometimes Earth itself, from being destroyed. Using white-tailed deer as a study animal, I had been working since 1996 to get people to understand there is something seriously wrong on our planet. If we do not get to work and save the living things here on Earth, humans will not survive. We do not have a Stargate or another livable planet available. Unfortunately, saving all life on Earth doesn't happen nearly as fast in real life as it does in fictional television shows.

The male fawn I named Teal'c had been hit by a car, which badly shattered a hind leg. Sadly, it did not heal properly, even with my giving him cell salts in his milk each feeding, so Teal'c had to be euthanized. That did not bode well for my deer fawn SG1 team. They were down by one member from the beginning. A study I found later said that transport of calcium into cells is seriously disrupted by endocrine disrupting toxins. The paralyzing summer of 2003 was not a good time to have a broken bone, since toxins were the likely cause of the paralysis episodes.

The female fawn (Sugar) came from Potomac, Montana, and was named prior to my receiving her. It is important that Sugar came from about 100 miles away from the Bitterroot Valley. She survived long enough to raise a single fawn and then four sets of twins, adding a significant supply of new genes into the white-tailed deer gene pool in northern Ravalli County. Because she had a lot of white on her legs above her hooves, Bob called her White-foot. She was one of his favorite deer of all those we raised. Of the six deer we released in 2003, Sugar, alias White-foot, was the only one to survive for seven years. My SG1 deer did not die saving the planet. They disappeared one by one over several hunting seasons, likely ending up in the neighbors' freezers. White-foot, to our dismay, vanished during the 2010 hunting season, the last of the group to go.

At night, I put Sha're back in the pen. Being small for her age, I didn't think she would be able to outrun coyotes or roaming dogs. She was always ready to go out in the morning, but did not hesitate to follow me back in at night. I fed Sha're as much goat milk formula as she would eat four times a day, hoping to help her catch up in size to the other fawns before the cold and snow of winter. She had her bunny friend, Sunny, to keep her company at night. The two were always together when Sha're was in the pen. When they lay down together to sleep, Sunny was usually snuggled tight under Sha're's chin.

At the end of September, I stopped putting Sha're in the deer pen at night. All of her normal-colored winter hair had grown in and she had not had a health problem of any kind in September. She stayed with Jack most of the time during October and November. He had learned to take care of himself quite well and was a good teacher for Sha're. Even the very cold weather at the end of October and first part of November didn't bother her. She survived hunting season, but poor Jack didn't. He was still a small fawn, but a neighbor shot him the last week of hunting season. After that, Sha're and Daniel were almost inseparable and remained together until spring. That was interestingly appropriate because in the SG1 TV show, Daniel and Sha're were husband and wife. By then, Sha're was a beautiful yearling doe with no evidence of the immune system dysfunctions that had plagued her as a youngster. Sadly for me, because I had become much too attached to her while working so hard to save her, she did not survive hunting season that fall.

About the time Sha're was killed in November 2004, my neighbor's 12-year-old daughter was diagnosed with Inflammatory Bowel Disease, which her doctor said was incurable. His prognosis was that it would be a problem for the rest of the girl's life. I told my neighbor Sha're's story and about her recovery after giving her the electrolytes and homeopathic cell salts. They decided to try what they called the "deer recipe." After taking one tablet of each of the cell salts every three hours and drinking a glass of the liquid electrolytes three times a day for a week, the girl was much better. Her original blood test had shown her primary health problem was liver damage. Three weeks later, a new blood test showed her liver had completely recovered. In a very grumpy tone, the doctor said she would likely get sick again. The girl continued taking the cell salts and her liver remained healthy. A few months later, the mother moved her family of two girls and a boy to London, England. The girl is now a young woman. The grumpy doctor was wrong in his prediction that she would again become ill with what he called Inflammatory Bowel Disease, because she never did.

Just like Firefly, Sha're proved that caring for deer fawns could do far more than provide deer for hunters to shoot. Caring for fawns and other wildlife can teach us how to help ourselves, and even more importantly, help others.

Clouds from the west bring
more than wind, rain, sleet, and snow.
They are clouds of death.

WHAT IS DEFORMING THE DEER

Enlarged hearts, underbite, and
Malformed reproductive gear;
For many years we've tried to
Find what is deforming the deer.

What happened to the porcupines?
Why did the toads disappear?
Rabbits and mink are declining,
And what is deforming the deer?

Rodents are dying painful deaths,
Their dying is nothing to cheer.
Damage to lungs and livers, caused
By what is deforming the deer.

Bird songs change so mates won't mate
And soon no songs will we hear.
What is deforming beaks and legs?
Find what is deforming the deer.

Less buzzing is now heard in spring.
What is making the bees disappear?
Pollinators are being killed
By what is deforming the deer.

Some children have trouble learning
What they need for their life's career.
To find the cause of damaged brains,
Find what is deforming the deer.

And what is harming children's lungs?
Please listen, and you will hear
Their tortured gasps for breath and ask,
If the cause is deforming the deer.

A baby's death soon after birth
Makes us stop and shed a tear.
To find why baby's life was short
Find what is deforming the deer.

Some insist there is nothing wrong,
To others it is quite clear
That all life is compromised
By what is deforming the deer.

We must not act in haste, you say?
It will be too late, I fear,
When no one is left to ask,
What is deforming the deer?

Males being born
now are affecting the rates
of reproduction.

House mice get severe nerve damage causing them to be unable to remain upright. Since 2007, I have found many deer mice, house mice, and meadow voles lying on their side unable to get up, often several a month.

This is a red squirrel eating while lying on her side photographed in 2013. She could not sit up to eat and tipped over when she tried. She remained on her side while eating. I tried to catch her to possibly mitigate the nerve damage. She escaped into a brush pile and I never saw her again.

Both before and after my short acquaintance with Elkie, the male elk calf with a crooked right front leg, I saw and documented many types of malformations in young of multiple mammal and bird species from western Montana. Some of them had crooked or otherwise malformed legs like Elkie's. Some were missing toes. Others had swollen or weak joints like both of Elkie's hind legs and the hind legs of several deer fawns. Interestingly, if only one leg was affected, it was most often on the right side. However at least a few always do the opposite of what is done by the majority.

Several years ago, a white-tailed deer fawn was born on our land with no toes on her left hind foot. I first saw her as a newborn with her mother. The young doe eventually grew a short strip of keratin along the top edge where her toes should have been. She limped, but managed to survive for four years. A friend sent me photos of a doe born in another part of Ravalli County with the same malformation. It was her right hind foot on which toes had not formed, following the usual pattern of the malformation being on that side. Occasionally, only the right front leg on a mammal is affected, usually being crooked or bowed because of disrupted bone development.

Some animals, especially young birds, have nerve damage causing them to be unable to open and close a foot. Since 1995, rehabbers have received a number of birds with nerve-damaged or malformed feet and legs. The right leg or foot was typically more seriously deformed or had more severe nerve damage than the left. When wings were malformed, both were often similarly affected. Some birds, such as ducks and geese, have weakened tendons causing the wing tip to point out to the side; when only one wing was affected, it was usually the right side. The same was true when only one wing of a fledgling had underdeveloped feathers.

Since 1996, individuals of several bird species were observed with an entire leg not formed during development. On every bird reported to me or that I personally examined with that malformation, the right leg was missing and there was no stump or projection where the leg should have been. The species I observed with their right leg missing included Mourning Dove, female Ring-necked Pheasant, Black-billed Magpie, Rock Pigeon, American Crow, and most recently in winter 2015-16, Slate-sided Junco. All were adults who were surviving despite having to hop and perch on one leg, apparently after learning to do so as fledglings. Additionally, on all the hatchling birds who came to me to be rehabilitated with legs or feet on both sides malformed, the right leg or foot was more severely affected than the left.

The right side was also more often deformed on toads I saw with birth defects. One young western toad found in our yard in 1997 had no foot formed on the right hind leg; another in 1998 had almost no toes on the right hind foot. Researchers studying frogs who were missing portions of a hind leg, foot, or toes, found far more with malformations on the right side than on the left. Even the underdeveloped, malformed eye in a western toad who lived in our yard in 2013, 2014, and 2015 was on the right. The toad was an adult when I first found it, so was at least four years old when I last saw it in spring 2015.

Humans reported their right side being affected by neurological damage on several occasions. For example, one morning in 2001, my father called to say my mother was not feeling well, asking me to take her to the hospital. She could not get out of bed because her whole right side was paralyzed. I drove to their house, which was not far from the hospital in Hamilton, Montana. By the time I arrived, she was beginning to have mobility in her right arm and leg, so she could walk with a person on each side to support her. Dad and I both thought she might have had a stroke, but the emergency room doctor couldn't find anything wrong with her. Her right side was continuing to recover motion and feeling. By the time we returned to my parent's home, Mom's right arm and leg were working normally. She was 88 years old at the time.

In a phone conversation the next day, a friend who also lived near Hamilton told me her right side was completely paralyzed when she tried to get out of bed the morning before, at exactly the same time my mother's right side was affected. My friend was 55 years old. She simply remained in bed until the problem went away in a short time. We never found what caused the paralysis. I eventually heard about one other person, a woman in her 20s, who had the same problem on the morning of the same day. Interestingly, even though age didn't seem to be a factor, all the people I knew of with those symptoms on that particular day were female.

Even more astounding to my scientist friends, was the malformation John Faust found on stone fly nymphs in spring 1997. Approximately 5% of those he caught along the Bitterroot River for his study on Squalla Stone Flies had much shorter legs on one side, almost always on the right. The left legs on the malformed nymphs were normal in length. All three segments found on a nymph leg were completely formed on both right and left legs, but on the abnormal legs, all segments were shorter than normal. When nymphs with short legs on one side changed into adult stone flies, they retained the shortened segments.

It is quite concerning that mammals, birds, amphibians, and insects all would have the right side more severely and/or more often affected than the left side, and in such a similar manner. Since the left side of the brain directs limbs on the right side of the body, it seems to be predominantly targeted. It appears something in the environment is able to disrupt specific gene signals and severely affect normal growth and nerve function, particularly on the right side. This phenomenon is especially interesting and deeply concerning because young and adults of so many species are being similarly affected, often causing damage that lasts for life, if they survive to have a life.

**Developing young
plus multiple pesticides
equals birth defects.**

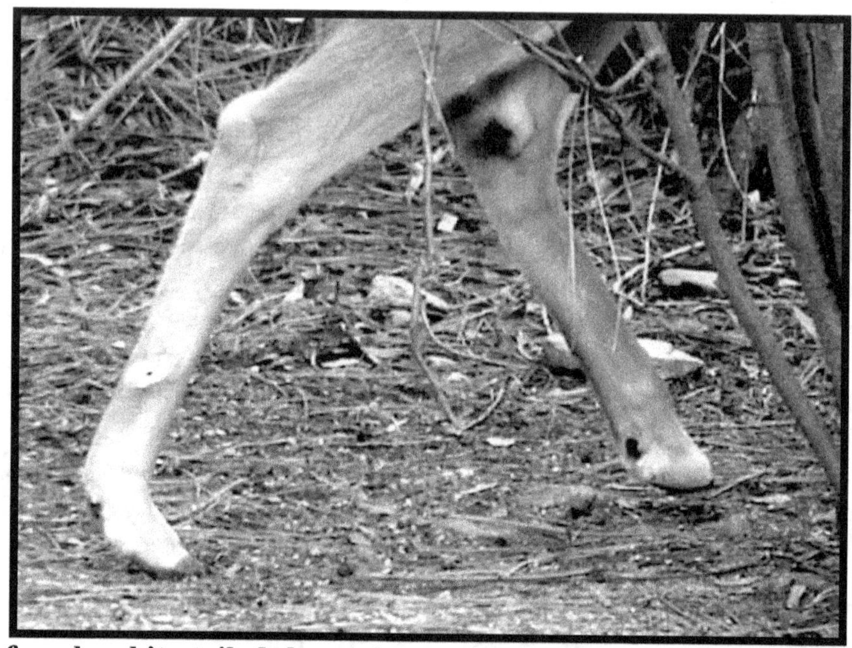

A female white-tailed deer who was born on our land with no toe bones on the left hind foot. There was a short strip of keratin at what should have been the top of the hoof wall.

CHAPTER 18
PERCHES AND COLD HUMMINGBIRDS

Early one cold morning in spring 1983, Bob discovered something was happening to hummingbirds who came to drink at our feeders. Like most bird lovers, we had hummingbird feeders on our porch and delighted in watching the Rufous, Calliope, and Black-chinned Hummingbirds who come to nest here in western Montana each spring. All of our feeders had perches on which birds could sit while drinking sugar water from holes in the feeder. Like everyone at that time, we assumed using commercially made feeders with perches helps the birds, and certainly would not harm them, as long as the mixture provided is fresh and contains only one part sugar to four parts water. More sugar causes liver and kidney damage.

As early risers, we had noted Rufous Hummingbirds were also early birds, often coming for their breakfast of cold sugar water during the coolest time of day, sometimes an hour and a half before sunrise. We did not often see Calliope and Black-chinned Hummingbirds at the feeders until just before the sun came up.

At about 5:30 one cold morning, when it was barely light enough to see, Bob watched as a male Rufous Hummingbird sat on the feeder perch and gorged himself on ice-cold sugar water. Then, to Bob's amazement, the bird fluffed up, slowly tipped over backward, and fell to the ground. Bob rushed out and carefully picked up the tiny bird, finding it still breathing but very cold. He warmed the bird by holding it in cupped hands and blowing warm breath into the bird's feathers. After 10 or 15 minutes, the hummer had warmed enough to regain its ability to fly normally and Bob released it. Always curious, I followed the bird around from a distance, watching it through binoculars as the sun began to show over the mountains to the east. The little bird's behavior appeared natural and its flight was normal, showing no ill effects from its likely brush with death.

After the sun came up that morning, I looked all around the house and yard in case there were any more hummingbirds on the ground. Sadly, I found one who appeared to have died the morning before. We had to warm three or more birds each morning during the following week of close observation from 4:30 to 7:00 a.m. They would land on a perch, drink cold sugar water, and then either hang upside down from the perch after tipping over, or fall from the perch to the ground. We couldn't find any reason for their behavior except being too cold to fly.

Bob decided to remove perches from the feeders. He wanted to see whether forcing birds to hover while drinking cold sugar water would keep them from becoming hypothermic. He continued to watch from 4:30 till after sunup to see what effect the lack of perches would have on the birds' behavior. The hummingbirds seemed to have no trouble feeding while hovering. They would take a few sips of the cold fluid and fly to their favorite branch to sit and preen between feeding trips. When they wanted more sugar water, they flew back to hover while pulling the cold fluid into their crops with their long thin tongues, then zipped back to their branch or flew out of our sight in the bushes. In the all the years since removing perches, we have not observed another cold or incapacitated hummingbird at our feeders.

Curious about injured hummingbirds I had received for care, I checked my records, finding mostly Rufous, with a few Calliopes. The injuries were predominantly caused by being bitten by cats or dogs, usually early in the morning in spring. That was an ominous pattern.

Hummingbirds hover when feeding on natural foods in the wild. When they fly from flower to flower, they get only a small drop or two of cold nectar from each one. That is much different than drinking a cropful of cold fluid from a feeder containing an unlimited amount of chilled sugar water. Actually, the tiny birds can ingest several cropfuls of cold sugar water without ever moving from a feeder perch, resulting in a significant drop in the bird's core temperature and acute hypothermia, often leading to their death.

Humans added perches to feeders to allow for easier viewing, with no consideration of consequences to hummingbirds. Birds who remain perched while drinking two or three cropfuls of cold sugar water are not generating heat energy needed to warm the fluid or their muscles. In addition, they are ingesting much larger quantities than they can obtain from a flower. Obviously, when they fly from flower to flower, their muscles produce enough heat to maintain a normal body temperature and warm the small amount of nectar they get from each flower.

If sugar water and outside temperature are in the 30s or low 40s, a hummingbird's temperature is lowered as much as 10 degrees or more by each drink from the feeder. After two cropfuls without flying to generate heat and warm their core temperature, it is lowered enough to affect their muscles. The birds are then no longer capable of normal flight, so are unable fly enough to warm themselves. Soon they are suffering from severe hypothermia and can't fly at all. When they become hypothermic, many remain motionless on the perch or tip over to hang upside down from the perch. Some fall to the ground, becoming easy prey for crows, magpies, cats, dogs, or other predators. We named this phenomenon Perch Hypothermia.

We surmised that Rufous Hummingbirds, who usually feed early in the morning, are more likely than other hummingbird species to experience Perch Hypothermia. However, several others, including Calliope, Ruby-throated, and Anna's Hummingbird have been reported with it by observers throughout the United States and Canada.

A hummingbird who becomes so hypothermic it cannot maintain normal flight or falls to the ground, unable to fly at all, is apt to end up dead. They can be accidently stepped on by large mammals or become breakfast for a cat, magpie, or crow. If they lie on the cold ground too long before the sun comes up and warms them, or if the weather is cloudy, thus remaining cool long after sunrise, the birds will eventually die of hypothermia or starvation, even if they are not found by a predator. That is what appeared to have happened to the dead hummingbird I found when we first observed Perch Hypothermia at our feeders. People usually do not get up early enough to watch hummingbirds feed between 4:30 and sunrise, so they do not observe them exhibiting Perch Hypothermia. Because hypothermic hummers are usually snatched up and eaten, no evidence remains by the time most people get up.

An early-rising biologist who taught at the University of Montana reported watching a Rufous Hummingbird feeding right outside his office window, while drinking his morning coffee. It was 7:00 on a cool, cloudy spring day. The bird sat on the perch and drank several times. When it tried to fly, it went downward, almost to the ground and out of sight around a corner. Being a biologist, the man thought he should find the bird and determine why it wasn't able to maintain flight. Before he could even put his cup down, a cat came into view around the same corner where the hummingbird had fluttered just above the ground out of sight. The cat had killed the incapacitated bird and was carrying it in its mouth. The biologist related this observation to me soon after it happened.

Another man from an eastern state wrote a letter to a magazine for bird watchers, saying he found what he thought was a dead Ruby-throated Hummingbird on the sidewalk under his feeder. He was on his way to his car to go to work, so was in a hurry. Without checking to see if the tiny bird was actually dead, he dropped it into a nearby garbage can and closed the lid. After reading about Perch Hypothermia, he was devastated to think the little hummingbird he had put into the garbage can may have still been alive. Being put in a closed garbage can is much like being buried alive. Even if the hummingbird warmed up and became active, without food it would not have remained alive for long.

Having rehabilitated wildlife in Montana for over 45 years, I have cared for quite a number of Rufous and Calliope Hummingbirds. Over that time period, I have observed hundreds of hummingbirds in the wild and several dozen in captivity. One observation is that Rufous Hummingbirds nearly always go into their torpid state at night, even when they are in a warm room or provided with extra heat, such as a heating pad on low under their box. Calliope and Black-chinned Hummingbirds do not usually go torpid when they are kept warm. They simply go to sleep at night.

I found, by doing a simple experiment with two different, permanently-injured Rufous Hummingbirds, how easy it is to initiate hypothermia in this species, causing the birds to quickly become unresponsive. Neither of those I used for the experiment could fly because one wing was badly damaged. Both eventually had to be euthanized when it became evident they would never fly again. I tried the experiment on the first bird in 1997 and repeated it when I received the second permanently injured bird in 1998. I wanted to make certain the behaviors I observed with the first bird were unequivocally caused by cold sugar water and not because of a health issue.

I tried to do everything the same with both birds, with the sugar water and outside temperature as close to the same as possible each time. For both trials, I took the hummingbird outside on a cool, cloudy day when air temperature was between 40 and 46 degrees Fahrenheit. I put the bird on a low branch of a bush, so it would not be hurt if it fell. After just one drink of 45-degree sugar water, the hummingbird's feathers quickly fluffed up and it became quite lethargic. In both trials, the bird ceased to look around or pay attention to its surroundings. It just sat motionless with its bill pointed upward. In 10 minutes, I allowed the bird to drink more cold sugar water. After the second time, it became completely unresponsive and didn't move even when I touched it.

In both trials, as soon as the bird became visibly hypothermic and didn't respond to movement, sound, or being touched, I took it into our house to warm it. Obviously, it was also important to determine whether the affected hummer could regain normal behavior after being warmed. With both birds, it took nearly 15 minutes of sitting on a warm cloth over a heating pad before the bird was warm enough to resume normal behavior. After each bird had warmed, it fluttered up onto a small branch I had pushed through the sides of the box for a perch and began to preen its feathers. After preening, the bird went to the syringe containing approximately 79-degree sugar water and began to feed as usual.

After two hours inside to make certain each bird had completely recovered, I again took it outside and put it on the low bush. When the hummingbird being tested wanted to feed, I let it drink from the syringe filled with 45-degree sugar water. Again, with one drink the bird fluffed up and pointed its bill upwards, becoming much less alert and somewhat unresponsive. As in the first test, after the second drink the bird became completely unresponsive and had to be taken inside and put on the heating pad to warm it.

When each bird was acting normally again, I put it on the branch outside for another experiment. For this test, I took a syringe of 80-degree sugar water for it to drink. The bird's behavior remained completely normal even after several drinks and over a half hour sitting outside in the cold. They did not fluff their feathers and both continued to look around at the wild birds and other things of interest to them. After each had fed six times on warm sugar water, with no observable adverse effect, I took it back to its box in the house.

The purpose of doing the same experiment with each of the two flightless, but otherwise healthy, hummingbirds was to determine whether it would become hypothermic if it remained quietly sitting on a perch while drinking more than one cropful of cold sugar water. The results of both experiments with different hummingbirds in different years were the same. They became cold, with feathers fluffed, and were completely unresponsive after just two drinks of the 45-degree sugar water, which was close to the same temperature as the outside air. I kept both birds for several days after the tests to be certain there were no adverse effects from the experiments or a health problem that might have affected their behavior during the experiments.

People in many states have observed hummingbirds who fell directly to the ground, tipped over to hang upside down from the perch, or fluttered frantically just above the ground because their wings did not work properly. Even if the hypothermic condition does not result in the death of a female hummingbird, it can result in the death of embryos developing in her eggs or of her hatchlings left cold and unprotected in the nest. Being hypothermic until the sun warms a bird so it can fly prevents female hummingbirds from returning to nests to warm eggs or hatchlings in a timely manner. The resulting mortality to young birds and consequent nesting failures could significantly contribute to declines in our hummingbird populations. Perches on hummingbird feeders may be responsible for thousands or even millions of hummingbird deaths each year. Simply removing them from feeders completely eliminates this horrific and totally unnecessary danger to the birds.

Another consideration is that each species of hummingbird has slightly different thermodynamics, as does each individual bird, depending upon its condition and whether it has been exposed to hormone disrupting environmental toxins. This does not justify causing those individual birds to incur an unnecessary premature death or serious injury as a result of feeding while perched, the only purpose of which is to make birds easier for people to see. Providing hummingbirds with supplementary food in feeders is supposed to help them, especially when nectar from natural flowers is in limited supply and while adults and juveniles are fattening up for their long migration. Attracting hummingbirds by supplemental feeding can provide many hours of enjoyable bird watching, and can be beneficial to hummingbirds if their welfare is always the primary consideration.

In 1988, I launched a crusade to inform the public about Perch Hypothermia. I wrote to ornithologists, outdoor magazines, bird magazines, and local newspapers. I was ridiculed and called unpleasant names; even some scientists said Perch Hypothermia could not possibly happen. Eventually, I found and consulted with hummingbird researchers in Texas. They had done studies that showed scientifically, under completely controlled laboratory conditions, that the flight muscles of Ruby-throated Hummingbirds were adversely affected by sitting motionless on a perch while consuming cold fluid; as a result, the birds could not maintain flight. Many people still claimed there was no

When a lively, healthy, but permanently flightless Rufous Hummingbird was given cold sugar water to drink while sitting on a branch on a cloudy day with a 42 degree outside temperature, it fluffed up its feathers and became unresponsive, a condition we named Perch Hypothermia.

scientific proof of our "Perch Hypothermia hypothesis." Hypothermia has long been a proven physical fact and has not been a hypothesis for centuries. It was well understood by ice age people.

Why is it so difficult for modern humans to admit that hypothermia can happen to a tiny bird? Why do not companies who manufacture and sell hummingbird feeders have to prove feeders with perches are safe for hummingbirds? That should have been done prior to putting them on the market.

Something that was not around to affect humans or birds during the ice age, and likely a major factor affecting a present-day hummingbird's ability to maintain adequate body temperature, is exposure to pesticides. Simultaneous combinations of herbicides, fungicides, and insecticides are especially disruptive to a bird's cellular functions. In studies done on adult chickens (much larger than hummingbirds) deliberately exposed to pesticide combinations (especially herbicides and insecticides, or herbicides and fungicides, or all three simultaneously) the chickens became paralyzed or died. Pesticide exposure has also been shown by studies to cause mitochondrial dysfunction, affecting an animal's ability to maintain normal heat and energy. Thus, it would be reasonable to assume a hummingbird recently exposed to pesticide combinations would be more susceptible to hypothermia than a healthy, unexposed bird.

In spring 1983, when Bob first saw hummingbirds becoming hypothermic, many calves were dying of Weak Calf Syndrome. Also, I received many hatchling birds of a variety of species with severe developmental malformations each spring between 1981 and 1985. Some of the worst I observed occurred in 1983, the year Bob discovered that Perch Hypothermia was seriously affecting hummingbirds at our feeders. The malformations at that time happened during development in the egg and included malformed or missing legs, feet, wing bones, bills, and eyes. The EPA banned two extremely harmful pesticides in 1985. One was a cancer-causing herbicide, 2,4,5-T, and the other was an insecticide called endrin that was found to cause brain damage, birth defects, and cancer. After that, problems with hummingbirds becoming hypothermic at feeders with perches appeared to lessen, judging by the number I received with injuries caused by cats and dogs. Most telling was that not one young bird of any species I received for rehabilitation between 1986 and 1996 had a malformation. This strongly indicated that endrin and 2,4,5-T were most likely responsible for the malformations rehabbers had observed in hatchling birds in the early 1980s. They also were likely instrumental in mitochondrial disruption, especially in small birds, causing hummingbirds to be more easily affected by hypothermia.

Endrin is a chlorinated hydrocarbon closely related to DDT, which was banned in 1972 after nearly causing the extinction of several bird species, especially our national bird, the Bald Eagle. Extensive use of endrin on forests and fields was extremely concerning to officials of the U.S. Fish and Wildlife Service, bird hunters, and bird watchers. It caused multiple adverse effects in Whooping Cranes, all waterfowl, Bald Eagles, falcons, game birds, and other birds. High levels of endrin were found in the meat of waterfowl and game birds harvested and used for food by hunters, which affected hunting license sales and businesses who sell to hunters. There were also concerns about the levels of endrin in meat from beef cattle.

When complaints were made concerning the public not being informed of the widespread nature of problems caused by endrin, Gordon McOmber, director of the Montana Department of Agriculture, denied the accusations against endrin and said there was "no need to notify the public immediately." He also stated the charge of birth defects in children "that they can't prove" was used by opponents of herbicide and insecticide use. And he said the problem should not be viewed in terms of "what endrin might do to a fish" because "if endrin had not been sprayed, the cutworm could have devastated Montana's agricultural economy by destroying the wheat crop." Obviously, he considered the

An immature hummingbird with an underdeveloped upper bill photographed by Amy Farrell in Stevensville, MT in summer 2010.

wheat crop to be far more important than the millions of humans, domestic animals, and wildlife, including fish, adversely affected or killed by exposure to the excessive amounts of endrin used on wheat crops at that time.

The poisoning of animals was likely compounded by simultaneous extensive use of two herbicides, 2,4-D and 2,4,5-T, better known as Agent Orange, which was blamed for, and eventually proven to be the cause of, cancers and health problems in U.S. soldiers and Vietnamese civilians. Many people exposed to Agent Orange, including American soldiers, also later had children with debilitating, life-threatening birth defects.

Picloram, another herbicide, was mixed half and half with 2,4-D for use in Vietnam as Agent White, which was sprayed extensively in the same areas where Agent Orange had been used to achieve more complete defoliation. In the early 1980s, the Agent White combination was applied on pastures and roadsides throughout western United States. Not likely a coincidence, there were extremely high rates of Weak Calf Syndrome in cattle herds in all the states where endrin, 2,4-D, 2,4,5-T, and picloram were used simultaneously, as well as in states downwind of where those chemicals were used.

The problem of Perch Hypothermia seems to have again become more prevalent in hummingbirds since 1994. This coincides exactly with extensive use of multiple fungicides, especially chlorothalonil in summer 1994, and the sudden exceedingly high use of Roundup® in spring 1996. Malformed bills on hummingbirds indicate they are not immune to what is causing multiple symptoms of thyroid hormone disruption in mammals and birds since 1994. Besides causing developmental defects, hypothyroidism seriously affects an animal's ability to properly regulate its body temperature because it disrupts normal mitochondrial functions. Therefore, it is obvious that hummingbirds exposed to multiple hormone disrupting toxins would more quickly become hypothermic after ingesting cold sugar water when outside temperatures are cool.

Many people who have built homes in urban and rural areas maintain large numbers of hummingbird feeders with perches in their yards. Everyone, especially in northern United States and Canada, should remove all perches or not put up hummingbird feeders at all. Also, those who deliberately attract hummingbirds to their property should never use pesticides of any kind to avoid harming their tiny guests. Planting a variety of nectar-containing flowers that bloom throughout summer and fall is especially good for the hummingbirds and also helps native pollinators and honeybees thrive.

Unfortunately, after 30 years of trying to have the problem of Perch Hypothermia addressed, companies that make hummingbird feeders still have not removed perches and have refused to put a warning on the feeder. Since 1983, the Rufous Hummingbird population has declined precipitously and if they continue to decline at the present rate, sadly they will likely be extinct by 2037. If anecdotal reports are correct, individuals of several other hummingbird species are also succumbing to Perch Hypothermia. Unfortunately, money talks much louder than dead hummingbirds. Dead hummingbirds can't even squeak.

**When hummingbirds drink
cold fluid while perched, chilled wing
muscles stop working.**

CANARIES

Killed in April, nineteen ninety-six
But not one of Mother Nature's tricks,
A buck with no scrotum met its fate.
In life, it could not successfully mate.
One of the more serious malformations
Now being observed in many nations.
Spread everywhere by rain and snow,
Hormone disruption is easy to show,

With amphibian researchers all agog,
Action was swift for a malformed frog.
When DDT caused malformed shells,
It was banned. But something smells,
When only a few have made a fuss about
Malformations in mammals like us.
 Sadly, the cover-up has been extensive
And proving cause is quite expensive.

Few people listen to what deer say,
As they watch their loved ones taken away
By cancer, diabetes, or heart disease.
Pay attention to the "canaries" please.
We have only one planet for all to live.
If it is poisoned, what will we give
To the next generation, to be passed on?
And what will be left when we are gone?

Canaries drop dead,
alerting miners their lives
are in grave danger.

CHAPTER 19
CHANGING BISON

It has been estimated there were once between 40 and 60 million bison living on the North American continent. Extensive massacres of these magnificent animals occurred because some people decided it was great sport to kill them for no ethical or even logical reason. Shooting bison just to watch them fall, market hunting, and hide collecting almost drove them to extinction by the late 1800s. Similar to what was done to the Passenger Pigeon and the Eskimo Curlew, all those millions of bison were slaughtered with little or no objection from people who did not actively engage in the wanton destruction. By 1900, plains bison were severely endangered, with just over 50 remaining in all of North America. That the population of a large mammal was deliberately decimated from 50,000,000 to 50 in just a few years is a tragedy that has been difficult for me to understand since I learned about it as a child. It is still incomprehensible that people would not want their children to see, enjoy, and learn from the same wild animals that they had. Even now, over a hundred years later, reckless greed and inexplicable stupidity still prevail over concern for future generations.

The 350,000 plains bison (*Bison bison*) alive today on ranches and in national parks and preserves are descendants of those last remaining few. Today, some herds are not genetically pure, having been contaminated by cattle genes in attempts by ranchers to cross bison with domestic cattle (*Bos taurus*). The intention was to develop a hardier breed of cattle who could better survive the harsh conditions on North American plains.

Twenty-three of the original surviving bison took refuge in high-mountain back country in what is now Yellowstone National Park. In 1880, explorers who observed bison living in the Lamar, Pelican, and Firehole valleys called them mountain bison and their descendants are still often referred to that way. At least 300 of them are thought to be now living between Pelican Valley in the winter and Mirror Plateau in the summer. It is likely those bison are descendants of the original 23 survivors who remained in the park.

After almost all bison were annihilated, 21 of the so-called plains bison who had been saved were released into the Lamar Valley in the northern part of Yellowstone Park. The ones referred to as mountain bison are shy and much more afraid of people than those introduced into Yellowstone from the plains. Bison living in high mountain habitats remain in their remote range year around. In recent years, the park has allowed human encroachment to reduce their once isolated range to about half what it was.

People concerned about the unique characteristics of mountain bison are recognizing that they should be conserved and protected because they look different physically, live in a forested, high mountain habitat, and have their own unique behaviors. Because of these factors, some have regarded them as a distinct subspecies. However, if there are actual genetic differences between mountain bison and plains bison, they were not found in genetic studies of several different herds in Yellowstone National Park. Conducted by Wilson and Strobeck in 1999, their study found no genetic difference between those identified as mountain bison in Yellowstone and descendants of the plains bison who were introduced to the park, and are now the most common bison in Yellowstone. Their paper stated, "If mountain bison existed and made a significant contribution to the gene pool of the bison at Yellowstone National Park, we would expect this population to be on a branch by itself or amongst the wood bison populations, as both mountain bison and wood bison were considered *Bison bison athabascae*. The genetic distances between the Yellowstone bison and the other populations would also be expected to be larger. As neither of these is supported by our results, the bison indigenous to Yellowstone were probably not mountain bison, but rather plains bison driven to the area by hunters." The "area" referred to is the forested high mountain habitat.

One of the purposes of this book is to show how epigenetic changes can influence the appearance and abilities of an individual as much or more than genes inherited from its parents. One hypothesis, with which I agree, is that the animals called mountain bison have changed their behavior and have a visible difference in taxonomic structure from bison living on the plains because of the long-term influence of their high mountain habitat, including adverse weather conditions. Similar epigenetic changes in other animals are well known and extensively documented. Adaptive changes without changing the actual genetic makeup would be expected to take place in herds of plains bison who had lived in a cold, mountainous habitat for many generations. Such epigenetic changes could easily include differences in both appearance and behavior, but would not be expected to cause changes in the bison's DNA.

The most recent epigenetic changes in looks and abilities of individual bison in Yellowstone National Park are not conducive to long-term survival of affected animals. Such changes, caused by a combination of Sonic Hedgehog and other gene disruption, mineral deficiencies, and thyroid hormone disruption during fetal development have resulted in the same birth defects we documented on other ruminants. For example, Yellowstone now has a higher number of male bison with a short, misaligned scrotum than with a normal-length, bilateral scrotum.

In addition to genital malformations, there is a high prevalence of underdeveloped facial bones in bison. In 2002, a man who cleaned and bleached bison heads to resell said that at least one-third of those he received for cleaning had an underbite. Many of the heads came from Yellowstone bison who were either hunter-killed or rounded up and taken to slaughter after leaving the park during winter. These observations indicate bison fetuses are being exposed to biologically significant levels of environmental toxins. If enough members of a species are simultaneously affected by such adverse epigenetic changes to their biological makeup, the survival of the entire population could be in jeopardy. Fortunately, that threshold has not yet been reached for Yellowstone bison, since the population is still increasing.

Animals who descended from the 21 introduced plains bison often migrate out of the park during harsh winters. In some recent years, they have been slaughtered in record numbers. During winter 2008, almost half the total number of bison in Yellowstone National Park were rounded up and sent to slaughter or died. Butchered bison were probably not examined for malformations. If they had been, birth defects should have been observed and reported. Ideally, bison with normal bite and genitalia should never be sent to slaughter. Only animals with malformations should be culled. That would hopefully help keep adverse epigenetic changes from being passed on to new bison generations.

Each year for over 20 years, Bob and I have gone to Yellowstone during spring and fall. Beginning in 2007, I tried to locate and photograph a bison with a normal scrotum. I have seen a few normal males, but they were always moving too rapidly or were too far away to photograph with my small camera. I have taken photos of many large male bison with almost no scrotum, and even more with the now extremely common misaligned hemiscrota, in which the left side is formed directly forward of the right one. In 2017, in a total of 17 different photographed bison, six (35%) had no scrotum, seven times higher than what is supposed to raise a red flag concerning a birth defect. The scrotum on a male bison used to be easily observed because, prior to 1995, it was long enough to hold the large testes away from the body wall. Also, the two hemiscrota on all male bison used to be bilateral with the midline of the body running between the two sides. A scrotum with normal configuration on a male bison is now difficult to find in Yellowstone National Park.

Calves born to bison in Lamar Valley are particularly affected by both underbite and malformed male genitalia, and thus some may have one or more of the other adverse epigenetic changes documented in newborn mammals. The so-called mountain bison living in high mountain habitats in Yellowstone are not readily visible, so there is no way for me to know whether they are being affected. Quite often, I have seen malformations on calves and adult bison in documentaries filmed in Yellowstone, but there is no mention as to whether those pictured are the bison considered to be mountain or plains varieties.

A documentary made by a biologist who spent many days each year observing and filming bison in all seasons in Yellowstone recorded food preferences, travel routes, and seasonal habitats of various herds. In a portion of the documentary, a calf walking beside its mother had an underbite so severe it could not close its mouth. I took a photo of that calf on our television screen on pause, so I could view it better. Besides having an easily observed underbite, the protruding incisors at the front of the calf's lower jaw were extremely crooked and widely spaced. Abnormal placement of the lower incisors is caused by disruption of specific Sonic Hedgehog genes, which dictate the location of tooth buds in a developing fetus.

It is hard to understand how the youngster was able to suckle and even more so, why the biologist who took the video did not see its severe underbite. The calf likely did not survive to adulthood because it would have been difficult for it to bite off enough forage to thrive after weaning. Fortunately, predators usually select weakened animals, which tends to eliminate many of those born with adverse epigenetic changes. Over 80% of the predator-killed big game animals found between 1998 and 2010 by Gary Cargile had a fairly severe underbite. He is a friend and naturalist who collects skulls and antlers from predator-killed adult male cervids (deer species). This suggests that wolves and mountain lions are selecting prey with an underbite during the winter.

Gary Haas is a wildlife biologist who cleans skulls for big game hunters. When he worked with us on our study to determine rates of underbite in game animals, Gary found between 40% and 60% of the heads from hunter-killed male animals (including elk, white-tailed deer, mule deer, pronghorn antelope, bighorn sheep, and moose) brought for cleaning in recent years have underdeveloped facial bones resulting in either underbite or overbite. Haas's examination of adult big game heads shows that many animals born with undesirable epigenetic changes are surviving to adulthood. Thus, surviving adults may be passing underbite to their young, since epigenetic changes can be inherited through several generations without changing the DNA. Even a mild underbite in large numbers of a wild grazing animal population is not advantageous to the survival of that population.

Serious symptoms of fetal hypothyroidism in Yellowstone's bison are extremely concerning. If the last 300 genetically pure bison with epigenetic adaptations for living in high mountain habitat are being affected similarly to bison adapted to living on the plains, it is an indisputable tragedy. In the deep snow and harsh winters high in the mountains of Yellowstone National Park, being unable to procure adequate nourishment because of underbite could result in extirpation of the bison who have epigenetically adapted to living in that habitat.

It also doesn't help for a high percentage of mature male bison to be unable to produce viable sperm because they were born with a short, malformed scrotum. Lower temperatures are required for spermatogenesis in mammals; a short or absent scrotum results in testes remaining too close to the higher temperature of the body wall, reducing sperm production and/or viability. On mature males born with underdeveloped external genitalia, the testes are normal in size and produce normal testosterone. Thus, a bull may grow large enough to defeat other males and become a herd bull, while being unable to produce calves due to infertility. Cows bred by such males often do not get pregnant so are bred again a month or sometimes almost two months late. If a bull with viable sperm eventually breeds such cows, the resultant late calves are more susceptible to predators immediately after birth. Also, they are often unable to grow large enough or put on adequate fat in time to survive the harsh Yellowstone winter. This is especially true in high elevations where deep snow is present for much of the year.

Estrogenic or anti-androgenic toxins, and especially a combination of those, cause another birth defect that affects reproduction by reducing testes size and often preventing them from descending away from the kidney area where they are first formed in a fetus. Having small or undescended testes affects the animal's testosterone production, and is the type of hormone disruption most often researched and therefore discussed by the news media. Malformations in bison and other mammals with the specific reproductive birth defects we have documented are not consistent with sex hormone disruption. The misaligned, malformed hemiscrota are consistent with disruption of Sonic Hedgehog genes. Scrotal underdevelopment is caused by zinc deficiency and thyroid hormone disruption.

Beginning in 1995, our study animal, white-tailed deer, had a sex ratio in favor of males at an average of 60 males to 40 females through 2003; it then returned closer to the normal 48 females to 52 males. In bison herds, having high numbers of large bulls competing with cows and calves for food, especially in winter, does not enhance the survival of young calves or the growth and survival of fetuses carried by pregnant cows. Fortunately, bison in Yellowstone do not appear to be affected by the serious population declines observed in mule deer, moose, mountain goat, and bighorn sheep.

Possibly wildlife managers and park superintendents have chosen to ignore the birth defects in the Yellowstone bison herd because their population is not in decline and, in fact, appears to be increasing each year. In fall 2002, I personally handed the park's head wildlife biologist a copy of our study concerning the high rate of underdeveloped genitalia and skewed sex ratio in white-tailed deer. I explained to park biologists at that meeting, and on several occasions since, that I continue to see similar malformations in park wildlife, especially the very visible bull bison. I also gave them our 2011 study concerning underdeveloped facial bones in ruminant species. They appear to have completely disregarded what our studies reported, even though wild ruminants, including bison, mule deer, bighorn sheep, pronghorn antelope, and moose in the park have the same easily observable birth defects. At least they are easy for me to see.

Photographed by Eugene Beckes at the National Bison Range, Moiese, Montana, this bull has a barely visible short bump rather than a normal bilateral scrotum that hangs down to hold testes away from the heat of the body.

On one of our park visits, right after photographing a bull with an extremely short scrotum, I showed the photo to a park biologist who was standing near his spotting scope waiting for a wolf to make an appearance. He simply said, "Wow, that is short." He didn't ask me if I knew why the bison was born with ectopic testes nor did he seem to want to discuss the issue at all. When I directly asked another park biologist, he assured me the male bison are not being neutered. Obviously, the large bulls with a short bump in the groin area (because their testes are in a horizontal position between the skin and the body) were not neutered. I had asked just to hear what he would say. Clearly male bison with ectopic testes have a birth defect that should alarm wildlife managers.

Several years ago, during our winter trip to Yellowstone, I took a photo of a small herd of bison who were silhouetted in a side view against the snow. Several of the bison, mostly cows and calves, had an easily visible underbite with the lower lip forward of the upper lip. I sent

257

the photo to a bison rancher, marking those with underbite; he agreed with my assessment.

Biologists in other states are becoming concerned about declining populations of mule deer, moose, and bighorn sheep, including those in Wyoming and Yellowstone. If there are no large mammals for tourists to see, it is likely fewer will visit national parks where viewing wildlife is one of the primary attractions. Fewer tourists will result in fewer businesses and fewer jobs. If this scenario does eventually occur, it will be partly because most people do not recognize abnormal facial development or malformed male reproductive organs in large mammals. This is concerning, but it is far more disturbing that trained professionals, who should immediately recognize birth defects in wildlife, often can't state the malformations are present or do anything about them for fear of losing their job.

A high prevalence of multiple birth defects in wild bison populations should be a major concern for all who care about their conservation. Bison living in high mountain habitats have special adaptations for that ecosystem. If those vital adaptations are lost, they can't be replaced. Ignoring debilitating malformations in hundreds of bison calves each year is inhumane and sadistically criminal. Just as when bison were almost annihilated, everyone who does nothing to stop this atrocity is an accomplice.

Wild bison deserve respect for their abilities and their important contributions to the ecosystem. They evolved unique features to enable them to survive the harsh conditions in which they live. Every one is a special and valuable individual. We must demand better management that adequately protects both the wild bison and their habitat. That must include protecting all bison who belong to the people of the United States from the effects of mineral chelating and gene and hormone disrupting toxins. Exposure to such toxins is changing the bison, and the changes are *not* for the better.

I sincerely hope when people visit our parks where bison live, especially Yellowstone National Park, Custer National Park in South Dakota, or the National Bison Range in Montana, that they pay closer attention to bison and other grazing animals. If enough people take photos and report individuals they see with birth defects to park officials, the officials will no longer be able to ignore the malformations or pretend they do not exist. This would greatly help in determining the toxins responsible and having them banned. If they are no longer used, hopefully bison will change again, returning to how they used to be. An added benefit of helping to save the bison is the possibility of saving people, especially newborns, maybe even your own child.

People kill bison
to save cattle from disease
cattle gave bison.

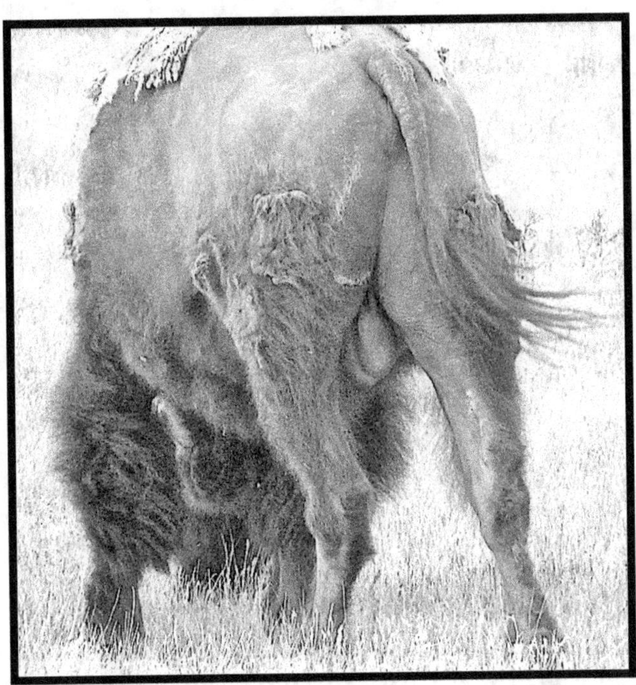

This adult bison photographed in Yellowstone National Park has a normal length scrotum but the left half of the scrotum (hemiscrota) was formed (during development in the womb) directly forward of the right hemiscrota. A male mammal scrotum should be formed with the hemiscrota containing the testes in a bilateral (side by side) configuration.

This photo of a bison calf with obvious underbite and short upper face, born in 2012, was taken February 18, 2013 in Yellowstone National Park.

CHAPTER 20
FALLING DOMINOES

Everything on Earth is interconnected. Consequently, one event can precipitate another, like one domino hitting the next, causing all to fall. A succession of events that occurred on the opposite side of the planet from us caused a related series of events in our region, clearly demonstrating that interconnectedness.

In 1991, when Mt. Pinatubo (located near the equator on the island of Luzon in the Philippines) blasted enormous amounts of ash and sulfur gases into the atmosphere, dominoes began falling faster than usual. That large eruption was fundamental in causing extremely high ultraviolet radiation over the northern portion of the Northern Hemisphere. It was even higher over the southern part of the Southern Hemisphere, especially Antarctica. Beginning in early spring 1993, ultraviolet radiation levels remained from 10% to 20% higher than normal for nearly two years. The effects of that helped instigate a progression of worldwide biodiversity-damaging effects that were both natural and human caused.

One of the consequences of those events was that wildlife and domestic animals suddenly had unprecedented rates of birth defects. The malformations and other adverse health symptoms were consistent with multiple disruptions of normal development prior to and after hatching or birth. Consequent mortality in mammal fetuses and newborns nearly every spring since 1995 resulted in a decline in many big game populations across North America. Wolves, bears, and mountain lions were blamed, which resulted in many being killed. Hatchlings of many species of birds have been observed with disrupted development, which can cause mortality and population declines. Mortality was and is even greater in amphibian populations, resulting in worldwide extinctions.

Except for poaching, most declines in animal populations are not because of predators, but are very likely because of manmade toxins in the air, in the water, and on foliage throughout the world. Destruction of habitat is nearly always given as a major cause of animal declines; in some parts of the world this is true because of increasing human populations and their effects. Where the environment has not been visibly changed, habitat destruction shouldn't be considered a primary factor. Toxins that disrupt basic biological functions are invisible, but they are deadly to developing young, even where the habitat remains relatively intact.

To truly understand the consequences of the falling domino events, we need to look at Earth's vitally important atmosphere, without which most life forms could not survive. Much of the animal life on Earth requires oxygen to live and breathe. A layer of a special form of oxygen called ozone is located in a region known as the stratosphere in Earth's upper atmosphere. The ozone layer is essential for complex forms of life, including humans, to exist.

A typical oxygen molecule is made up of two oxygen atoms (O_2). But when bombarded with cosmic radiation, some molecules break apart into individual atoms. Since an oxygen atom isn't stable alone, it binds to two other oxygen atoms to form an ozone molecule (O_3). Fortunately for complex living creatures, ozone molecules are very effective in absorbing the most damaging ultraviolet (UVB) portion of radiation given off by the sun. For every 1% increase in stratospheric ozone, 2% of the UVB radiation is blocked from reaching Earth's surface.

If a lack of ozone allows too much UVB radiation to reach the planet, a multitude of unfavorable chemical reactions can result. Exposed skin sunburns more quickly and seriously. When damage occurs in the photosynthetic portion of plants, it is said the plant sunburns. In both plant and animal cells, high radiation can cause epigenetic changes to cells and to organ growth during development. Good examples are the numerous unnaturally white or white-spotted animals and white flowers observed by many people in the late 1990s. Also, because a plant or animal's immune system can be severely damaged by exposure to high UVB radiation, it leaves them much less able to detoxify chemical pollutants and resist infectious or opportunistic microbes. Without protective ozone in the stratosphere, complex life on Earth would cease to exist, leaving only the microbes that first inhabited Earth more than three billion years ago.

In the 1970s, several chemists made the alarming discovery that man-made chemicals known as chlorofluorocarbons were damaging Earth's protective ozone layer. Soon thereafter, scientists working with the National Aeronautics and Space Administration (NASA) discovered the formation of a large thinning area in the stratospheric ozone over the

South Pole. Fortunately, scientists and political leaders quickly recognized the critical threat to humans and to the continued existence of complex organisms. Officials from many countries met and signed the international treaty known as the Montreal Protocol, phasing out the widespread use of chlorofluorocarbons.

Regrettably, some ozone-damaging chemicals are still in use. It takes several decades for the chemicals to travel to the stratosphere from where they are released near Earth's surface. Also, each rocket that goes through the ozone layer causes damage. Recently, more countries and private companies have been sending rockets through the ozone layer into space. Fortunately for us, the protective ozone layer has been recovering, even in the Polar Regions.

Ozone thinning can be compared to wearing out your jeans. A hole forms where the cloth has worn away completely, but cloth around the edges is thin and ragged, enlarging the hole as it continues to deteriorate. Each Southern Hemisphere spring since the late 1970s, an ozone hole has developed over the South Pole, with thinner, ragged areas extending far to the north over Australia, South America, and all the southern oceans.

There is also thinning of the ozone layer over the Northern Hemisphere, though not as extensive. Each spring after 1992, a larger area of thinner ozone formed over the North Pole, extending south over North America, Europe, and Asia. Each spring since the mid-1990s, an area of somewhat thinner ozone has formed over the North Pole, extending south over North America, Europe, and Asia. Fortunately, stratospheric ozone over the Northern Hemisphere has recovered since the extremely high ultraviolet radiation found by Canadian measuring stations in 1993.

In 1982, 10 years before the eruption of Mt. Pinatubo, there was a massive eruption of a Mexico volcano called El Chichon. Scientists discovered then that sulfur gases spewing from large volcanoes could work together with manmade chlorofluorocarbons to destroy global atmospheric ozone. Gases from the substantially larger eruption of Mt. Pinatubo in 1991 caused the ozone layer to thin even more, an additional 4% worldwide. Consequently, ultraviolet radiation reaching Earth's surface increased by an average of 8% in the years immediately after Mt. Pinatubo's eruption, with the area under thinner ozone layers experiencing even higher UVB radiation. Immune systems of animal life exposed to the sun in areas of high UVB radiation were harmed, especially in the extreme Southern Hemisphere.

In addition, oceanic and atmospheric warming from natural and human-caused greenhouse gases has been accelerated. This is in part because of the effects on plants of toxins released by people, reducing the ability of plants everywhere to remove carbon dioxide from the atmosphere. Billions of dead and dying trees, the elimination of soil micro-organisms from billions of acres of farm land, and far less phytoplankton in all the oceans result in the removal of considerably less carbon dioxide now than prior to the widespread application of multiple pesticides in the 1940s.

Like a line of falling dominoes, simultaneous exposure to high UVB radiation and environmental chemicals results in more infectious diseases and higher mortality in many plant and animal populations. Ironically, high ultraviolet radiation can be advantageous to some living things, including oomycetes, fungi, lichens, blue-green algae, and a whole suite of microbes and other primitive microorganisms. Microbes represent the earliest colonizers of Earth, developing before the planet's atmosphere had free oxygen or an ozone layer. Ultraviolet radiation often causes organisms to mutate, and while many mutations are fatal, some can be beneficial. In microbes, with their single-celled forms and high rates of reproduction, mutations are often advantageous, allowing new and improved microbes to rapidly increase in number. However, mutations in more complex organisms like mammals and other vertebrates can cause developmental defects and cancer.

Here in western Montana, I observed in 1993 that both blue-green algae and lichens (symbiotic associations between blue-green algae and fungi) began to grow at what seemed astounding rates. At the same time, sudden high rates of infection by potato blight and plant-damaging fungi, such as wheat rust, had farmers in much of Canada, the northern portion of the United States, Europe, Russia, the United Kingdom, and other countries struggling to protect their crops. They were advised to use more and stronger fungicides.

Potato blight was called a fungus, but it is an oomycete, whose physiology is closer to that of multi-celled organisms like humans than of fungi. Failure to appreciate this relationship may prove to be a costly error, if birth defects, loss of life, lost jobs, and burgeoning health care needs are considered. Blight oomycetes quickly mutated to be resistant to fungicides previously used to protect potato crops. Consequent yearly use of the fungicide chlorothalonil to control rapidly spreading potato blight in states upwind of western Montana rose from a pre-1994 total of a few thousand pounds to several million pounds by 1997, continuing to increase until 2001.

Chlorothalonil is classified by the U.S. Environmental Protection Agency as a "General Use Pesticide" of moderate toxicity. Superficial exposure causes eye irritation and dermatitis. While nearly all toxicity studies performed on chlorothalonil were based on ingestion, the inhalation study using rats showed a high toxicity rate when breathed. Glutathione, an important defense mechanism against toxic chemicals within the liver, binds with chlorothalonil and its metabolites; the bound toxin is then transported to the kidneys where it is excreted. This allows simultaneous exposures to other toxins, especially the glyphosate in Roundup®, to more seriously damage cells in developing young. It is important to note that initial studies conducted on pesticides of all kinds to determine any adverse health effects prior to registration by the EPA were, and still are, mainly done on adult rats, most often males, and not on embryos or fetuses.

Synergistic or sequential effects of toxins are seldom considered or tested. However, in a study of pesticides commonly found in a typical human diet, Italian researchers learned that combinations of pesticides at very low levels, as well as low-level exposure to chlorothalonil alone, caused oxidative damage resulting in misreplication of DNA. Chlorothalonil alone also induced genetic (DNA) damage in human and mouse cells. Those effects, especially misreplication of DNA, can result in cancer. Chlorothalonil should have been declared carcinogenic and immediately banned as a result of such studies, but it wasn't. It remains the most used fungicide worldwide. Is it any surprise that cancer is now extremely common, even in young people and other young animals?

On March 17, 1999, I collected melt water from snow that fell into glass pans in our yard, and sent it for analysis to Energy Labs in Billings, Montana. They found chlorothalonil at 0.03 ppb and two similar chemicals at 0.39 ppb. The lab technician told me the other two chemicals were likely metabolites of chlorothalonil or were contaminants. Hexachlorobenzene, the main contaminant of chlorothalonil, was banned by the EPA because it is highly carcinogenic to humans. Producers of the newer fungicide simply attached two cyanide atoms to the hexachlorobenzene ring and gave it a new name, chlorothalonil, but the two chemical molecules remain very similar in structure, thus likely have similar effects on exposed animals. The question is why was such a dangerous fungicide even registered for use?

Maybe it was because chlorothalonil was registered for use by the EPA without any testing for its ability to cause hormone disruption and cancer, which is proving to be a costly mistake. Chlorothalonil and its metabolites appear to be thyroid hormone disrupting, likely because they replace thyroid hormones in receptors of an animal's cells without performing the vital functions of those hormones. Also, recent studies have determined that, with a simultaneous or sequential exposure to glyphosate and chlorothalonil, damage to animal cells increases significantly. For example, exposure to cyanide in chlorothalonil would enhance glyphosate's ability to deplete vital amino acids and minerals.

In summer 1994, biological systems of all plants and animals were impacted by high ultraviolet radiation, in addition to the new applications of many millions of pounds of chlorothalonil. It appears to be just a horrific coincidence that only two years later, in 1996, genetically modified Roundup Ready® crops were approved and planted. The synergistic effects on animals throughout the United States from exposure to millions of pounds of Roundup® suddenly applied to crops modified to be resistant to glyphosate, in addition to exposure to high UVB radiation and excessive applications of chlorothalonil and other fungicides, were astounding. In spring 1997, birth defects in vertebrates that were first observed in 1995 were unprecedented in number. Disrupted development was even documented in a study of insects in 1997. All I could do was observe and take notes while an unbelievable procession of biological dominos all began toppling at the same time.

Birth defects and other adverse health issues continued to increase dramatically through 2001, then began going down and continued to decline through 2006, likely because of far less use of chlorothalonil on potatoes and measurable recovery of the protective ozone layer. Then, most concerning, in spring 2007, a major increase in prevalence occurred for many birth defects and, for some, the prevalence doubled. Interestingly, spring 2007 was the one immediately after formulas were changed for multiple herbicides being extensively applied to fields throughout the United States. The question must be asked: Was any testing done on those new formulas before they were released for use?

In 1992, the EPA registered several compounds made with synthetic nicotine, called neonicotinoids or neonics, for use as insecticides. All pesticides must be registered with the EPA before being sold in the United States. A registration application requires an exact list of components and other information, as listed on their website under pesticide applications. The EPA evaluates material provided to determine safety to humans, animals, and the environment. The company producing the pesticide must provide data from studies conducted on it, leaving a wide opening for misinformation and outright fraud, as has been demonstrated.

In the 1970s, information surfaced that more than 800 safety studies done by one laboratory (Industrial Bio-Test) on chemicals, including the most-used herbicides, insecticides, and other pesticides, were "nonexistent, fraudulent, or invalid." In 2017, 100,000 pages of chemical industry secrets (called the Poison Papers) were found stored in an old barn in Oregon. The Poison Papers show many more testing laboratories were involved and that the EPA worked with pesticide makers to register products that were not actually tested or on which tests were completely faked. They show the EPA also worked to keep products on the market when it was evident they were causing serious environmental harm and damaging human health.

Neonicotinoids were one of the pesticides shown by the Poison Papers to have been registered using fraudulent tests. The use of neonics has risen steadily, making them currently the most used insecticides in the world, like DDT once was before being banned. And like DDT, they should never have been registered as acceptable for use. Similar to chlorothalonil and glyphosate, neonicotinoids travel great distances in moist weather fronts, falling in snow and rain far from where they are applied. And like chlorothalonil and glyphosate, they work synergistically with other pesticides, especially those two, causing extreme harm to all living organisms exposed.

To compound the effects on embryos and fetuses, especially in grazing animals in our area, planting Roundup Ready Alfalfa® resulted in a massive increase use of glyphosate on newly planted alfalfa fields here and in states upwind. At the same time, large amounts of various neonicotinoids began being used in summer 2006, both to coat seeds prior to planting and to apply directly to crops after the plants come up. For wild and domestic grazing animals, eating sprayed Roundup Ready Alfalfa® significantly increased their exposure to glyphosate. Thus, several factors regarding pesticide use likely contributed to the drastic increase in the most commonly observed birth defects like underbite, as well as the sudden appearance of new malformations not observed prior to 2007.

Domestic bees and wild pollinators have been dying at unprecedented rates since the increase in use of neonicotinoids, especially Clothianidin®, fungicides such as chlorothalonil, and glyphosate on Roundup Ready® crops. With millions more people to feed each year, we absolutely cannot afford to lose pollinators and thus one third of the world's food supply. It appears that too many humans, combined with declining pollinator populations, are two more falling dominos we need to immediately address if we plan to be around much longer.

While scientists throughout the world have studied various defects such as reproductive malformations in fish, amphibians, and reptiles, the fairly recent developmental defects in other vertebrate species have been largely ignored, particularly in wild mammals. Montana State and County Health Departments considered 0.42 ppb of the chemical combination found by Energy Labs in our snow water in 1999 too low to be of concern regarding effects on development. They also paid no attention to the July 1999 test of Bitterroot River water (the main water source for our valley) that showed 0.53 ppb of the highly estrogenic herbicide Alachlor®, which is not even used here.

Chemicals found in these tests were carried here in moist weather fronts and are probably present year around, likely at much higher levels during summer and fall. Those and many other pesticides are used in states upwind of us. Every air breathing animal (including humans) has been inhaling multiple toxic chemicals with each breath before and after 1999 when the tests were done.

Most animals are much better designed to neutralize and detoxify chemicals when they are ingested than when inhaled or absorbed through the skin. This is because, before humans began developing a wide range of toxic organic chemicals, animals were much more likely to eat a toxic plant than to breathe a toxic chemical. The hepatic portal system, part of digestive circulation in animals (including humans), directs blood from parts of the gastrointestinal tract to the liver, which processes nutrients and fluids before they travel to the rest of the body. All compounds absorbed from the small intestines, including toxins, pass first through the liver where they are metabolized before going back to the heart and on to the rest of the body.

Thus, the liver acts as a filter, picking up toxins in order to protect the rest of the body from exposure to them as much as possible. When these are normal environmental toxins, it is able to clean the blood without being damaged, except in extreme cases such as when poisonous mushrooms are ingested. However, with all the pesticides we add to our air, water, and food, the liver is unable to keep up with the extreme quantities. It can become damaged by toxin overload or by specific toxins, making it less efficient. Toxins in air are absorbed directly through the lungs, without being filtered by the liver, a possible reason why some pesticides are more damaging when inhaled. The effects of many chemicals are enhanced by inhalation or skin absorption. Medical researchers today are using knowledge of this to deliver more effective dosages of medications by inhalers, nasal sprays, and skin patches.

Concerned citizens attempted in vain to convince health department officials that if the pesticides found in the 1999 tests, which weren't used here in Ravalli County, were present in our air and water, other pesticides not used here were also likely being deposited by rain and snow year around. In addition other hormone-disrupting chemical combinations are transported by weather fronts, including PCBs and multiple heavy metals. These toxins are carried on dust particles in rain and snow, and accumulate on foliage, soil, ice, snow and surface water all over the world. Transported heavy metals include mercury, arsenic, lead, barium, cadmium, aluminum, and others. Some, such as mercury, lead and cadmium, bio-accumulate becoming extremely toxic to animals higher in the food chain. Many are also toxic to essential organisms at the base of the food chain, especially phytoplankton in oceans and microorganisms in soil.

Toxins in dust carried by weather fronts fall or run off into streams, rivers, and the world's oceans. Herbicides are especially harmful to plants with only one cell or just a few cells. The consequent depletion of vital populations of phytoplankton and soil microorganisms significantly contributes to the decline of photosynthesis. That in turn increases atmospheric and oceanic carbon dioxide levels shown by researchers to be contributing to a warming global climate. Global warming is considered by many to be a natural phenomenon, but it is actually closely related to human activities. The application of billions of pounds of toxins worldwide is quite definitely a human activity and is accelerating the warming of the planet in multiple ways.

Such visionaries as Rachel Carson, Thomas Detwiler, Douglas Seba, Eugene Shinn, and many other researchers began recognizing in the early 1950s that global depletion of photosynthesis is a serious problem that would upset Earth's natural balances. They and their colleagues tried to warn us of the consequences of poisoning one-celled plants from the 1950s through the 1980s, when there was still time to reduce the damage. At that time, scientists were already showing, through numerous studies, how human actions were upsetting our planet's natural balances. Ignoring human-caused depletion of global photo-synthesis, combined with increasing human populations and the consequent increase in pollution, pesticide use, and green-house gases such as carbon dioxide, methane, and others, we are now experiencing precisely what those scientists tried to warn us would happen. Unfortunately, many people, including high government officials, are still denying the obvious.

Even though our local and state officials dismissed airborne transport of toxic chemicals as unlikely, it has been well documented scientifically. The ability of chlorothalonil to travel long distances from where it was initially applied was demonstrated in a U.S. Dept. of Agriculture study of the Bering Sea. Chlorothalonil was found in every fog sample and most seawater samples collected. The tests were done hundreds of miles from potato fields in Russia, where chlorothalonil was being used at the time of testing. Multiple studies of Roundup®, 2,4-D, and neonics have shown similar long-distance transportation.

After large amounts of glyphosate, chlorothalonil, and neonics began being used in states upwind, Bob and I often observed damage to native plants, garden crops, and ponderosa pine trees immediately after a rainstorm, especially in summer. The tops of plants and young pine trees would bend completely over, pointing toward the ground. Leaves of some garden vegetables quickly developed spots or turned yellow or brown the day after rain fell.

In summer 2007, all the gladiolas in a large flower patch my nieces had planted to earn school money were blooming and ready to sell at the local Farmer's Market. A weather front came through the valley the night before market day, causing a light shower. The next morning all the gladiolas were dead. Every blossom on every stalk was shriveled and brownish in color. My brother and his family are all chemically sensitive, so they did not use any pesticides on their garden. Whatever killed their entire large patch of flowers in one night had to have been in the rain that fell on them. If toxins in rain, and thus in the air, did that much damage to plants so quickly, imagine how much harm it did to the lungs of animals who were outside in the rain.

When USGS researchers tested snow in Glacier National Park, they found it had higher levels of a variety of pesticides, as well as sulfates, nitrates, and heavy metals, than any other of the eight primary national parks tested. The researchers said the only way for such biologically significant levels of toxins to get into snow and lake water on the tops of Glacier National Park mountains was to travel on dust in weather fronts from fields in states upwind of the park. I had suggested to local scientists who worked in Ravalli County that pesticides coming from states upwind were causing birth defects and adverse health issues on many vertebrate species, including newborn human babies. They said it wasn't possible for atmospheric transport to bring enough pesticides to our area to affect the health of animals. Sadly for the damaged newborns, they were wrong and the USGS researchers proved it.

Tiny specks of dust also carry many kinds of bacteria, viruses, and fungi, in addition to toxins. Some of those organisms not only survive the trip, they thrive on chemicals carried on the particles and minerals of which dust is composed. When specks of dust are inhaled into an animal's lungs, bacteria, viruses, and fungi also go into the warm, moist environment. There they can grow relatively unimpeded, because chemical toxins also present on the dust compromise the animal's immune system. In addition, the animal may have other factors affecting its well-being and health, causing a classic domino effect. When the last domino falls, the individual dies or, in a worst-case scenario, the proverbial dominos keep falling, resulting in mass die-offs or until the entire species goes extinct.

Chemicals coming here from other states aren't always the most damaging. During most of the 1990s, mint fields were scattered throughout the northern half of Ravalli County. The primary chemicals used on mint were several herbicides (including Terbicil®, Bentazone®, and Copyralid®) and two insecticides applied to kill mites (Propargite® and Acephate®). The estrogenic power of this mixture of ingredients was insidious. I sent two neutered, three-and-a-half-months old, completely normal male Saanen goats and one two-year-old Nubian female to join the goat herd used at the local wildlife refuge in their weed-eating program. A large complex of mint fields adjacent to the entire east side of the refuge was treated with all of the above, plus other chemicals regularly sprayed or applied through sprinkler systems. When I brought my goats home after five weeks at the refuge, the two young males coughed almost continuously, both were emaciated, and most

My nieces' dead gladiolas the morning after toxic rain fell on them during the night.

significantly, both had grown udders. Male goats are not supposed to grow an udder!

I had a veterinarian verify the two young males' mammary development and then began treating them for chemical exposure. The treatment relieved their coughing and enabled them to gain weight. However, they retained their mammary development for over six months and acted like females the entire time. Eventually, when they were over a year old, their enlarged mammary glands finally receded and they resumed normal behavior for neutered male goats.

Interestingly, while those chemicals were being applied on mint fields in the Bitterroot Valley, there were many reports of girls and boys from five to eight years old with breast development. Doctors gave the boys a shot of androgens and their breasts returned to normal. The question remains whether the children suffered permanent damage from the hormone disruption they had experienced that caused breast development at such a young age.

In 2001, because of a decrease in mint prices, those fields were plowed under and other crops were planted. Fortunately, the extremely estrogenic combination of chemicals was no longer used. Since mint field pesticides stopped being used in Ravalli County, I have heard no more reports of little children with abnormal breast development in the Bitterroot Valley, nor have I seen or heard of any young male goats with udders.

For many years, composites of herbicides have been consistently sprayed as a result of our state and county officials declaring a "War on Weeds." Undocumented amounts of 2,4-D, picloram, glyphosate, MCPP®, Dicamba®, and other hormone-disrupting, mitochondria-damaging, cancer-causing herbicides are sprayed every spring and summer by the Forest Service, Bureau of Land Management, State and County Highway Departments, railroad companies, and thousands of Montana citizens, in addition to pesticides applied in states upwind. The many so-called inert ingredients in pesticides used here and in the millions of acres of fields throughout the U.S. and other countries must also be considered. Many additives are far more toxic, DNA damaging, or hormone disrupting than the primary ingredient, as are many of the breakdown products called metabolites.

Both sides of many county and state roads are sprayed at least once a year. Consequently, nearly every organism in the area of application and downwind is exposed at biologically significant levels to combinations of those herbicides and many others, plus their so-called inert ingredients and metabolites, for hours or even days. Bees, birds, sheep, and goats have been the most often reported casualties found dead after roadside spraying.

Additionally, hatchling birds and young goats, completely normal at birth, have been observed to suddenly exhibit lethargy, diarrhea, and inability to digest food. Then, a day or two after the exposure, they have an underbite as a result of interrupted growth of their upper facial bones. Animals are not supposed to be able to develop such defects after they are born or hatched. Those symptoms, and disruption of feather growth in birds, were observed to occur immediately after exposure to known applications of 2,4-D combined with picloram or other herbicides in the area where the young goats or hatchling birds lived. Birds in nests where there are many sprayed lawns often have an underdeveloped upper bill. Four of five young House Sparrows and several hatchlings of other species I received for care in 2011, all from different towns, had a short upper bill. The prevalence of this defect in hatchlings appeared to decrease in 2016 and 2017.

According to a 200-page report by the President's Cancer Panel released in May 2010, exposure to pesticides, especially two or more in mixtures, are very harmful to young children. That children are allowed to play on recently sprayed lawns should be of great concern. Many commonly used pesticides, including those used on lawns, cause damage to mitochondria, the power packs of cells. Many, especially Roundup®, also cause oxidative DNA damage. Such cellular damage often results in cancer, heart disease, strokes, autoimmune diseases, neurological diseases, diabetes, osteoporosis, and many other conditions. These health issues have been increasing significantly in children in the United States. Actually, calling the symptoms of chronic or acute poisoning a disease is completely disingenuous. If poisoning by pesticides stopped, most such "diseases" would become far less common.

Unfortunately, more people and sprawling subdivisions continue to add impurities to the air we breathe: increasing amounts of pesticides of all kinds; wood smoke from stoves; smoke from trash and slash pile burning; increasing vehicle exhaust; and chemical-laden dust from sprayed, unpaved roads. The total number of chemicals living cells currently have to deal with is difficult to comprehend. When combined with fluctuating elevated natural and human-caused radiation, it is surprising that animals are still able to survive and reproduce. The health of individual animals of different species throughout the planet, from sensitive microbes and insects to larger mammals including humans, has likely been more seriously impacted during the last 20 years than at any other time in recorded history.

Simultaneous stimulatory and suppressive immune and brain cell changes, cellular oxygen depletion, and mitochondrial damage result in a reduction of electron flow between cells. All of those factors in turn cause a drastic disruption of cellular communication. Reduced electron flow and disrupted cellular communication interferes with cellular transfer of positively charged minerals, called cations. This results in minerals remaining in the blood stream rather than going into cells that require them. Just the interference with efficient cellular uptake of calcium has many negative effects on an animal's body. Copper is another mineral essential to cellular function. Electron flow between cells depends upon the correct balance of copper and other minerals in both enzymes and proteins responsible for cellular communication. A multi-celled animal can't function normally if its cells are unable to communicate. Other important, positively charged minerals can be similarly inhibited from performing their vital functions in cells, including selenium. It is necessary for production of six or more enzymes vital to the proper functioning of the immune system in vertebrates. Selenium is also necessary for normal thyroid function. Serious disruption of many cellular activities will result when selenium is not available to cells. This is why exposure to Roundup®, a patented mineral chelator, causes numerous and obvious detrimental effects in exposed animals.

In more sensitive animals, hypersensitivity reactions are enhanced by exposure to environmental toxins such as pesticides and exhaust from snowmobiles, diesel trucks, and other vehicles. Transference of oxygen to cells is consequently compromised by inflammation of lung tissue. Lack of oxygen drastically reduces a cell's energy, as does mitochondrial damage and consequent disruption of cellular production of enzymes essential in aiding the mitochondria in changing sugar into heat and energy. This reduction in cellular energy results in even more drastic disruptions of function and communication. If cellular energy and normal electron flow are not restored, administering large doses of calcium or other minerals, vitamins, or liquid electrolytes, such as Lactated Ringers® solution, does little to return the animal to health. It is a domino effect in the animal's body directly related to the domino effect in the environment. For an affected animal, the last domino to fall is premature death. A culmination of the environmental domino effect is falling survival rates in many species of animal. Viruses, bacteria, and parasites are nearly always blamed for animal die-offs. The true cause, lethal poisoning by toxins in their environment, is seldom held responsible.

I examined and documented hundreds of wild and domestic animals, especially amphibians, birds, and mammals, with malformations very similar to those reported in human newborns in western Montana. Between 1995 and 2001, I learned of many human babies born with malformations, one of the most common being developmental bone deformities involving the skull and limbs, including hydrocephalus, no eyes formed, cleft palate, underdeveloped skull and maxilla, and malformed or missing limbs or digits. Other problems reported were hypospadias*, micro-penis (abnormally small), and scrotal malformations, several of many types of heart defect, and a much higher than normal incidence of damage to chromosomes 13, 18, 21, and 24. It was reported to me that a cluster of eight babies with chromosomal damage, plus one other with a heart malformation, were born in western Montana the last weekend of July 1997. Several people and domestic animals in Ravalli County had sudden renal failure in 1996 and 1997 and five babies with no renal organs at all were born in Lake County between 2001 and 2002. Unfortunately, the Missoula doctor who publicly promised to look into the increasing birth defects in human babies was tragically killed in a vehicle accident before he could begin the study he had planned.

*(Hypospadias is a birth defect in which the opening of the urethra is on the underside of the penis instead of at the tip.)

According to CDC records, the incidence rates of obesity, diabetes, and autism have gone up significantly since 1994. These health issues have been shown by recent studies to result from epigenetic changes to the fetus during development. That coincides closely in time with the sudden expression of malformations in young of mammals and birds in spring 1995. I helped with a study ("The High Cost of Pesticides: Human and Animal Diseases," published in August 2015), which examined birth defects and health issues, as shown by CDC records, in newborn children and humans of all ages throughout the United States that corresponded to the birth defects and health issues in wild and domestic animals. We found an astoundingly close correlation between the increase in adverse health issues in people, especially newborns, and the increase in use of glyphosate on Roundup Ready® crops.

The autism rate by birth year in children has gone up steeply since 1994 and nearly doubled between 2007 and 2013. There have been several new studies showing autism is the result of epigenetic changes in the brain during development, and that some mice and other animals are born with autism. Therefore, it is not surprising that we also found the prevalence of autism in children closely correlates with the increasing prevalence of multiple birth defects, including symptoms suggesting autism, in other vertebrate young. Most astounding is the 98.5% correlation between the increase in autism in children and increase in the use of glyphosate.

In addition, the incidence rates of cancers in fatty tissue such as brain, prostate, breast, and colon increased significantly immediately after 1994. Montana went from rating near the bottom into the top 20 states with the highest cancer rate per capita. In 2003, Montana was the only western state in the top 20, at number 17. By 2013, Montana was number two in cancer deaths of all the western states, exceeded only by the state of Washington.

Liver function is seriously disrupted in numerous ways by chronic exposure to toxins. The liver is one of the most important organs of the body. One of its jobs is to remove toxins, microorganisms, and many other unwanted substances from the blood stream and change them into a form that can be excreted. It seems obvious that if the liver were constantly dealing with toxic chemicals that inhibit lipid metabolism, it would be triggered to increase production of lipid precursors. Cholesterol is a lipid precursor. That is why the liver produces it. Interestingly, the increase in cholesterol levels has been vilified by modern medicine as an indicator of susceptibility to many serious health problems. Another important consideration is direct damage to the liver from exposure to pesticides. In our 2015 study, increase in liver cancer in humans of all ages correlated by 93% with increased use of glyphosate.

In a study done many years ago, goats were deliberately exposed to cyanide during development in the womb to determine its effects on developing human newborns. The young goats who survived to be born had high cholesterol and diabetes at birth. They also had many of the observable symptoms of fetal thyroid hormone disruption, including underdeveloped upper facial bones and underbite. Obviously, being exposed to cyanide caused fetal livers to produce more cholesterol to deal with the extremely toxic cyanide. High cholesterol should not be treated as if it were the problem. It would make much more sense to consider high cholesterol an easily tested indicator that the body is being adversely affected by chronic exposure to environmental toxins, especially cyanide in the most used fungicide, chlorothalonil.

One of the most severe effects of such toxins is disruption of the immune system. There are now over 80 human autoimmune disorders recognized by doctors. Once considered separate diseases, they are now beginning to be recognized as related symptoms of immunosuppression. Over 20 million people in the United States have been diagnosed with autoimmune disorders. Most autoimmune disorders were once thought by many in the medical profession to be symptoms of aging, or simply a figment of the patient's imagination.

According to several well-publicized studies, babies born in wheat producing areas are more likely to have malformations than those whose parents live in areas where wheat is not produced. This was stated to be due to the specific pesticide combinations used on wheat fields. Many other well-publicized studies have shown that farmers exposed to the herbicide 2,4-D or other pesticides, and all people living in farming areas, had a much higher cancer rate than those in areas where pesticides were not used as much. Each year, millions of acres of agricultural fields, especially wheat fields, are sprayed at regular intervals by aircraft, in addition to pasture and forest land being aerial sprayed to control weeds. As little as 20% of the pesticides delivered from an aircraft lands on target plants, with the rest carried off site by the wind..

International scientific papers state that a child's fundamental right to healthy development is being compromised throughout the world. The same is happening to other animal young. Disruption of basic cellular function in living organisms is causing adverse health effects in the young of vertebrates and is implicated in causing animal populations worldwide to decline significantly, with many going extinct. It is also seriously compromising the ability of many species of plants to survive, and verifies the interconnectedness of all life on Earth. The series of events we have observed, occurring one after another like falling dominos, have resulted in altered appearance and declines in diversity of plant and animal life in the valley in which I live, throughout the United States, and all over the planet.

Another domino fell in the form of dangerous radiation from the tsunami-damaged nuclear power plants in Japan in March 2011. It took approximately eight days for the radiation to travel across the Pacific Ocean to the California coast. In 1997, when we told health officials the fungicides and other pesticides sprayed in states upwind of western Montana could travel for 150 miles, most said it isn't possible for them to travel that far. It is very strange no one said it isn't possible for radiation to travel thousands of miles from Japan to North America. It took only two more days for radiation to come inland from California to western Montana. People here bought nearly all available potassium iodide pills several days before the radiation arrived in California.

Those same people paid no attention when we suggested in 1997 that our sudden increase in cancer and other health problems might be because of airborne toxic chemicals carried here from states adjacent to Montana and directly upwind. It is quite obvious that pollutants of all kinds can travel for thousands of miles and even more obvious that toxins would be far more damaging if they travel for only a few hundred miles and are not as diluted by dissipation. There is indisputable scientific evidence that chemical pollution alone represents a serious threat to the health of children, adults, and future generations, threatening the survival of mankind and most other complex species. We also know that simultaneous exposure to radiation can greatly compound adverse effects of toxins on living cells.

The lives of children and all other young, and their basic right to healthy development, should not in any way be a political or financial issue. Political and religious beliefs of parents have no bearing on whether their child will be adversely affected in the womb by hormone disrupting toxins, having their lives disrupted by the effects of global warming, or left without a future in an environment that can no longer support life. As residents of Earth, we have been presented with very clear and poignant options. We must immediately stop poisoning complex life on our planet and use less toxic ways to deal with weeds and pests. Or we can continue to follow our present course until the last domino falls, that domino being the extinction of complex life, including mankind.

**Hear the splash of frogs
as they jump from lily pads
into extinction.**

DANCE OF LIFE

Earth whirls through space
Dressed in sparkling blue,
Sprinkled with cloud sequins.
A lovely ballerina, whirling,
She pirouettes around the Sun
And the dance of life begins.

Benevolent Sun slips radiantly
Through the darkness of the universe,
Sharing freely her light and heat.
Like a midwife, she extracts
Life from Mother Earth's womb
And hearts begin to beat.

Pulling at Earth's ocean skirts,
Playful Moon joins their ballet
Whirling barren and carefree,
Creating estuaries, teeming with
Life and new species evolving
Where the rivers meet the sea.

Life comes from the living Earth.
Balancing on her water and soil,
Too much life is not a plus.
If we continue to poison her skin,
To destroy her breath, so vital to life,
She will dance through space without us.

Viewed from space, Earth looks
like a small, round, blue marble.
Some still claim it's flat.

CHAPTER 21
SYNDROMES AND SYNERGY

Each year, millions of newborn animals die or fail to thrive because of exposure to toxins. There seems to be extensive deception in a massive attempt to keep people from knowing about these losses and understanding the causes. People who make money poisoning all life on Earth have been extremely good at covering up what they are doing. One way the deception is achieved is by giving the same symptoms in newborns of each species a different name, usually ending with the word syndrome. For example, veterinarians, medical doctors, and researchers have an endless assortment of names for the symptoms of thyroid hormone disruption that many animals now have at birth. Newborn domestic animals have the same symptoms as those in wild young, and newborn human babies are similarly affected. Our babies often show even more symptoms than other animals, because many symptoms of fetal thyroid hormone disruption are easier to detect in a child.

The most common names for the symptoms of Congenital Fetal Hypothyroidism (CFH) on two species of domestic young are Weak Calf Syndrome (WCS) for cattle and Mare Reproductive Loss Syndrome or Early Foal Loss for horses. I have not heard the name for the same condition in domestic goats or sheep, but they likely have one. Newborn domestic goats and lambs frequently have the same symptoms as calves and foals, often even more acute than the larger animals.

In wild mammals and birds, the symptoms of fetal hypo-thyroidism were once called Chronic Wasting Syndrome. That name is not often used now because it is easily confused with Chronic Wasting Disease, which is caused by abnormally folded prions in brain cells. The function of normal prions is to protect brain cells from various types of radiation. Both Chronic Wasting Disease and Chronic Wasting Syndrome appear to be caused by environmental toxins, with different ways of initiating each of those diseases in an animal, although immune system damage occurs with both.

Similarly, a variety of terms are used for CFH symptoms in human newborns. For example, when a pregnant mother is a smoker, if symptoms of thyroid hormone disruption occur in her newborn, it is called Fetal Tobacco Syndrome, rather than fetal hypothyroidism. When a pregnant mother who drinks alcohol has a child with symptoms of thyroid hormone disruption, her newborn is said to have Fetal Alcohol Syndrome. There are many names for organ damage in human newborns, even though the resulting malformations are completely consistent with disrupted thyroid hormones during embryonic and fetal development. They are also strikingly similar to symptoms we have documented in high prevalence in other newborn mammals and hatchling birds.

Symptoms consistent with disruption of thyroid hormones during development should obviously be called Congenital Fetal Hypothyroidism for all newborn vertebrate species. Doing this would avoid confusion and make clear what is actually wrong with the babies. If livestock owners, biologists, researchers, and medical doctors called these conditions by the correct name, simultaneous outbreaks of CFH in livestock, wild animals, and human babies would be easily recognized. For example, if large numbers of sheep, goats, calves, and foals born on multiple ranches in a certain year have underbite, as well as abnormal weakness at birth and other CFH symptoms, it would be a strong indication of a serious, widespread environmental problem. Any environmental cause of CFH in wild and domestic animals is likely to also affect human newborns. Thus, the cause of CFH in other animal young should be recognized and mitigated as quickly as possible to minimize those effects on human fetuses and newborns.

Because of identical symptoms, WCS appears to be the same condition as CFH. **All ranchers need to recognize that Weak Calf Syndrome is Congenital Fetal Hypothyroidism and understand that there is an environmental cause.** This has made it much easier for those who do understand this connection to prevent WCS from happening to their newborn livestock.

From 1969 through 1985, WCS was a serious problem in cattle herds in Ravalli County, the rest of Montana, and other states. Veterinarian Jack Ward diagnosed the first case of WCS in winter 1964 on a ranch in Ravalli County. During calving season 1969, WCS became epidemic in western Montana and throughout the west and mid-west, with occurrences remaining high through the early 1980s.

In 1969, large amounts of endrin, a deadly insecticide, were used early in spring on wheat fields throughout Montana to kill cutworms and on forests to kill tree beetles here in Ravalli County and in the states directly west and upwind of Montana. At the same time, use of herbicides 2,4-D and 2,4,5-T, the two components of deadly Agent Orange used in Vietnam, was greatly increased on fields and forests in western states to combat weeds. In addition, DDT, an insecticide, was sprayed almost daily from spring through fall in western Montana towns to kill mosquitoes. DDT was banned in 1972, but discontinuing heavy spraying of that poison did not appear to reduce the epidemic of WCS, which continued to kill calves at high rates. The EPA banned both endrin and 2,4,5-T in 1985 so neither was used in the United States after that date. It was very telling that beginning immediately after use of endrin and 2,4,5-T ended, WCS became almost nonexistent in western Montana cattle herds.

After being absent for 10 years, WCS began occurring again in spring 1995, with many calves affected and high mortality on some ranches. As I have repeatedly stated, spring 1995 was when many species of newborn wildlife, domestic animals, and most importantly, children in western Montana began having multiple symptoms of CFH, including serious birth defects. One of those in domestic calves is underbite, not often detected because almost no one checks the mouth of newborn calves; few ranchers will admit their calves have this defect if they do see it.

The main conditions said to result in WCS include nutritional deficiencies, specifically selenium, and low forage protein, in addition to cold weather and bacterial or viral infections. The reason those same conditions did not cause widespread Weak Calf Syndrome prior to 1969 and between the years 1986 through 1995 was not addressed. Another consideration is why the prevalence of WCS in certain regions suddenly increased from 2% to 6% in some years to more than 50% in other years, with no evident change in the conditions veterinarians have implicated as causing WCS. However, there were major changes in the combinations and amounts of herbicides and other pesticides being used in those time periods.

Cold weather is another condition commonly associated with WCS. However, low temperatures, deep snow, or long winters did not result in cows producing weak, immuno-suppressed calves with underdeveloped facial bones and resultant underbite in the time period prior to 1964. Cattle had been raised in the United States for many years before 1964. From 1940 through 1963, I lived on my parents' ranch in South Dakota where spring temperatures were very cold and we sometimes had blizzards in May. On our ranch and neighboring ranches, no WCS ever occurred. After 1969, when Weak Calf Syndrome had become a widespread problem, a study of over 80,000 calves at Clay Center, Nebraska stated that "even without rain or snow, the number of calves that died increased rapidly below 50 degrees Fahrenheit and as little as 0.10 inches of precipitation caused the calves to have visible symptoms."This clearly indicates that the calves had severe mitochondrial disruption resulting in their being unable to maintain normal body heat.

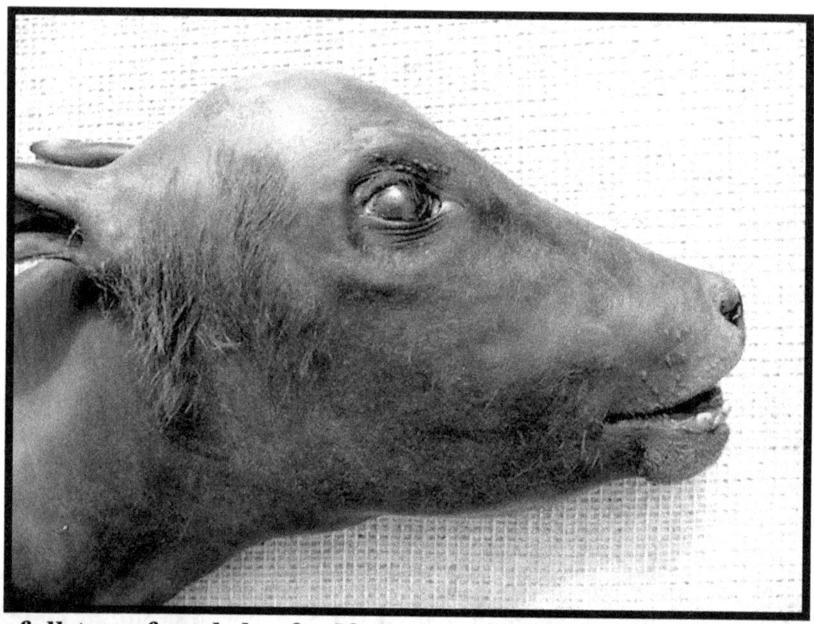

This full-term female beef calf was born in 2006 with almost no hair, and severe craniofacial malformations including underbite, malformed teeth, and small, misplaced eyes. She died soon after birth.

It also suggests there may have been toxins in the rain which, when inhaled, can directly interfere with a calf's normal cellular functions. Low levels of combinations of toxins can volatilize from sprayed pasturelands for months and toxins are in the precipitation itself. Most importantly, it doesn't take more than a few parts per billion (even less of some toxins) to disrupt cellular functions in a fetus or a newborn.

Low quality food during pregnancy is another factor associated with WCS/CFH, usually resulting in the pregnant cows being in poor condition. Cows with insufficient nutrition give birth to calves with less vigor who are unable to maintain their heat and energy, so are slower to stand and suckle. Research done on sheep clearly showed that malnutrition alone causes CFH, with all the resultant health problems and malformations. Not surprising, WCS research on cattle showed that as malnutrition increased, the incidence of WCS increased. Research conducted in Wyoming showed that undernourishment in cows resulted in smaller calves who were more susceptible to diseases like scours and death. Jack Ward's research here in Ravalli County showed that thinner cows resulted in higher winter-feeding costs, lighter calves at weaning, and calves requiring more veterinary care.

Between 1997 and 2007, I examined 21 calves with veterinarian diagnosed WCS and all had an underbite. The high incidence of underbite in beef calves was a likely cause of the reduced weight gain reported by multiple ranchers in that time period. Another consideration for ranchers is that if heifers with underbite are kept for breeding, they will be more susceptible to being undernourished because they can't graze efficiently. Thus, those heifers will be more likely to produce another generation of calves with underbite and other symptoms of CFH.

Wolves, which were first reintroduced in Yellowstone National Park in winter 1995-1996 and in Idaho in 1995, have spread throughout western Montana. They either interbred with wolves already here or replaced them. After their reintroduction, they became a scapegoat, blamed for losses of newborns in both wild and domestic grazing animals. They were even blamed for decreases in weight gain in beef cattle on summer ranges when there were no wolves in the area and no livestock deaths from predators. While I have often heard ranchers blame wolves for loss of calves and weight loss in their cattle herds, I have never heard them blame the toxins they, their neighbors, and farmers in neighboring states use in copious amounts for causing the high prevalence of CFH/WCS, calf mortality, and weight loss. Livestock owners began blaming wolves as soon as they were reintroduced and have continued to completely ignore the actual cause of CFH/WCS, calf deaths, and declines in weight gain.

In the 42 years since 1969, during the years of high calf mortality, the collective cost to the livestock industry included the loss of millions of animals and billions of dollars. Ironically, a huge fuss is made about wolves killing between 200 and 300 cattle per year throughout the entire United States, for which most livestock owners are compensated. Ranchers are not reimbursed for calves lost to toxins, natural or man-made. If wolves kill a calf, the objections are loud and long. But not once in the 42 years while calves here in western Montana were dying by the thousands because of fetal thyroid hormone disruption, have I ever heard a rancher swearing at him- or herself or the neighbors for poisoning their calves, even when losses were up to one third of their calf crop. For mankind, denial seems to be the longest stream of thought there is. It remains in full flood stage regarding the horrific effects of toxins on newborns.

In 2017, a study by R. Ashauer, I. O'Connor, and B.I. Escher ("Toxic Mixtures in Time – The Sequence Makes the Poison" published in *Environmental Science Technology*) showed that sequential exposure to multiple toxins is as damaging and as important as the dose of each toxin to which an animal is exposed. The authors stated, **"We provide the first evidence that carry-over toxicity occurs among chemicals acting on different targets and when exposure is several days apart. It is therefore not only the dose that makes the poison but also the exposure sequence."** In actuality, a horrific, unplanned, planet-wide study on sequential exposures has been going on since the first organophosphate and organochlorine pesticides began to be widely used soon after World War II. As more and more kinds of pesticides were developed and used, birth defects, syndromes, cancer, and multiple other adverse health issues increased, often resulting in early death.

In 1994, when the new deadly combination of pesticides began being extensively used in states upwind, our Western Toad populations declined drastically by late summer. The next year in summer 1995, Minnesota's frog population was discovered to have a high number of malformations, most often of the limbs. Researchers in Minnesota collected more than 13,000 northern leopard frogs over several years and found deformities in 6.5%. The usual rate of deformities in frog populations is between zero and 2%. Because of the extensive publicity, reports of malformed frogs from many states, including Montana, began being received by researchers.

A literature search shows that health problems, including immunosuppression and malformations in many species of vertebrate wildlife throughout the Northern Hemisphere, were identified in 1995 and in the years since. For example, the life expectancy of North Atlantic right whale females declined from approximately 52 years in 1980 to only 15 years after 1995, a highly significant change. Also, expected reproductive events during a female's lifetime declined from five in

1980 to one in the years since 1995. Other species of ocean mammals, such as sea otter, southern right whale, and orca, have experienced significant population declines since 1995. Pollution, diseases, immuno-suppression, and accidental net drownings were listed as causes of mortality in those species. Pollution by heavy metals, pesticides, and other chemicals is well known as a primary cause of immunosuppression and much higher susceptibility to disease.

The southern resident orca population off the North American west coast initially declined significantly between 1982 and 1985. This was the same time period that Ravalli County wildlife rehabbers observed developmental malformations in local bird species, and WCS was epidemic in calves throughout Montana and other western states. It was also when reproductive malformations were first found in Sitka black-tailed deer in Alaska. The southern orca population began to decrease again in 1995 and the decline has continued, leading to a recommendation that this population be listed as threatened.

At the same time, there was a decline in sea otter populations along the west coast of North America. Studies investigating the declines showed that 70% of carcasses recovered and examined were prime-aged animals, mostly female, who had died from unknown causes.

Elephant seal populations along the west coast had a skewed sex ratio in favor of males, also beginning in 1995. We observed a similar phenomenon that began with white-tailed deer fawns born in spring 1995. Their sex ratio averaged 60 males to 40 females in over 500 examined fawns in the eight-year period from 1996 through 2003. Goat ranchers throughout the U.S. reported high ratios of males, with some ranches having up to 80% males in the early 2000s. This was not beneficial for dairy goat owners, since males are worth less than females.

Reproductive malformations are not listed as a clinical symptom for WCS or Mare Reproductive Loss Syndrome, although I have observed them in male foals, calves with WCS, newborn lambs, and domestic goats. Disruption of the normal formation and growth of the genitalia is now common in newborn male mammals, especially those who have one or more of the other symptoms of fetal hypothyroidism. Reproductive malformations have been documented in increasing numbers of mammals worldwide. A review done in 2008 by Gwynne Lyons for *CHEM Trust*, "Male Wildlife Under Threat," reports a planet-wide increase in prevalence of malformations of the male genitalia in multiple vertebrate species since 1995. Also, in 1995, scientists began finding both male and female reproductive malformations at a rate of 3% in four species of mice at the Kesterson National Wildlife Refuge in California. By 1998, the rate had increased to one-third of the 87 field mice, house mice, harvest mice, and California voles examined. Mice are mammals like us, but there was no publicity about this very alarming study, while frogs with malformations made headlines around the world.

All of these serious effects in multiple species corresponded exactly in time to when we began seeing reproductive malformations and other birth defects in multiple mammal species in western Montana. For example, in white-tailed deer fawns born from 1995 through 2001, one-third of the 250 male deer I examined and measured for our prevalence study had malformations of the scrotum including none, very short, or only one hemiscrotum present. On those, one or both testes were in a horizontal position between the warm body wall and the skin, which causes heat damage to the sperm. Such a high rate of those specific reproductive malformations was unparalleled in medical history.

According to Alaskan biologist and hunting guide Jake Johnson, male Sitka black-tailed deer living on Kodiak Island, Alaska, had a disturbingly high incidence of a different male reproductive malformation, with over 60% of the male deer he examined having undescended testes and consequently no or half a scrotum. On the Sitka black-tailed deer, one or both testes had failed to descend away from the kidney area. Their testes were also severely underdeveloped, being from one-fourth to one-half normal size. The oldest reports of this problem are from Uganik, Alaska, in 1983. Johnson saw his first deer with no scrotum in 1990 and another in 1994, preceding the birth defects and wildlife declines that began in 1995. The rate then increased dramatically, with 10 (48%) of the 21 male Sitka black-tailed deer taken by hunters he guided in 1999 and 14 (74%) of 19 in 2001 having this reproductive malformation.

Other mammals are being similarly affected. Young river otters with high body burdens of toxins showed a significant decrease in penis size. Males of several rodent species I have examined and photographed here in western Montana (including deer mouse, house mouse, fox squirrel, red squirrel, chipmunk, domestic rat, and domestic hamster) had either no scrotum or a short, misaligned scrotum; also, many have a very short penis sheath on the external skin. A week-old male chipmunk brought to me for care had no penis sheath at all. He also had a disrupted immune system and other symptoms of chemical exposure, and did not survive.

In western Montana, introduced eastern fox squirrels live primarily in urban areas, depending on food supplied by people, such as pet food, birdseed, fruit, and berries. Several of those I have examined had no or almost no scrotum; young squirrels received by other rehabbers for care were missing toes or part of the tail, with some showing signs of neurological damage. As reported in our 2015 study, on a total of 27 male fox squirrels I examined between the years of 2010 and 2014, 21 (78%) had no scrotum and two (7%) had only one hemiscrotum formed, all with ectopic testes. Just four (15%) had a normal scrotum containing both testes. In addition, on 24 (89%) of the 27 the penis sheath was less than half normal length. That is an alarmingly high prevalence of reproductive birth defects, even with a small sample.

Because fox squirrels usually live in urban yards, they run around on lawns that are frequently sprayed, resulting in pregnant females and their fetuses having sequential exposures to multiple toxins that work synergistically. Children play on those same lawns, and to feed themselves and their young, parent birds hunt for insects in the contaminated grass and soil. Dogs in towns spend much of their time on lawns sprayed with pesticides and many dogs that are not bred to have an underbite are now born with one. A friend's dog was born with a misaligned scrotum, indicating that canines are being born with that reproductive malformation. Perhaps most concerning are the statistics showing increasing numbers of our dogs now die of some type of cancer, apparently the price they have to pay for supposedly being man's best friend.

Reproductive organs in humans are also being adversely affected. Growing evidence from a large number of studies points to an increase in the incidence of human male reproductive problems corresponding to those in other male animals. Genital abnormalities, testicular cancer, reduced semen quality, and sub-normal fertility in human males is referred to as Testicular Dysgenesis Syndrome. The recent rise in the prevalence of Testicular Dysgenesis Syndrome is thought by researchers to be caused by genetically susceptible individuals being exposed to endocrine disrupting toxins. This strongly suggests the symptoms of Testicular Dysgenesis should be called chemical poisoning instead of being referred to as a syndrome.

Other serious health problems in human babies and young people have also increased dramatically. These include premature birth, asthma, autism, chromosomal damage such as Down Syndrome, obesity, diabetes, issues related to calcium deficiency (e.g. rickets, brittle bones, or fractures slow to heal), multiple types of cancer, and others. There are now hundreds of health problems in newborn children that have a variety of names, many ending in the word "syndrome." Irritable Bowel Syndrome is common and is often caused by fairly severe damage to the child's liver, interfering with their ability to digest certain foods. Since the liver is frequently damaged by exposure to toxins, it would seem prudent to find what toxins are affecting the child rather than prescribing a drug for them that is actually another type of toxin. Such symptoms as liver damage, mitochondrial disruption, and metabolic acidosis in people of any age usually result in their doctor prescribing medications. Prescription drugs can cause the same type of damage that exposure to pesticides inflicts on cells, cellular functions, and often to the liver and kidneys, resulting in mitochondrial disruption and metabolic acidosis, as shown in our study (Swanson N, Hoy J, Seneff S, 2016) listed in References.

The symptoms of fetal hypothyroidism, disruption of intercellular calcium and other mineral levels, damage to mitochondria, disruption of enzymes necessary for maintaining heat and energy, metabolic acidosis, and thymic atrophy with its consequent immuno-suppression and autoimmune reactions, are not conducive to the perpetuation of any species. Such symptoms in multiple species of all families of vertebrate in the same time period should be considered strong evidence that widespread exposure to increasing levels of environmental toxins is causing unprecedented damage to animals, particularly developing young. Contaminants, especially pesticides, end up on food sources, in surface water, and on skin. Thus, animals experience many sequential, synergistic exposures to a variety of unknown combinations of chemicals by several processes, which varies according to season and the types of toxins used nearby and upwind. In addition, spraying large areas with numerous pesticides one after another results in sequential exposures, recently recognized as a major factor in the amount of damage caused to an exposed organism.

Cyanide, nitriles, nicotine, and glyphosate are all severely damaging to thyroid glands and disrupt normal thyroid hormone function. Most importantly, they work synergistically to cause more severe cellular damage than any one of those alone. An example of such synergy occurred in summer 2006, when the formulas of several popular herbicides, including Roundup®, 2,4-D, dicamba, and others were changed. Also during the growing season of 2006, there was another huge increase in use of Roundup® on new, genetically modified crops and a massive increase in the use of neonicotinoids, which act synergistically with glyphosate in Roundup® and cyanide in chlorothalonil.

Immediately after sequential exposures in adult animals to those new, more deadly toxins, there was a steep increase in the prevalence of birth defects in newborn vertebrates. For example, in spring 2007, underbite doubled and overbite more than doubled in examined deer fawns; also, heart defects, severely damaged lungs, and tumors became common in birds and mammals of all ages. After 2006, heart defects became the number one birth defect in newborn children, and autism doubled in just 10 years from 2007 to 2017.

The shocking increase in deadly changes in health that are clearly connected to fetal exposure to multiple environmental toxins is being heartlessly ignored, especially those in wildlife. I have been repeatedly told that because of greed, no one cares, which I sincerely hope is not the case. I have to believe the deceptions used in the extensive attempts to cover up the epidemic of often lethal effects on health and survivability that are clearly caused by massive over-use of multiple pesticides will soon become evident. There are better and healthier ways of controlling pests and growing crops. The young of all species have a right to normal development and healthy, productive lives. **We need to address this issue immediately so far fewer children are born with health problems that disrupt their lives and the lives of their entire family.**

**Intelligent life
is endangered by toxins
damaging brain cells.**

THE WISH

When a man went to the hospital
Room, a small boy with brain
Cancer said he was going to die.
When told that he could have a wish,
He thought for a moment, and with
A smile, said he would like to fly
In a hot air balloon or a glider so
He could see what the world is like
Looking down from way up high.

Suddenly his expression changed,
And a tear fell from his eye.
He said his best wish would be to
Stop using things that cause cancer
So children would not have to die.
The man said it might not be possible
But he hoped that people would try.
They shook hands and the man quickly
Left, so the boy wouldn't see him cry.

On a sunny day, he received his wish
For a ride in a hot air balloon.
Though he can no longer know it,
It is painfully clear that his "best wish"
Won't be granted any time soon.
Although the boy was able to look at
His world from way up in the sky,
Many children, like fragile flowers,
Are still destined to wilt and die.

CHAPTER 22
LIVING A HORROR MOVIE

Almost everyone has seen a horror movie with a build-up of increasingly strange and scary scenes until heroes and heroines subdue the villain, cure the disease, or at least survive natural or sometimes completely made-up unnatural disasters. Try putting several of those scenarios into one movie, pile on hundreds of bodies with an ever-increasing prevalence of debilitating malformations, itching blisters, scaly sores, hideous tumors, and live animals literally disintegrating before your eyes. This is what I have been watching live and in color on a regular basis in the years since summer 1994. I have been living a very long horror movie that was not scripted and is definitely not make believe. What I have been seeing on a regular basis for over 20 years is much too real. To someone with a scientific leaning, it is comparable to living inside a gigantic test tube while viewing an appallingly disastrous experiment. Unfortunately, this planet-wide experimentation is on people and almost all other living things. What should be most concerning to everyone alive today is that this extensive, uncontrolled experiment does not appear to have any safety measures.

I know many people call those who report events far less extreme than what I have observed a Chicken Little. Chicken Littles are accused of insisting, "The sky is falling!" when nothing drastic is actually occurring. I am not saying the sky is falling. But the pesticides, radiation, heavy metals, and many other toxins we are releasing into the atmosphere do fall back to Earth in rain and snow, contaminating surface water, plants, and all living things. I guess technically some of the sky *is* falling and the results *are* serious. What is so amazing is that there has been little concern shown for what those toxins do to plants and animals, especially children and the grazing animals we use for food.

After the high ultraviolet radiation in 1993 and 1994, a natural disaster to which few in our area paid the slightest attention, the horror scenarios began occurring faster and faster. By 2007, I had necropsied multiple animals with health problems that were quite unsettling to see. For example, several of the 20 to 30 animals I necropsied each year had single large tumors or multiple small ones. Some were more frightening than anything conjured up for scary movies. Even very young animals, especially fledgling birds, had ugly-looking tumors. Some were diagnosed as cancerous and some weren't, but they were all deadly.

Another extremely disturbing cause of death I observed in wild and domestic animals, especially young ones, was for them to suddenly drown in their own blood from massive hemorrhage in the thoracic cavity. One of the more recent was an interesting adult male white-tailed deer with a short lower jaw who lived on our land. I saw him in our yard occasionally and photographed him several times. At the age of three, he made it through the 2015 hunting season even though he had a nice, medium-sized rack with a drop tine (pointing down) on the left antler. Antlers with drop tines are highly sought-after trophies. I continued to see him frequently after that hunting season; in fall 2016, his antlers were even larger, but without the drop tine. Late that November, after he had survived three winters with a fairly severe overbite and a fourth hunting season, a neighbor found him dead the day after the 2016 hunting season ended. There was not a mark on him, so I knew he hadn't been shot or hit by a vehicle. My necropsy found that a blood vessel had burst near his heart and he died almost instantly when blood filled his lungs. At least that is a quick death and the animals do not suffer as they do when dying slowly of cancer or starvation.

In dissecting several hundred animals prior to 1995, I had not seen any of those multiple bizarre health issues, but they have since become quite common. Just when I thought I had seen almost every possible disturbing adverse health scenario, in spring 2007, symptoms in newborns became even more concerning. When I necropsied dead newborn elk, deer, and domestic goats, I found they had strange-looking dilated vessels on the surface of their hearts. Most also had an enlarged right ventricle, causing the heart to look like something conjured up for a movie prop, much different from those I was used to seeing. By 2010, animal hearts were back to a more normal appearance, no longer having the strange-looking dilated lymphatic vessels on the surface. Not surprising, in 2007 prevalence of birth defects such as underbite, overbite, herniated umbilicus, and others in newborn mammals also went much higher.

The most frightening scenes in this real-life horror movie were the fast-growing tumors I began seeing in hatchling and fledgling birds especially between 2007 and 2009. A developing altricial (helpless at

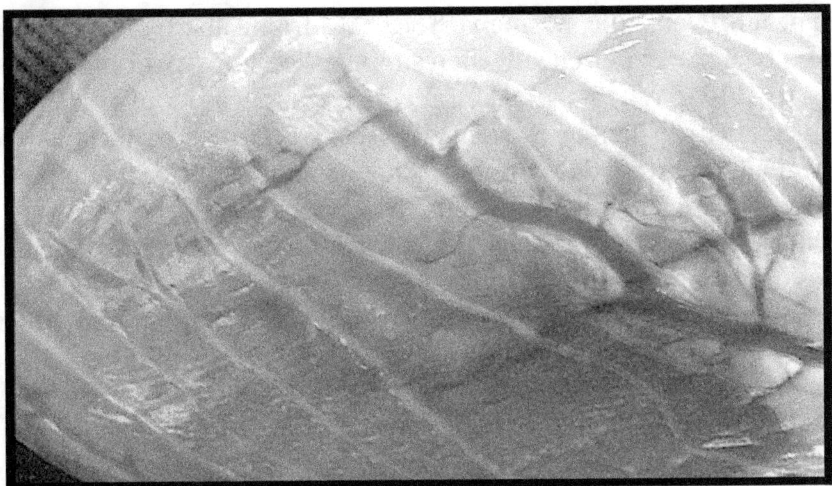

The white lines are extremely dilated lymphatic vessels on the surface of a newborn deer heart.

hatching) bird, which spends the first three to five weeks in a nest, is only five to 10 weeks old from its entrance into the world in a newly-laid egg to when it leaves the nest as a fledgling. Young birds of all sizes, from larger ones like raptors to small songbirds, had multiple tumors in the neck and face or throughout their internal organs when brought for care. It was also fairly common for injured adult birds brought for rehabilitation to have tumors. But it is especially distressing to see that such extensive cellular damage can happen to a hatchling in their short life. Movies about zombies are not nearly as disturbing.

In addition to the increasing cancers, chemical blisters are another health problem we have seen since the birth defects first began occurring. Chemical blistering increased in summer 1994 and has been observed on many individuals of all ages in a wide variety of mammals. Squirrels, deer fawns, goats, domestic dogs, domestic cats, and people, especially children, were those most often affected. During certain times of the year, Jenny, our chemically sensitive Corgi, would suddenly develop blisters inside her ears, on her toes, and sometimes on her back and legs. We avoid using pesticides and almost all other chemicals, including common household products. Jenny would often get multiple blisters immediately after a weather front passed through, so most likely she was reacting to something in the air, or in rain that fell on her.

A chemical blistering occurrence that confirmed the serious effects of moisture in passing weather fronts happened to a young woman who lived near Stevensville, Montana. She told a friend about the blisters and strange rash she experienced when snow fell on her wrists and hands in February 2003. When she called me at the suggestion of her friend, I arranged to meet her in Stevensville to take photos of the rash. We connected about five days after the blisters and rash had first appeared. The area where snow had contacted her skin was still red and swollen, but the blisters were nearly healed. Scabs indicated where they had been. It was quite amazing that snow could have such an acute effect by simply falling on human skin. As with the gladiola-killing rain, I had to wonder what damage breathing the toxic snow had done to sensitive lungs of animals. I could only surmise the plot of the horror movie I was living was about insidious chemical warfare that damages living things upon which rain or snow falls, or any animal that breathes the air while the deadly moisture is falling. A major problem with this scenario is that there is no way to know if raindrops or snowflakes falling from the sky are deadly or harmless. It is like "weather roulette."

In 2010, I received a male white-tailed deer fawn for care who was similarly affected health-wise, as evidenced by his symptoms. However, he was exposed to 2,4-D by direct application on the wetlands where he was born. He had chemical blisters and multiple chemical poisoning symptoms, with such severe neurological damage he was unable remain upright, stand, or walk. He was brought to me by a man who found him in a riparian zone on land belonging to his neighbor. The area where the fawn was born had been heavily sprayed with 2,4-D, a common herbicide, to kill cattails the summer before and was again sprayed with it soon after the fawn was born. His mother's exposure to 2,4-D the previous year, in combination with all the other toxins that fell on plants she consumed before and during the fawn's development, was likely responsible for his multiple birth defects (including abnormal genitalia, underdeveloped upper facial bones, and malformed teeth). His lower incisors were leaf shaped, pointed on the top, and had small tooth-like projections on the sides. In spite of his birth defects, the fawn could stand, suckle, and run, and appeared to be doing quite well for the first two weeks after he was born. Then the landowner again sprayed with 2,4-D, including the place where the fawn was bedded. Soon after that final application of 2,4-D, the rescuer observed the fawn with severe neurological damage.

The person who brought the fawn for rehab had been watching the mother for two or three years and had seen the normal-acting fawn several times after he was born. Immediately after exposure to fresh 2,4-D, the rescuer saw that the two-week-old fawn fell down each time he tried to stand and suckle. It was likely he was predisposed at birth to be especially sensitive to 2,4-D as a result of his mother's exposure the previous year. According to the data on 2,4-D, it is not supposed to cause extreme neurological damage. It is also not supposed to be used in riparian areas to avoid contaminating surface water.

Fearing the fawn would die, the man brought him to us, hoping I could do something to save him. Unfortunately, giving him cell salts, electrolytes, and MSM did not make the little guy's legs work properly. I fed him every three hours and worked with him for over two weeks, but the neurological damage to his legs grew steadily worse. Finally, I had to make the sad decision to euthanize him. Necropsy revealed that, in addition to external birth defects, he had an underdeveloped thymus, a very enlarged right heart ventricle, and large white areas on his lungs indicating dead tissue, so his chance of surviving for long were not good even if he had not developed extensive neurological damage. So many adverse health issues on one little fawn is far worse than any scene from a horror movie because they were all too real.

One young fox squirrel who was brought to me rivaled the deer fawn in multiple ugly symptoms of chemical poisoning. Besides large, repulsive-looking chemical blisters on his left ear, his right front foot had no toes, and severe neurological damage caused him to run in circles, always to the left. Fox squirrels living in urban areas where they spend a large amount of time on sprayed lawns (as do children) seem particularly susceptible to chemicals. Some young squirrels also do not develop in a normal manner, remaining undersized and dwarfish as adults.

Occasionally, domestic animals who die are brought to me because the owner has heard I necropsy them or because they want me to add their animal to the data I keep. Those have included foals, calves, lambs, baby goats, and newborn pigs, all with birth defects. Three or four of the goats, including newborns, had large goiters, a common symptom of thyroid hormone disruption. However, in the hundreds of wild animals I necropsied, the thyroids were usually close to normal in size and shape or even somewhat small.

Acute bone disintegration, especially around the roots of incisors in the lower jawbone is another strange issue I have observed in live or necropsied animals. The bone becomes extremely thin and porous, causing teeth to loosen and fall out. A grazing animal cannot bite off forage without lower incisors, so their loss results in malnutrition, a lowered quality of life, and often death from starvation, a real-life horror plot.

Several livestock owners brought carcasses of their goats, sheep, calves, and llamas after the animals died suddenly with no indication of prior illness. Some had blisters on their muzzles. The one with the worst blistering was a neutered male Nubian goat with so much damage to the muzzle area it looked like something had eaten away his skin. He also had a fairly severe underbite and an enlarged heart. Like many other animals who died unexpectedly, he had died of sudden lung hemorrhage, causing him to drown in his own blood. Is it any wonder that I find zombie movies extremely boring? Make believe zombies aren't nearly as frightening as the bizarre symptoms in animals I have necropsied.

Obesity and diabetes in children and adults is usually blamed on diets high in fat and carbohydrates or on the person for not controlling their eating habits. Thyroid hormone disruption will also cause these health problems, even when a person is eating a healthy, low fat, mostly plant-based diet. This was sadly illustrated by Honey, my pretty gold and white Nubian milk goat. Of all my goats, Honey was the most sensitive to chemicals in air, rain, and snow. Besides having the bottom edge of her ears fall off after exposure to rain dripping from them, painful-looking chemical blisters occasionally broke out all over her muzzle. During the winter Honey was three and one-half years old, at the same time more of her ear tips was being eaten away by rain and snow, the bone at the front of her lower jaw deteriorated, allowing her lower incisors to tip far forward. By early spring, after even more bone loss, the lower incisors began to fall out one by one. After she had lost all of them, Honey could not eat normally, but she still appeared to be in good condition, even a bit fat. She ate weeds, the tall green grass in the goat pasture, and the small portion of grain I gave her each day. By late summer, she was looking even fatter. It was perplexing how she could become so fat with no lower incisors to bite off grass and other plants. As summer progressed she appeared to be in good shape, but more blisters appeared on her muzzle and she acted like she didn't feel well.

The blisters on Honey's muzzle became worse and nothing I put on them helped, so I had her blood tested at the local veterinary lab. Results showed she had leukemia, the human kind, which is rare in goats and quite different from goat leukemia. Because of her illness, the only humane option was to euthanize my beautiful, sweet goat. When I necropsied her, I was extremely surprised to find she had very little muscle left, like a starving animal. Most perplexing, a two-inch-thick blanket of fat completely encased her abdominal region. It appeared that much of the food she had eaten during spring and summer had turned to fat, becoming a strange, thick layer of adipose tissue. She wasn't sitting around eating potato chips and Twinkies, but she did spend much of the day lying down. There appeared to be a close connection between her extreme sensitivity to chemicals and having a disrupted metabolism that resulted in leukemia, simultaneous obesity and malnutrition, and a major decrease in bone density resulting in the loss of her lower incisors.

Health statistics from the Center for Disease Control (CDC) show that obesity rates and consequential diseases linked to obesity, including heart disease and diabetes, have dramatically increased since 1994, and are now considered to be epidemic in children and adults. The increase in obesity was and still is claimed to be because of life style, such as spending a lot of time watching TV or playing video games while eating fatty snacks. Very young children are often obese before they are old enough to choose a lifestyle or consume anything other than milk, water, fruit juice, and eventually baby food. Some are obese when they are born, even though their mothers did not drink carbonated or alcoholic beverages and ate as much healthy food as possible. The rates for cancers in fatty tissue, such as brain, breast, and prostate, in addition to leukemias and lymphomas in both young people and adults, have also been increasing quite rapidly since 1994, according to the CDC web site. Many goats with underbite (some with chemically blistered muzzles), which were brought to me to necropsy, had died of either cancer or thoracic hemorrhage. Most were young animals, usually less than five years old.

Goats, birds, and humans are not the only animals I have observed with tumors. One of the most repulsive, and at the same time most colorful bright pink and white, fast-growing tumors, was around the incisors at the front of the lower jaw of an adult female sheep. She had been born with underbite, indicating she had fetal hypothyroidism during development. It is likely that thyroid hormone disruption during development may predispose an animal to be more susceptible to some kinds of cancer. That is a logical conclusion because the majority of the mammals I have necropsied that had diagnosed cancer or tumors not

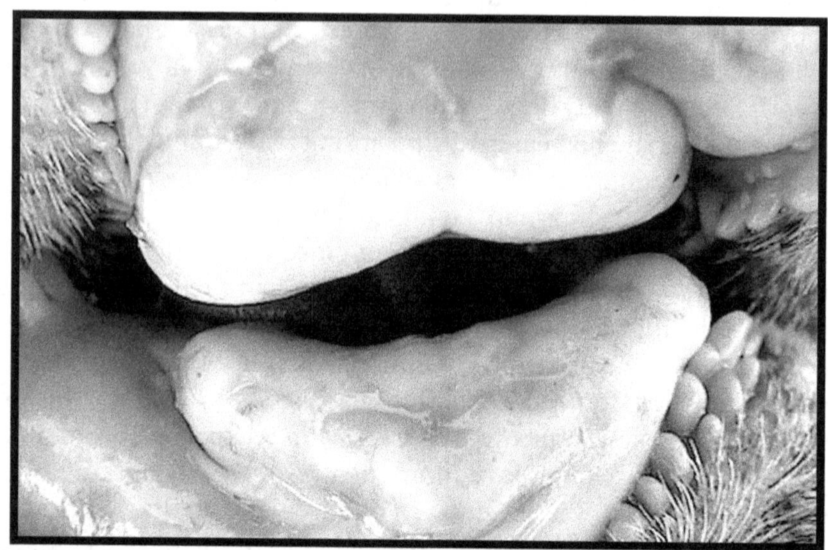

Honey's mouth at the time of her death, after all of her lower incisors had fallen out.

verified as cancer also had an underbite or other symptoms of thyroid hormone disruption.

Many toxic chemicals damage the cells' mitochondria, the power packs that turn sugar into heat and energy. If sugar in the bloodstream is not turned into heat and energy, it causes a higher than normal glucose level until the body is able to deal with it in some other way, usually by storing it as fat. Some animals I have necropsied have been quite obese even though they had extreme lung damage, including symptoms of emphysema and white, dead lung tissue. Many of the toxins now present in air can cause inflammation of lung tissue, resulting in shortness of breath and lung damage. Besides adverse effects on the lungs, the right ventricle of the heart (the chamber responsible for pumping blood through the lungs) is usually enlarged and thin-walled.

Symptoms listed for people resulting from chronic exposure to low levels of pesticide combinations includes burning eyes, shortness of breath, skin rashes and blisters, extreme fatigue, joint pain, muscle pain and spasms, incoordination, digestive problems, abdominal pain, urinary incontinence, depression, lethargy, dehydration, and loss of ability to think clearly and function in a normal manner. People, especially children, who feel tired and depressed all the time and who can't move

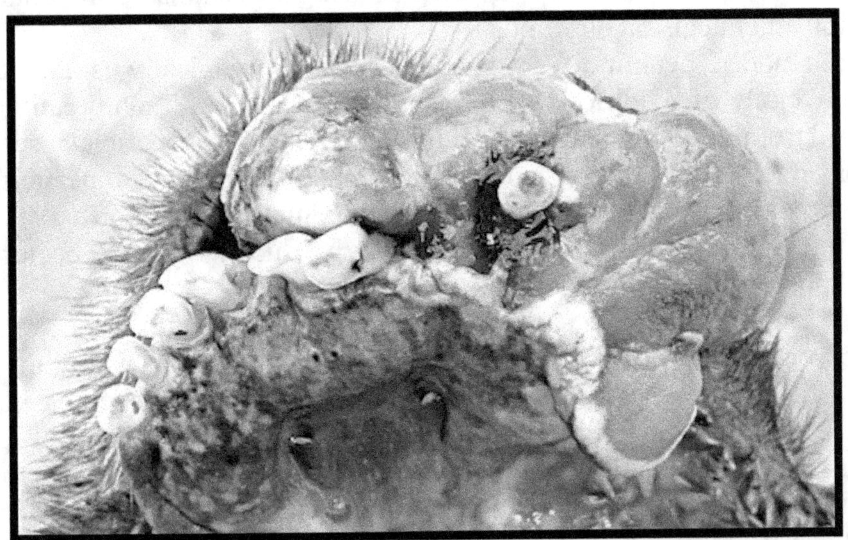

This shows the top view of the fast-growing, ugly tumor on the lower jaw of a female sheep born with an underbite.

without pain, will resist exercise. Often, the affected children sleep much more than normal or prefer activities where they can sit still because they do not feel like moving. Activities children normally enjoy, such as running and playing, cause shortness of breath, fatigue, and muscle and joint pain, so are avoided as much as possible. Is it a coincidence that obesity and diabetes rates in the United States were reported to have more than doubled in the years since 1994? That is the same time period during which wild and domestic newborn animals have suffered and often died because of specific new types of birth defects and other adverse and often strange health issues. Watching children and other young animals suffer is far more disturbing than watching a horror movie because it is not fiction. It is excruciatingly real!

It is also very likely, based on the evidence, that there is a direct connection between chronic low-level exposures to pesticides, prescription drugs, and other toxins, and the obesity, heart disease, and diabetes epidemic. It is similar to a runaway train speeding down the tracks. No one will do anything to stop the train or even tell people about the mortality it is causing. Before that train is brought to a halt, the body count will be extremely high. The monetary cost of health care and resultant deaths will also be exorbitant, much higher than the cost of growing crops organically as opposed to using unsustainable amounts of deadly chemicals on our food.

An added benefit to growing everything organically is that the biodiversity of wildlife is significantly increased, with many animals saved from extinction, including birds, butterflies, and beneficial insects. Conversely, if people continue to spread massive amounts of pesticides over the entire planet, we will soon have a quiet Earth, not just a silent spring. The life forms most likely to survive such as viruses, bacteria, and possibly lichens do not make much noise.

I can certainly relate to the meteorologist who tried his best to warn everyone of how deadly and destructive Hurricane Katrina was going to be. Unfortunately, too many people did not listen or did not believe him, and many ended up living a real-life horror movie. Because many people want to continue using deadly chemicals like pesticides, or make money from their use, not enough is being done to determine the cause or causes of the astronomically high rates of birth defects, cancer, and other now-common adverse health issues. As a consequence, people will become unhealthier, they will continue to lose their children, pets, and livestock to cancer, and wild animal populations will keep declining.

Cancer and a whole list of health problems caused by thyroid hormone disruption, mitochondrial dysfunction and chronic sub-clinical metabolic acidosis (often considered a normal consequence of aging) are becoming very common in older people. When I was young, almost no one died of cancer, because hardly anyone ever got cancer. In the ranching area where I grew up, people mainly died from accidents with machinery or occasionally from heart attacks or strokes. I had not even heard of a child having cancer until I came to Montana in 1963 and began teaching elementary school here. Even then there were only a few children reported to have cancer in all of Montana.

Interestingly, the national media reports, at least for a few days, when studies show that a pesticide causes cancer in humans. For some reason, they have said almost nothing about the very visible, high prevalence of birth defects in mammals and nothing at all about finding the cause or causes. This is extremely concerning because our children are one of the species of mammal often born with those birth defects.

Most adverse health issues children are born with as a result of fetal exposure to toxins, especially multiple synergistic pesticides, require extensive periods of hospitalization. Just consider what it is like to be a child in a hospital undergoing chemotherapy, being constantly poked with needles, having dangerous operations, losing their hair, and all the other ghastly experiences connected to having severe birth defects or cancer. For the child to whom this happens, it could indeed be described as living in a long, terrifying horror movie.

Please be one of the super heroes who help save newborns and all others from the deadly chemical warfare that is perpetrated on them, and finally bring this alarming real-life horror movie to an end.

**Toxic rain creates
lovely flowers, green grass, and
fast growing tumors.**

A young fox squirrel with chemical blisters in his left ear had missing toes on his right foot and severe neurological damage when he was found.

303

Fledgling starlings fed only dog food as hatchlings grew white malformed feathers and couldn't fly. The person who raised the starlings because a friend brought them to her after finding them on the ground looked on the Internet for the correct food to feed hatchling starlings. It said to feed them moistened dog food. Unfortunately, many kinds of dog food have been found to contain high levels of glyphosate from the grain they contain. Glyphosate chelates the minerals needed for normal feather growth. This leads to the question of whether the dog food is adversely affecting pets.

Our beloved dog Jenny was only 13½ years old when we had to have her euthanized in July 2015 because her legs no longer functioned. She could not stand or walk even after extensive veterinary tests and treatment. Jenny became progressively worse and completely stopped eating because her digestive system no longer worked. Even when I offered special foods she had always liked, she wouldn't eat. All of her life she had been a veritable toxin meter. Unfortunately, her cellular reaction to toxins did not indicate to which chemicals she was exposed.

As everyone knows, a testing laboratory is necessary for identifying specific chemicals and their levels in the environment. However, officials responsible for the health of people, their livestock, and wildlife have paid little attention to my friends or me when we asked for testing (especially for glyphosate levels) of rain, snow, surface water, and foliage here in Ravalli County.

It is quite apparent that problems connected with maintaining good health and a clean, livable environment nearly always come back to conflict of interest. Just follow the money. It appears there is a deadly conflict between making huge profits and doing what is best for sustaining life. Big game hunters spend a considerable amount of money in Montana, in both large and small businesses. Obviously, to maintain an adequate tax base, our state and local officials are more in sympathy with protecting businesses than with protecting the health of newborns. After over 20 years of trying, we haven't been able to convince state officials or business and livestock owners to even acknowledge, let alone do something, about birth defects and other health issues in the animals on which their livelihoods depend.

Governors and other officials in the United States and Canada who have resisted addressing this issue are responsible for creating revenues from license sales and maintaining sufficient wildlife populations for hunters. They are also supposed to be responsible for protecting the health of humans and wild and domestic animals living in their state or province. Unfortunately, creating revenue prevailed over maintaining health and saving lives. I have asked them if everything dies, what good is money? They do not seem to see beyond tomorrow with those gigantic dollar signs blocking their vision. To be kind, we should forgive this behavior by state and local officials. However, it is extremely difficult for me to be forgiving, because so many children and newborn animals have been and still are being killed or maimed for life by disruption of their health and normal development. All this suffering and death is occurring so businesses, especially corporations and their stockholders, are able to generate larger profits. We all must stop putting business as usual ahead of working together to protect the newborns. Without viable young of all species, life as we know it will go extinct and we will soon follow.

Twenty years ago, when I began documenting birth defects and keeping notes on what I observed, little was known about the gene disrupting effects of pesticides. Studies of how genes work and how toxins can affect normal gene function have been providing researchers and medical doctors with an enormous amount of new knowledge in this field. Glyphosate has been one of the most studied pesticides regarding its ability to disrupt genes. Once they have been properly tested, many other pesticides will likely be found to have similar effects. This is especially alarming when it results in life-changing developmental defects and multiple health issues that can be passed on to future generations without actually altering DNA.

While adverse effects on human health are an important consideration, domestic animal health, wildlife health, and maintaining viable populations of our native animals and plants are crucial to our own survival. Also, raising and selling domestic animals is essential to our economy, especially here in Montana. Without ranchers, livestock owners, and the animals they raise, Montana's economy would likely collapse. And without Montana's varied wildlife populations there would be far less money spent here by people who enjoy watching our native animals, those who hunt and fish, and tourists who come to Montana from other states and nations.

I was told that if officials admit the air, water, and plants are so toxic they cause many Montana grazing animals to have a high prevalence of birth defects and many to have cancer, chemical blisters, heart and lung damage, and other major health problems, people would not want to come here. Thus, state and county government agencies have done their best to cover up the birth defects and suppress information concerning increases in adverse health issues, especially in newborns.

What the giant cover-up of health problems in Montana is supposed to accomplish over the long term is unclear. Animals throughout the United States, Canada, and much of Mexico have many of the same developmental defects and so-called diseases caused by pesticide exposure. Thus, the cover-up of the multiple kinds of defects in Montana animals is pointless and not at all helpful in stopping the use of what is so seriously affecting newborns, causing cancer in all ages of animals, contributing to mass extinctions in wildlife, and resulting in the unnecessary deaths of millions of people. Unfortunately, these are just a few of the most devastating effects.

Prior to 1995, mountain lions, bears, and coyotes were not considered significant factors in causing population declines in wild ruminants. Wolves were seldom seen in the United States, except for Alaska, until several years after the birth defects began. By then, big game populations were already declining as a consequence of increased thyroid hormone, gene, and retinoic acid (Vitamin A) disruption; mineral deficiencies and resultant disruption of mitochondrial functions; and severe metabolic acidosis. Those and other disruptions of normal fetal development have been shown by hundreds of studies to be caused by exposure to pesticides, particularly Roundup® and all the other highly used pesticides that work synergistically with the chemicals in Roundup-type products. In the years after use of Roundup® sharply increased in 1996, the continuing disruption of normal development in wild young has resulted in a simultaneous decline in wild ruminant, bird, amphibian, and beneficial insect populations.

Roundup Ready® crops are genetically modified to survive being sprayed directly with Roundup® instead of surviving only when it is applied to the soil before planting crops. The purpose is to kill all other plants without killing the genetically modified ones, but it means our food crops contain even more glyphosate than before. In a letter to USDA Secretary Tom Vilsack, pathogen researcher Col. (Retired) Don M. Huber, an Emeritus Professor at Purdue University, presented Secretary Vilsack with strong evidence that increased use of Roundup® on genetically modified crops is resulting in deadly side effects. Most importantly, recent studies have shown that ultra-low exposure to glyphosate, the main ingredient in Roundup®, causes craniofacial and neural defects in embryos of mammals, birds, and amphibians. Even more alarming was finding the damaging exposure levels were much lower than the EPA allows in human foods.

A comprehensive review of the effects of exposure to glyphosate ("Glyphosate's Suppression of Cytochrome P450 Enzymes and Amino Acid Biosynthesis by the Gut Microbiome: Pathways to Modern Diseases," written by Dr. Anthony Samsel and Dr. Stephanie Seneff) was published in *Entropy*. In the abstract, authors stated, "Negative impact on the body is insidious and manifests slowly over time as inflammation damages cellular systems throughout the body." This is the first time I have seen the word insidious used in a review abstract. In my opinion, its use is decidedly warranted; the effects on developing young are especially insidious. Dr. Samsel and Dr. Seneff have written several more papers showing the effects of glyphosate on various organs in people, which are available on the Internet.

Another scientific article written by Dr. N. L. Swanson and published online April 24, 2013, ("Genetically Modified Organisms and the Deterioration of Health in the United States") provides multiple charts. These clearly show a close correlation between the increase in use of glyphosate and food crops genetically modified to be resistant to glyphosate with increases in many serious human health problems, especially diabetes, autism, and heart defects.

A very important factor is that glyphosate is always used with surfactants and adjuvants, called Roundup-type products. Low levels of such products have been found to be one thousand times more toxic to cells than glyphosate alone. A comprehensive review by Dr. Michael Antoniou and his colleagues published in 2015 ("Dr. Michael Antoniou: Roundup Causes Massive Kidney and Liver Damage at Low Doses") can be found online in *Environmental Health Journal*. This review leaves no doubt concerning the effects of Roundup-type products on the liver and kidneys of humans and other animals. Of course, severe liver and kidney damage have very adverse effects on digestive processes, resulting in lack of appetite due to inability to digest food. Many of the animals people brought to me to necropsy had damaged livers and often were reported to have stopped eating before they died.

The numerous, extremely painful health issues that occur in domestic animals as a result of eating feed contaminated with Roundup® products are appropriately being considered animal abuse. The article "Without Prejudice – Glyphosate" published online July 17, 2017, on the DOCTOR TED website (http://doctorted.ca/animal-production-news-

/without-prejudice/) reports and shows photos of severely damaged organs, especially the liver, from cattle and sheep fed glyphosate-contaminated feed. Nothing was said in this report about the slow, debilitating, painful deaths experienced by wild animals as a result of similar exposure to glyphosate and Roundup-type products, which certainly should also be considered animal abuse.

For people who want to avoid foods with biologically significant levels of glyphosate (as they will after examining the photos of animal organs on that link), there is a wonderful new book available that gives the names of numerous food products and the glyphosate levels found in each. Author Tony Mitra worked long and diligently to obtain test results and put them in an easily understandable format so everyone can find the glyphosate levels in foods they buy. His book, *Poison Foods of North America*, is available online through Amazon.

What has been so exasperating regarding the birth defects we have reported in our studies and with photos, in addition to actual animals (alive and dead), is that most government officials claim there are no malformations. They also say exposure to Roundup-type products does not cause birth defects. Or they claim the birth defects we point out to them are normal variations, no matter how bad the defect is and even when it causes mortality. Those same officials ignored all other scientists, many of whom were medical professionals or biologists, who reported the same birth defects in animals or verified those we reported were definitely malformations. Here is an important question: How could I take hundreds of photos of animals with birth defects if there aren't any birth defects? If there actually were no malformations in domestic animals and wildlife, other people would not be able to take photos of them or post them on the Internet, as thousands of people have done.

In the years since we first reported birth defects in wildlife, the only motive my colleagues and I have had is to prevent animals, including humans, from being chronically poisoned. Fortunately, in the last five years, many people began to work together to get Monsanto to take their poisonous products off the market. One such organization is Millions Against Monsanto. In addition, many top-level scientists from a number of different countries have been working for years to prove that pesticides are causing great harm to entire ecosystems.

An example is the extensive review concerning glyphosate use and birth defects that result from exposure to it in developing young. Also written by Dr. Michael Antoniou and his colleagues, "Roundup® and Birth Defects: Is the Public Being Kept in the Dark?" was published by *Earth Open Source*, 2011. The authors state, "The EU Commission has known since 2002 that glyphosate causes malformations." They continue, "The public, in contrast, has been kept in the dark by industry and regulators about the ability of glyphosate and Roundup® to cause malformations. In addition, the work of independent scientists who have drawn attention to the herbicide's teratogenic effects has been ignored, denigrated, or dismissed. These actions on the part of industry and regulators have endangered public health."

My colleagues and I are some of those independent scientists who have been ignored, denigrated, or outright dismissed. Additionally, if the actions of industry and regulators have endangered human health, it is obvious the health of most animals and thus the entire biodiversity of the planet have been endangered. Because millions of people and animals have died due to regulators' failure to protect them, this has far surpassed "endangering health" to actually being undeniable genocide and biocide.

Dr. Antoniou's review was stated by other scientists to provide, "a comprehensive review of the peer-reviewed scientific literature, documenting the serious health hazards posed by glyphosate and Roundup® herbicide formulations." The recent reviews and new studies connecting glyphosate directly to the alarming increases in multiple adverse health issues are observably correct, with evidence in these reviews strongly indicating that Roundup® should be immediately banned from all use worldwide.

Forced synergistic and sequential exposure to Roundup® and its primary ingredient, glyphosate, along with chlorothalonil (and the deadly cyanide it contains), neonicotinoids (made of nicotine), and all other highly used pesticides should be considered chemical warfare. Chemical companies made these disastrous products and promoted them until they were sprayed all over the world in massive amounts. Most of these toxic chemicals have been shown to travel thousands of miles by atmospheric transport from where they are applied. Many hundreds of studies show the multiple and very serious synergistic effects of pesticide combinations on vertebrates and invertebrates.

Alice M. Milner and Ian L. Boyd state in their paper, "Toward Pesticidal Vigilance," "The current assumption underlying pesticide regulation – that chemicals that pass a battery of tests in the laboratory or in field trials are environmentally benign when they are used at industrial scales – is false." There is now simultaneous exposure to developing young of every species in the world to industrial levels of the two chemicals (cyanide and nicotine) doctors have shown cause birth defects in children born to mothers who smoke. In addition, there are multiple sequential exposures to similar and sometimes higher levels of many other pesticides (especially glyphosate, which kills vertebrates, invertebrates, and plants). This is resulting in unprecedented cancer in animals of all ages, health problems in children and other newborn vertebrates, and extinctions in wildlife and native plants. This is not simple poisoning; it is far worse. These dangerous combinations are changing the configuration and epigenetics of millions of animals and are destroying the very fabric of biodiversity.

Children do not have choices, especially prior to conception and when they are in the womb. Exposure to these toxins not only disrupts a child's normal development; it disrupts their entire life and that of their family members. Caring for the epidemic of special needs children and those with cancer and other serious health problems, as well as providing special education for children whose brain development has been disrupted, has nationwide and worldwide economic and social consequences.

All people who care about wildlife, other animals, and most of all, care about the children now being born and growing up in a toxic world, must choose to work together and begin making better decisions. At the rate plants and animals are declining, and human health issues are increasing, we appear to be running out of time. We can find healthier substitutes for many of the hormone disrupting toxins now in use. We can collectively choose to immediately ban or at least properly regulate the pesticides and other toxins that are the most dangerous and causing the most harm. We can do extraordinary things if we all work together. **As President Obama continues to say, *"Yes, we can!"***

**Tiny wet snowflakes
in numbers great enough, can
topple tall pine trees.**

All young animals should have a right to normal development and to be born normal and healthy.

CHANGING FACES

From mountain tops to valley floor,
Short-grass prairie to ocean shore,
Growing cells are rearranging
So young faces now are changing.

Bird bills are often short or long.
And some can't sing their mating song.
Because their genes are rearranged,
Young birds' faces too are changed.

Many ruminants, like deer,
Are born with underbite each year.
Because their genes are rearranging
Mammal faces now are changing.

Newborn young with malformations
Are being born in all the nations.
Children's faces too are changing,
Because their genes are rearranging.

Pesticides in tiny traces
Cause newborns with changing faces.
Rampant corporate corruption
Covers up the gene disruption.

All the world should be concerned.
Forests of genes are being burned.
With gene expression rearranged,
More than faces can be changed.

To stop the illness and genocide,
It doesn't help the young to hide
The birth defects and biocide.
Report defects! Help turn the tide.

Then young ones can again be whole
Without the defects taking toll
On every aspect of their being;
The hopeful future we are seeing.